A VICTORY FOR HUMANITY

A VICTORY FOR HUMANITY

BY DICK TRAUM
& Mike Celizic

WRS
PUBLISHING

A Division of WRS Group, Inc.
Waco, Texas

Dedications

To Betsy and Joey, who supported me.
—*Dick Traum*

Text © 1993 by Richard Traum and Michael Celizic

First published in the United States of America in 1993 by WRS Publishing, A Division of WRS Group, Inc., 701 N. New Road, Waco, Texas 76710
Book design by Kenneth Turbeville
Jacket design by Talmage Minter

10 9 8 7 6 5 4 3 2 1

Library of Congress Catalog Card Number
Traum, Richard
Celizic, Michael

ISBN 1-56796-011-1

Acknowledgments

I have had an opportunity to partake in a wide range of life's experiences—joys and sorrows, successes and failures, laughter and tears. Without the negatives, you cannot fully enjoy the positives because it is the range of experience that makes life complete. The possibilities for these special opportunities did not come by luck, but from the interaction with and support of others. I would like to thank the following people who contributed to my wonderful life experience.

First, there are over 3,000 Achilles runners, a few of whom you will read about, who have made me look good and have supported my running. We have so many, that I could rewrite this book using an entirely different group of names and events.

Second, there are over 500 volunteers and supporters who have run with Achilles members, helped establish chapters, made introductions, and contributed meaningfully to my goals. Some I am actively working with now are: Bill Abelow, Norm Barham, Gary Blom, Vincent Bonacci, Alan Brown, David Block, John Childs, Roger Chin, Jen Clemente, Gary Clermont, Jerry Chmielak, Brenda Cole, Dan Coster, Ed Coyle, Jim Decker, Ralph Eckelman, David Edmonds, Arnie Epstein, Peggy & Martin Ferguson-Pell, Muriel Frohman, Nicole Formsel, Irv Gikovski, Bob Golinski, David Gonzalez, Terry Greenberg, Elaine Hall, Dan Hamner, Peter Herbert, Melissa Holden, Tess Hyman, Howard Jacobson, Michele Jones, Nick Katsounis, Evelyn Kaftan, Ben Kaiser, Virginia Kelly, Jamie Kempton, Paul Kiell, Hans Krauss, Bob Laufer, Eric Lee, Stan Levine, Irv Lipskind, Tom Litwin, Tom Madine, Lynn Manley, Deborah Mellinger, Carlo Morano, Gary Muhrcke, Jere Munro, Tom O'Connor, Carlton Odom, Larry Otis, Linda Paulmino, Dick Parker, Betsy Petrick, Jeff Pledger, Mark Pollard, Larry Rawson, Max Rhodes, Martha Ryan, Mike Ryckoff, Alan Satran, Paul Savage, Herman Schwarz, Richard Seton, Dave Shennan, Syl Schefler, Dennis Tabakin, Rob Tannor, Reuben Tavarez, Norman Vale, Vanessa Webb, Mark Weidenbaum, Daniela Zahner.

Third, I would like to thank people who have introduced me to running and different endeavors: Irv Bader, Norman Brickell, Joe Coppoletta, Joe Cruickshank, Patricia Dorff, Anne

Emmerman, Tim Erson, Joe Fetto, Bob Glover, Robin Griskus, Arthur Hamilton, Morris Hartstein, Helene Hines, Richard Koplin, Hans Kraus, Frank Land, Fred Lebow, Eda Lisi, Al Melleby, Ketil Moe, Patti Parmalee, Amy Reiss, Al Reyes, Mike Richards, Don Roberts, John Ross, Alan Roth, Peter Roth, John Seedor, Leszek Sibilski, Ken Sherrick, Bari Slatis, Murray Weisenfeld.

Fourth, the Achilles Board of Directors and Advisors has been there to provide guidance, make introductions, and provide support. Can you imagine an organization in which most of the gross income is provided by the Board? I have had no major successes without having been helped by a board member: Frederick Cook, Linda Down, Thomas Einhorn, Karen Gale, Albert H. Gordon, Carl C. Landegger, Fred Lebow, George Miles, William E. Phillips, Theodore C. Rogers, Stephen Roth, Allan Steinfeld, Andrew H. Tisch, Stephen D. Wald.

Finally, a tremendous amount of time has been spent on running and related activities. These hours would normally have been spent with my family. Thanks, for caring while I was off somewhere doing something else, to: my mother, Lilly; my son, Joey; and my wife, Betsy.

FINISH

Chapter 1

To strive, to seek, to find, and not to yield.
—Alfred, Lord Tennyson
Ulysses

Day doesn't so much break as ooze on the first Sunday of November in Staten Island, New York. The Greeks of Homer's time called it rosy-fingered Dawn. Here, at the foot of the Verrazano Narrows Bridge, Dawn comes with the fingers of a six-year-old—gray and grimy, with dirt under the nails.

Not that anyone's watching the sky this morning, November 1, 1992. New Yorkers aren't big on sky-watching to start with. People who stare at the sky in the Big Apple are tourists. Every mugger past the fourth grade knows that. New Yorkers keep their eyes focused straight ahead, on their destination, glancing down now and then to avoid stepping in any of the unpleasant substances that dot the sidewalks. Today, the thousands who are gathering on the grounds of Fort Wadsworth have another reason to keep their gazes riveted to what lies underfoot and ahead. It's marathon Sunday, and eventually the grounds of the old fort will be paved with the anxious bodies of the more than 29,000 runners who will thunder off across the bridge and through the five boroughs of New York in the city's greatest mass test of character and will.

There's no rainbow with a pot of gold at the end, no yellow brick road to follow, just a broken, painted blue line that starts at the bridge and continues 26.2 miles to the Tavern on the Green in Central Park. But it's a quest, if you will. People come to me seeking qualities that they don't think they have inside them and I send them off on this quest through the streets of New York. It's not easy. For many people, running a marathon will be one of the most difficult and painful things they've ever done. I know it was

for me. But I freely send others off in pursuit of that same
pain. My runners are a tiny fraction of those who run the
race, and every one of them is disabled in some way. For
them, the race is a double challenge, a challenge that many
of them never imagined they could meet. At the end, they
get a heavy hunk of metal attached to a loop of brightly
colored ribbon, and a diploma. The medal and diploma
mean they've finished the quest; conquered the New York
City Marathon. Both, though, are just symbols. Whatever
people discover along the way has been inside them all
along. So what the marathon does is introduce them to
themselves. Like the Oz characters, they aren't trying to
inspire others, and they're not trying to make the world a
better place in which to live by running a race. But that's
what happens. Others will be inspired by their efforts, and
the world will be better for their passing. The victories they
will win today are deeply personal, but they are for all of
mankind, as well.

The vast horde of runners starts arriving at Fort
Wadsworth on an endless procession of buses about 5:30 in
the morning. I don't take the bus myself. I drive to the fort
and park on a little access road just outside the main gate
and a hundred yards or so from the Verrazano Bridge toll
booths. That's the Achilles staging area. It's not big on
facilities. Inside the gates to the army base, where the growing
swarms of runners are greeted in English, French, German,
and Spanish, are seven big, striped tents providing an acre
and a half of cover, where runners can get away from the
frigid pre-dawn air. There's coffee, hot chocolate, bottled
water, ranks and ranks of porta-johns, and the biggest tourist
attraction of the marathon staging area—the world's longest
urinal. Outside, where 150 Achilles runners and twice as
many volunteers gather, are two porta-johns, one jumbo
container of coffee, a supply of bottled water, and one 1991
Chevrolet station wagon—mine—that can provide refuge
from the cold for six or seven runners.

It's almost always cold on marathon morning, but this
year is one of the coldest—not quite cold enough to freeze
water, but more than frigid enough to freeze fingers and
toes. Some of us in Achilles have an advantage there. We're
disabled. That's currently the politically correct word. Some

people still call us handicapped. Almost no one uses the word cripple anymore. By any name, many of us aren't all there, so we've got less to freeze. (But that's not what I tell people who ask me how the cold affects me. I tell them that because I have only one leg, the toes on that leg get twice as cold. Some of them believe it; others laugh. That's what they get for asking.) Anyway, we've got amputees who are missing anything from part of a leg or an arm to all four limbs. We've got paraplegics and quadriplegics. For them, the cold is a different problem. Since they can't feel their legs, they have to be especially careful when it's very cold or they could get frostbite and not know it. We've got blind runners and an autistic runner, several with severe arthritis, some with heart trouble, a few who've had strokes. Others have cerebral palsy, multiple sclerosis, cystic fibrosis, cancer, small bowel syndrome, diabetes, brain damage, heart transplants, and a few things even most doctors can't spell. That's why we call ourselves the Achilles Track Club; we're all vulnerable, we all have our weak spot. Mine is a leg; the right leg. The upper half of my thigh is original equipment. The rest of the leg is plastic and alloy. And, yes, jokes aside, we feel the cold like anyone else. But we'll deal with it. We've dealt with worse. We're athletes and we're here to run.

When I took my artificial right leg for a 26.2-mile run in 1976, I had no idea it would come to this. I entered the New York City Marathon that year because I was a runner and that's what runners do in New York. It turned out that no one without the standard issue of two legs had ever run a marathon before. I kept running anyway, and other amputees took it up. Terry Fox, a young Canadian, heard about me when he was in the hospital having his cancerous leg amputated. He decided if I could run a marathon, he could, too, and set off to run a marathon a day across Canada. He didn't make the full distance. The cancer came back and took him away. But he touched his nation's soul. He was a national hero when he died, and deserved to be. Although we never met, he returned the inspiration I had once given him with another inspiration for me: to form a track club for disabled runners.

By November 1, 1992, that club had been churning out the miles for 10 years and as many New York City Marathons.

Back in 1983, six Achilles runners had gathered at the starting line. The next year it was 13. Now it had grown to 148 who came not just from the United States, but from 15 foreign countries as well.

I'm not thinking about that now. There are too many things to do to spend time reflecting on where we came from or what we've accomplished. The runners are thinking about the challenge ahead. I have to worry about getting them to the starting line and making sure they have the support they need to finish something they've been training all year to do.

Marathon Sunday starts for me around 4 a.m. Like almost everyone involved with the marathon, I don't get much sleep the night before. We'd all like to, but it's just not possible. The adrenaline is pumping too fast to let anyone sleep much. Besides, many racers, including the 12,000 from foreign countries, spend the night in Manhattan, and a Saturday night in Manhattan, even marathon eve, is full of too many attractions to waste one's time on sleep. It's no different for disabled runners than for the able-bodied. Anyone with any experience gets plenty of sleep two nights before the race. It will be enough to carry them through until the night after the race, when sleep comes as easily as it ever will. So they stay out late and get up early. Marathon Sunday is probably the only morning of the year in which the majority of the guests in many Manhattan hotels are up and about at 4 a.m. On any other Sunday, anyone up that early is just coming in. This Sunday, they're going out.

Over at the West Side YMCA, on 63rd Street just off Central Park West, the scene is the same as at the hotels; only there, it is played out in communal bathrooms. I've been putting Achilles runners up at the West Side Y for years. Achilles is picking up the tab for about 80 runners this year and providing a per diem expense allowance of $20 per day per runner for a week. That accounts for the biggest chunk of our $40,000 race budget. For Achilles, that's a lot of money, and so we stay at the Y, where the bathrooms are down the hall and the rates are low.

In the early morning, the Achilles runners must present quite a surprise to any regular guests who go out in the halls. Doors are opening and people are emerging, some with guide dogs, some on crutches, some with artificial legs, others in wheelchairs. All are converging on the bathrooms in a babble of a dozen tongues. And the question probably arises in the mind of the regular guest: "What do I say?" It's amazing how many people can't figure out that what you say is: "Good morning." If you want to add, "Good luck in the race," go right ahead.

Once they're awake and dressed, the runners join the thousands making their way to the New York City Public Library at 42nd Street and Fifth Avenue to catch a bus to the start. Before boarding a bus, most Achilles runners rendezvous with their volunteers on the library steps. These volunteers are the unsung heroes of Achilles. Normally, we have two for each athlete. They help clear the way, get water and food along the route, provide companionship and encouragement, guide blind runners by means of a cord that both volunteer and athlete hold, and, most important, help set the pace.

Pacing is critical in a marathon. After a year of training, athletes get to the starting line gushing energy and enthusiasm. They feel as if they can run forever, and when the gun goes off, the natural urge is to take it out fast. But the marathon is dangerous to anyone, disabled or not, who expends too much energy too early. Whether it takes you two hours and 10 minutes or 22 hours, the last miles are tough. If you don't have enough in reserve, they're sheer agony. So the volunteers have to know what pace to keep to get their athletes in at their targeted times, and they have to rein the runners in early so they'll be able to finish and experience the rush of having that New York City Marathon medal hung around their necks at the finish line.

For the more than 29,000 regular entries in the marathon, the race starts at 10:47 a.m. The faster Achilles athletes set off at that time, also. But for some Achilles runners, the race starts sooner—and ends later. In some cases, a lot later. For that reason, we have three starts. The first is around 6:15 a.m., 4.5 hours before the official start. The second group goes off 2.5 hours later. The rest leave with the main body of runners.

My first job of the morning, after making sure everyone has their numbers and volunteers, is to get that first group off on time. The start is announced for 6 a.m., but I don't plan for it to go off until 6:15, and today that's how it works. One of our longtime coaches, Patti Parmalee, calls the roll and leads stretching exercises for the 15 early starters. When it's time to get to the starting line, city policemen stop outbound traffic on the bridge and a motley parade of runners and volunteers, bundled up against the cold, crosses eight or 10 lanes of toll plaza to get to the New York–bound lanes. A non-runner might think that they're incredibly cheerful for people who face a minimum of eight hours of hard work. But that's the bottom line on why we do this crazy thing. It's fun. It's a dream; a fantasy coming true.

It's also one of my only personal running rules. Don't worry about what running's going to do for you or think you have to do it at a certain speed. Do it because it's a great adventure; because it's fun.

At the same time, all that good cheer masks sheer terror, especially for a first-time marathoner. If you've never run one before, the anticipation is not half the fun. It's not like waiting to get on the roller coaster where you think about the fun. All you can think about—and wonder about—is just how much is this thing going to hurt, and can I do it? What happens if I get too tired? What happens if I get cramps? What happens if I get diarrhea? There's nothing wrong with all these questions and doubts. If it weren't that way, it wouldn't be a proper quest.

Among the 15 runners who are starting in the first group is Zoe Koplowitz. Zoe has multiple sclerosis (MS)—a progressive disease that attacks the nervous system—and needs two crutches to help her walk. For years, people with MS were told not to attempt strenuous exercise. Zoe has ignored that advice, just as has Jimmy Huega, a former Olympic skier who also has MS. When Zoe came to Achilles and said she wanted to run, we welcomed her. This year, she's setting out on her fifth marathon. Last year, she needed more than 23 hours to finish. This year, it will probably be 24. What she does is as incredible as the feats of the world's fastest runners. If you doubt that, try running for 24 hours, because that's what she does. I like to joke with her. I tell her the run will probably take all day.

Another of the early starters is Sister Mary Gladys, a

cheerful, gray-haired nun. Her T-shirt, which bears the inscription, "Cardiac Runner," says it all. She has angina and will need some eight hours to finish the marathon. That may be a world record for women with angina. She's a little worried this morning. Last December, she had foot surgery and lately her foot's been acting up. But she cut some padding for the area that's sore and is determined to go on. Then there's Dan Winchester, one of our first members. Dan—Doctor Dan, actually, as he has a PhD—has cerebral palsy and uses a wheelchair. Because his limbs are permanently contracted, he can't move his arms to push his wheelchair, so he kicks the chair backwards with his feet. It gets the job done. Several years ago, when he joined us, he could, with great effort, propel himself a couple of blocks. Now he can not only get around town, he can comfortably complete a marathon.

Another early starter is Rosalie Ames, who's in her 60s. Ten years ago, she was running with knees so arthritic she was told they would have to be replaced. The doctors told her to keep walking until she couldn't move anymore. She did, and a strange thing happened—at least the doctors found it to be strange. Instead of her getting worse, her arthritic pain subsided. I'm convinced the exercise is responsible. So is Rosalie, and today she's going to get a big dose of exercise.

Patti Parmalee gives the Achilles group one last pep talk before sending them off. She makes sure they know the importance of taking in enough fluids and that they have our emergency telephone number to call if they have any difficulties along the way. She also talks about the importance of pacing. By the time the blast of an airhorn pierces the early morning grayness, they're as cranked as they can be.

Then they're gone in a flurry of cheers and smiles, and I retreat to my station wagon to warm up. Patricia Dorff, our coach and newspaper editor, is there, along with Floyges Belgrave, a wonderful woman from Trinidad who is partially blind and will be starting her second New York City Marathon in a couple of hours. I have the car running to get the heat up, but Patti Parmalee bangs on the window and asks me to cut the engine. She says the exhaust fumes aren't good for the growing number of runners and volunteers in the staging area. I cut the engine, but think that this is a reaction that only a dedicated runner like Patti, who is world-class, could have. The staging area is right next to the toll plaza and vehicles are all over, spewing far more fumes than my station wagon. Add in the unending procession of buses and the thick New York air and it's hard to figure how one more car can make a difference. But that doesn't matter to a true runner. Smoke is smoke and you attack it anywhere and any way you can.

It gets kind of funny at times, in terms of what kind of behavior runners will tolerate. Before a big race, for instance, everyone has to go to the bathroom, sometimes more than once, as bowels get nervous. So you have this huge outdoor urinal at Fort Wadsworth, with hundreds of men at a time letting it hang out in broad daylight. Then you have people squatting behind the thin cover of shrubs because the porta-johns have long lines in front of them. And that's okay. But let one person get spotted sneaking a cigarette in the bushes— yes, some people actually smoke and run marathons—and he or she will not escape without an outraged lecture and nasty stares. Personally, I don't care what people do in the bushes. If they want to smoke, fine. I just want them to run, and, most of the time, once they start running regularly, they'll give up cigarettes without a lecture. Even if they don't quit, they'll be healthier for running.

I'm convinced that running can do more for the disabled than modern medicine yet knows. That's one reason I'm delighted to find an old friend, Jen Clemente, at the staging area. Jen's been volunteering for four years, but I hadn't expected to see her this year. She's studying to be a physician and had just spent the summer on a medical research project in San Francisco. I invite her into the car and she tells me she flew back to New York just to volunteer for the marathon.

"Volunteering for Achilles is my favorite thing to do all year," she tells a reporter who's joined us in the car. "When I run on my own, I always find a way to look negatively on it. Like I'm not running fast enough, or not meeting my goals. It's stressful. But when I volunteer, I'm doing it for someone who needs my help and everything is a positive."

The first year she volunteered to run the marathon, Jennifer ran with Matt Densen, a blind runner. Without having to worry about her own time, she and Matt ran a 3:52 marathon—more than a half-hour better than her previous fastest time. Since then, she's come with us to volunteer in Moscow and Poland. Today, she'll be running with a Polish runner who's missing an arm, so she'll probably get to run another fast race.

The research project she's working on at Stanford is a study of the effects of weight training on bone mass. I told her before she started that she would find that running builds bone mass better than weight lifting. I've had pain in my knee, which was diagnosed as arthritis in 1977. I have less pain now. I've been trying to convince people in the medical profession to research the relationship between running and arthritic pain, but haven't had a lot of luck. I mentioned it yesterday morning in a speech before the American Medical Joggers Association, but do not expect any feedback. Jen is moving in that direction and when she becomes a doctor, she'll almost certainly do more research.

She puts it as "if" she becomes a doctor. She confesses that the attitude she's encountered in med school is not encouraging. "A lot of my classmates are interested in surgery and they study all the time so that they're out of touch with people."

She'll make a great doctor and I tell her that. I hope she sticks it out. We need more people like her.

By 7 a.m., Patti Parmalee is leading the next group in exercises and the staging area is getting crowded. A contingent of eight Achilles runners from South Africa—the first official delegation from that country—has arrived and I call them over to the car to listen to a radio interview I taped with them earlier in the week. It was with Joe Cruickshank on a show called "New York Works." Explaining why they came to New York to freeze, one South African volunteer says, "We felt it would be a lot more fun running with new people from America rather than with the same old blokes we always run with."

I leave the South Africans to listen to the rest of the interview and go back outside to pass out windbreakers and do some cheerleading. There are dozens of small but important chores to attend to. Some runners and volunteers have either forgotten their race numbers or didn't receive them. I supply them with extras I have in the car. I also hand out safety pins to attach numbers to shirts and tubes of Vaseline which runners use to prevent chafing. A few runners can't find their volunteers and vice versa, and others don't know what to do with the equipment bags they brought to the starting line. I help pass out hot coffee. Various radio reporters keep stopping by for interviews. As I tend to these chores, I keep an eye out for old friends.

I see that Lois Schieffelin has arrived. Lois is 81 years old and will once again be the oldest woman in the marathon. She's wearing a red sweat suit that nicely matches her flaming red hair. Across the front of the shirt is printed "Big Red," her nom de track. When someone asks her why she's in Achilles, she laughs and says, "My age is my disability." Although she has arthritis, she started running when she was 75, and in her first New York City Marathon she ran with her son and her grandson. They've repeated that trifecta in following years. Last year, she finished in 6:32, a personal best for her at the tender age of 80. When somebody tells her she's sure to win her age group, she quips, "There aren't any people my age," thus echoing Casey Stengel's famous line of two decades ago: "Most of the people my age are dead."

Lois says this will be her last marathon. She said the same thing last year.

A little after 8 a.m., there's a stir of excitement in the staging area as Fred Lebow, the founder of the New York City Marathon and one of the most famous runners in the world, stops by to say hello. Fred has run dozens of marathons all over the world, but until this year he had not run once in his own marathon through the five boroughs. He had always been too busy organizing the race and making sure everything went well. Two years ago he was diagnosed with brain cancer and given six months to live.

But he cheated the odds.

In 1991, when he was too weak to run the race, the marathon was dedicated to him. This year, he worked hard and decided that he would run for the first time the race he created. Grete Waitz, the great Norwegian runner who has won New York a record nine times, asked to run with him. And together, Fred and Grete have been the story of this year's race.

As the Achilles runners see him, shouts go up. "Hey, Fred!" "Yeah, Fred!"

He passes through quickly, shaking hands, bestowing an encouraging word here and there, and then he's gone through the gates of Fort Wadsworth. It's not a long visit by any means, but it's a landmark. Fred himself admitted before the race that in prior years he was always so consumed with managing the event that he was barely civil. His passion for running had also estranged him from a large family of brothers and sisters, nephews and nieces. Now, after his battle with cancer, he realizes what he had been doing. For the first time in years, he got together with his family, and this year all of them will be waiting for him at the finish line.

Instead of brushing distractedly past people at the start, this year he mingles with them. For the runners and for him, these are special moments. Fred and I have a special relationship that stretches back 16 years. As a board member of the New York Road Runners Club, I am one of his bosses. He, in turn, is one of my bosses as a board member of Achilles.

By 8:20, the crowd in the staging area is getting antsy. People are hopping, jogging in place, rocking back and forth in wheelchairs. I'm not running today, yet I'm pacing up and down like an expectant father. Finally, at 8:30, Patti bellows into her electric bullhorn: "Achilles Track Club! Move it out!"

They don't need any more encouragement than that. At Patti's order, almost 200 people start across the outbound lanes of the toll plaza to the starting line. About a third of the crowd are Achilles runners. The rest are volunteers. Most of the volunteers will run with the athletes. The remainder act as marshals at the start and then patrol the course, performing whatever duties are needed. Most often, that involves taking over from a tired volunteer guide.

I'm particularly proud this year to have Cyril Charles working as a volunteer marshal. A native of Trinidad, Cyril joined us several years ago. He was blind. After he ran the marathon, we arranged for a cornea transplant operation that restored his sight. He came back the next year to run with a blind runner as a sighted guide. He now lives in New York and continues to work with and for Achilles. Other volunteers include Norman Barham, a partner with the

Insurance Brokerage firm of Johnson & Higgins; Norman
Friedman, a businessman who while in his late 60s ran a
three hour, 45 minute marathon; George Miles, the Chief
Operating Officer of New York City's Public Broadcasting
System station, Channel 13; after having had a great
experience last year, he joined the Board of Advisors of
Achilles; and Richard Stopel, president of New York Outward
Bound. Achilles and Outward Bound have jointly conducted
a number of runs and initiatives. I am working with Richard
to develop projects which integrate disabled people into
Outward Bound initiatives. Like so many of our volunteers,
they keep coming back year after year, finding that they have
as much fun doing the marathon as the Achilles athletes do.

By some miracle, as the runners spread out across the
starting line and Patti Parmalee gives her pre-race lecture
about pacing, hydration, and emergency phone numbers,
the sun finally breaks through the murk. Suddenly, New
Yorkers are reminded again why they live in this city: Because
on a Sunday morning, with the sun out and the air crisp, it
truly is spectacular from up here on the bridge. From a mile
up the road, at the crest of the bridge, the runners will be
able to see all of New York's vast bay to the left and the
open ocean to the right. The water is actually blue and it's
dotted with ocean-going ships and barges. Ahead is the
entire city, from Brooklyn at the far end of the bridge to the
towers of Manhattan. You don't get this view from a car
whizzing by in traffic; not like this, where you can suck it
all in, roll it around, taste it. It's still cold, but you don't
notice it any more now that the grimy dawn has surrendered
to the sun.

The runners who are listening to Patti's spiel are as motley
as the early group. Bunched in the center of the line is a
group of wheelchairs, including Diego Alcantara of the
Dominican Republic. Diego does not have a racing
wheelchair, so he's going to do the race sitting on a
homemade skateboard. It's nothing more than a few planks
about 18 inches wide that he's nailed together and mounted
on two sets of skate wheels. He propels himself by pushing
with gloved hands against the street—backwards uphill,
forwards downhill and on the level. After Diego finishes the
race, Carl Landegger—a volunteer and member of the board

of advisors of Achilles—will offer to buy him a racing wheelchair.

Some ask why wait until after the race. Why not get him the chair before? The answer is that the chair—or a cornea transplant or new prosthetic limb—is the reward. There are some people who, if they knew they were going to get a chair or limb or whatever, might not train as hard and might not finish the race. And I want them to finish, so it's race first, collect your reward later. Of course, if they are forced to drop out, I'm not going to say, "Tough luck. Try again next year."

It just means more this way because they've earned it.

I believe strongly in that. If I see any of New York's many disabled panhandlers working the lines of rush-hour traffic in a wheelchair, I never give them money, and I don't beg for money for Achilles. To illustrate the point, I joke about getting cups and having the Achilles runners collect money from the two million people watching the marathon on the sidelines. This would perpetuate the belief that the team is "handicapped."

One reason that the disabled don't like being called "handicapped" is because of the belief that the word comes from the old practice of disabled beggars holding out their caps in their hands to collect alms—"hand-in-cap." The origin of the word is actually somewhat different. It comes from horse racing, where odds were drawn from a cap. But the idea lingers that the disabled have their hats or hands out looking for help. The truth is that a disability is not necessarily a handicap. We who have disabilities can do most anything anyone else can, be it running a corporation or running a marathon. We don't need alms. We just need what anyone else does—opportunity.

Among the camera crews covering the marathon start is one from Japan, which has been filming a two-part story about Luis Flores, an athlete with cerebral palsy who will finish the race in 7:45. Along the way, the Japanese television crew will turn him into another Rocky, which is appropriate, since it's exactly the way many runners feel when they defeat the marathon.

The athletes include teams from 15 foreign countries.

Ketil Moe, founder of the Achilles Track Club of Norway, has brought a team of seven runners. Moe himself has cystic fibrosis, a disease of the lungs. He spends two hours every morning after he wakes up coughing up the phlegm that accumulates during the night. But he has done several marathons and trains regularly. He'll break 6:30 today. On Tuesday morning I'll be joining him and the Norwegian team when they meet with Boutros-Ghali, United Nations secretary general, to talk about international programs for the disabled. Also on the starting line are the South Africans, including three blind runners, one of whom is being guided by Bruce Fordyce, a runner famous in South Africa for winning that country's Comrades Ultramarathon a record nine times.

Three former Soviet Republics have sent teams: the Ukraine, Georgia, and Russia, which in turn has sent three teams, including one from Svedlosk, the hometown of Russian President Boris Yeltsin. One blind runner is President Yeltsin's masseur. There are two runners from Mongolia, five from Bulgaria, 11 from Poland, four from Switzerland, six from Trinidad and Tobago, seven from the Dominican Republic, and single runners from England, Mexico, Brazil, and France. Peti McReynolds from Harlem, who is autistic, is ready, as are Dave Gribbin and Jill Schreiber, who are recovering from severe brain injuries. I see Gary Blinn, who's running with his second heart and Al Reyes, who has had quadruple heart bypass surgery.

The tradition of starting disabled athletes earlier than the other runners began with my first marathon in 1976. Knowing that I would need more than seven hours to finish and that the majority of the runners in the race would complete it in about four hours, we decided that I should start early. These days, with thousands of fun-runners in the race, it's not quite as lonely seven hours after beginning, but the early start remains so that the Achilles runners can enter Manhattan and finish the race before the huge crowds lining the streets leave. The crowds cheer lustily throughout the race, and get especially enthusiastic when an Achilles runner goes past. Most people never get to hear the roar and applause of the crowd, and when they do, it's an experience they'll always remember.

About five minutes before the early start, Patti sends those volunteers who are with wheelchair athletes off across the bridge. This is a little secret about running with a wheelchair athlete: On the ascent that makes up the first half of the Verrazano Narrows Bridge, the wheelchairs struggle along slowly. But on the downslope, they can start whizzing along at speeds up to 40 miles per hour. So if you're running with a chair, you'd better get to the bottom of the hill before your athlete starts that downslope or you're going to spend a lot of time trying to catch up.

At 8:47, just on schedule, the airhorn is blown and the runners thunder off across the bridge. I do some more radio and television interviews. Then, about 45 minutes after they've left, I get in my car and follow the route, slowing down to shout advice or encouragement. The advice is usually to slow down. The encouragement is, "Have a good one." The streets of Brooklyn are pretty much empty of spectators at this hour and police are still letting cars through, so I also have to remind some runners to hug the curb. I do notice one early spectator, though, sitting near the curb just before Mile Seven at Fourth Avenue and 17th Street in Brooklyn. It's Tex, who was born with no legs and only one arm after her mother took a drug called thalidomide, which caused many birth defects some 30 years ago. Tex has done a marathon with Achilles, but today she's just cheering. I stop to chat and think about how small New York can seem at times like this.

Early on, it's quiet going. The bands that set up at various places along the route to serenade the runners haven't started playing yet, and the volunteers at the water stations are just getting organized. So the first three hours and 10 or 12 miles are fairly serene. Then, usually just past the halfway point at the 59th Street Bridge, the main body of runners will catch the lead Achilles runners. From then on, the race will be run in an ocean of noise and color and people.

Except for a few elite runners and wheelchair racers, who will go off with the main group of runners at 10:47, when you talk Achilles, you're not talking speed burners. These are ordinary Joes and Janes from all walks of life. Running cuts across a lot of class lines, and Achilles cuts across more than most. We have more minority representation than the marathon as a whole. We probably also have a greater percentage of poor runners. But we don't care what sex or age or color or religion you are. We don't care how many arms and legs you have. The disabled are such a minority in society that the tie among Achilles runners is stronger than any ethnic or class distinctions. I can identify more with a Russian amputee runner than his countrymen can, and vice versa.

We're all here for the same reason. The point of life is to do something. For too many years, the disabled were discouraged from being physically active. The fact that in 1976 I was the first amputee ever to run a marathon is proof enough of that. That's not to say the disabled did nothing. Wheelchair basketball's been around a long time. Before I started running I played tennis, skied, beat a golf ball around the course, played softball, and did whatever else came up. But for many disabled people, these are not viable activities. They lack either the time or the money or the opportunity. Running, though, is there for everyone. You don't need a court. You just need a strip of pavement.

The best thing about running is that it gives everyone a chance at success. No matter how slow or out of shape you are, you can get out and do what you can. Do it regularly and you'll soon be getting better. The learning curve is very long, and without extraordinary effort you can continue to improve for many years before you reach a plateau. Many Achilles runners have never experienced anything like that. For them, as for most people, day-to-day life doesn't necessarily reward one for effort. Anyone knows you can put in the hardest day's work possible and your boss may still yell at you or the contract may still fall through. If you're a doctor, you can perform a technically stunning surgery and still lose the patient. If a lawyer, you can present a perfect case and still lose the trial. That's what life as an adult is like. That's also what life is like in sports other than running. But in running, there is a greater degree of fairness. No matter how much you want to play major-league baseball or scratch golf, if you don't have the skill, you can't do it. But almost any able-bodied person who puts the same effort into running can run a successful marathon.

Running takes you back to your childhood, when the

more you worked, the better you got; there was a direct connection between effort and results. In the everyday run of things, life isn't fair. In running, life is fair. You put this in and you get that out. It's no coincidence that so many of the people who run in the New York City Marathon are doctors, lawyers, and teachers—people who don't always get that kind of return in their jobs.

For the disabled, life can be particularly unfair. For many, joining Achilles gives them the first opportunity to get full return on their investment of effort. The club is full of people who first put in their training and finished their marathon, and then realized that if they could do a marathon, they could do something else in life. Success breeds confidence. It raises your level of aspiration. So it's very important that a disabled person have a good chance of finishing any marathon he or she chooses to run. Rarely does anyone who has not run a half-marathon in the months leading up to the race run under the Achilles banner. I also try to personally watch as many runners as I can during a workout so I can judge their fitness. I want them to succeed, not fail. And most of them succeed.

But I can't dawdle now and take in much of the scene. I'm due back at the Tavern on the Green to go on ABC's live television broadcast with Jim McKay to talk about Achilles. I could live very nicely without ever doing another interview, but if Achilles is to grow, I have to get the word out. People tell me I'm fairly good at the public relations angle, so I take that on as my primary job and leave the organizing to Patti Parmalee, the coaching to Helene Hines, and the foreign chapters to Leszek Sibilski, a Polish sports journalist who got us going overseas and is one of Achilles' finest friends.

Besides, I've done all I can for the runners. I made sure they trained enough to be able to do the race, and then I sent them off on their quest. The rest is up to them.

*"Be ashamed to die until you have won
some victory for humanity."*
—Horace Mann

I believe in probabilities, not fate. If you'd asked me on
the last weekend in May 1965, I'd have told you the same
thing. And the probability is that each of us, in our lives,
will face several situations which can either end our lives or
change them, sometimes drastically.

In a lot of ways, when my one-in-a-billion shot struck, I
was lucky. Better what really happened to me than what
almost happened in high school. Then, I had been on the
track team at Horace Mann High School in New York.
Sprinting and weight events were my preference. On this
particular afternoon I was lounging on a stack of planks
that were to be used for a wooden track at Riverdale Country
Day School, where we were practicing before the track meet.
Elsewhere on the field, other members of the team were
warming up, but I wasn't paying attention to them. So,
when one of the javelin throwers got off the greatest toss of
his life, I didn't know a thing about it. Then, a needle-
sharp, steel-tipped missile came whizzing out of the sky and
embedded itself with a quivering and emphatic THUNK! in
the wooden plank directly between my splayed-out thighs.
Another six inches and he would have nailed me in a man's
most delicate piece of anatomy. Another two feet and I
would have been dead. Because of incidents like that, the
javelin would eventually be banned from most high school
track programs. At the time, all I could do was breathe a
heavy sigh of relief. It was a non-event.

So, when I lost my leg a half-decade later, it really wasn't
so bad. Better a leg than my life.

It happened on Sunday, May 30, the day before Memorial

Day, at a service area on the New Jersey Turnpike down by
Cherry Hill. It was a terrific spring day, the kind television
weather persons like to take personal responsibility for. It
was crisp and clear, one of those days when you can't help
thinking how great it is to be alive.

It was great to be alive. I was 24 1/2 years old and a
doctoral candidate at New York University. While completing
my written exams, I had a part-time job driving a delivery
truck for a beverage company. Made good money, too—
around $300 a week. In 1965, when the average factory
wage was just over $100 a week and a slice of pizza cost 15
cents, that was junior executive pay. Besides all of that,
earlier in the month, I had gotten engaged.

The engagement was the reason for going to South Jersey.
My fiancée, Rosalie, who was three years older than I, had
friends in Philadelphia whom I hadn't met. With the
wedding approaching in a few months, we were going to
take advantage of the long weekend to meet them. We
started early. I picked her up in my car and we stopped to
get coffee and donuts in the upper 40s on the East Side of
Manhattan. From there we cut across town on 45th Street
and took the Lincoln Tunnel to the Jersey Turnpike. The
heavy traffic on the Memorial Day Weekend occurs on Friday
afternoon and evening and Saturday morning. That's when
New Jersey's superhighways turn into parking lots as people
head south for the Jersey Shore. By Sunday morning the
roads are practically deserted, so we made good time on the
turnpike, better than I had expected. Because of this, when
we got close to our destination, we decided to stop at a
service plaza to let Rosalie go to the restroom while I got gas
so that we wouldn't have to stop on the way home.

Rosalie got out and went into the service building. I
pulled up to the gas pumps and told the attendant to fill
the tank up. While he did, I got out of the car to stretch my
legs and drink in the wonderful day. I wandered behind the
car and was standing facing it while the attendant manned
the nozzle on the side of the car to my left. I took no notice
as a big, old Chrysler full of people pulled up to the pumps
behind me. Like Rosalie, some of the people in the Chrysler
wanted to go to the restroom, but the woman in the front
passenger seat couldn't open the door. The driver, an older

gentleman, leaned over to open the door. As he did, the car started to roll forward. I wasn't aware of any of this, but I soon would be. Sensing that the car was rolling toward me, the man must have panicked. He jammed his foot on the pedal, only he missed the brake and hit the accelerator. The big pile of steel and chrome leaped forward, smashing into my legs and crushing them between the two bumpers. My head flew forward and I hit the trunk lid with my head, denting the trunk and cutting a gash in my chin. He hit me so hard that he drove me and my car—which was in park—some 10 feet forward. As I flew past, I clipped the gas station attendant with my arm and decked him.

We've all heard people say, "It happened so fast, I didn't know what hit me," and that's exactly what it was like. I didn't feel any pain. My body went into shock. My brain, meanwhile, tried to make sense of the sudden and enormous input of data by relating it to things that had happened before. Of course, nothing like this had ever happened to me before, so my first reaction to the impact was the same as if someone had come up behind me unseen and clapped me hard on the back.

While I was trying to restore mental order, the Chrysler still hadn't finished with me. There is a little-known fact about rear-end collisions: When a car hits you from behind and knocks you forward, it stops momentarily. Then, if the accelerator is still depressed, it leaps ahead again and gives you a second shot. That's what happened now, as the car hit me again, and then again a third time.

By then, I knew I'd been hit and my only thought was, "Okay, you've made your point. Why are you hitting me again? Enough already."

By the third shot, the man driving the Chrysler had finally found the correct pedal and stopped the carnage. A lot of women in the car that hit me were screaming. The Chrysler's radiator, broken from the impact, hissed as I sat and then lay on the pavement. I knew that my leg was broken, but even though the bone was sticking out of the leg of my pants, I didn't realize how badly I was hurt. I knew I had to get back to my beverage route Tuesday and I figured I'd probably miss work. I figured they'd take me to the hospital, put my leg in a cast, and I'd be able to go—in a wheelchair or on crutches—to the bachelor party my friends were throwing for another friend later in the week.

Somebody called an ambulance, and at some point my fiancée came out of the service building and saw me lying there in a large pool of blood. She was stunned.

The ambulance arrived quickly, although at a time like that you're almost in suspended animation and it's impossible to tell how long anything lasts. As they were packing me on a stretcher, I asked one of the attendants whether this sort of thing happened often. Somehow, it occurred to me that this was a volunteer ambulance squad and, being a New Yorker, I thought that maybe I should tip them for such quick service. After all, in New York, everyone expects a tip for everything. So I offered one of the guys $10 and asked if that was enough. He said it wasn't necessary and then I felt guilty for embarrassing him. That's about all I remember. I passed out in the ambulance, and by the time I got to the hospital in Camden, New Jersey, I didn't have a pulse. They got the pulse back, gave me blood, and rushed me into surgery to try to save my right leg, in which the veins were ripped and bones were shattered. I woke up in intensive care. My left arm was in a cast from having hit the gas station attendant. I realized through the fog that I wasn't going to be going to that bachelor party. I had been in the hospital only a day or two when they realized that the leg wasn't getting an adequate blood supply and they scheduled another surgery to transplant veins into the leg.

I received a letter from my sister, Joanne. It stated that she was shocked, but as a psychology major, she realized that these things were often greatly exaggerated. That was a mistake. When she visited, we laughed about the letter.

It was two or three days later that they decided they had to operate again immediately. You'll have to forgive me for not knowing exactly how much time had passed. I was barely there. The only way I knew I was going into surgery was that they put me on a gurney and started wheeling me down the hall. I remember they had trouble getting me through the elevator doors.

Then, suddenly, I had this feeling like I was going ZOOP! down a hole. It was like Alice in Wonderland and the rabbit hole. It only lasted a few seconds, but I was definitely going somewhere. Where I was going was out of this life. My heart had stopped, and as I fell down the rabbit hole, the doctors were beating on my chest and zapping me with the defibrillators. I guess I knew I was dying because I later reflected that it was like John Keats' "Ode on a Grecian Urn." In the poem, Keats contemplates an urn on which the people depicted are frozen in a moment of life and time. I thought that I would be frozen forever on this gurney, being wheeled into an operating room. I suspect that my experience of going down a hole, which others in near-death situations have also experienced, is where stories of heaven and hell come from. Others report seeing bright lights and god-like figures at the other end of the tunnel. I never got that far, because the doctors did their work well and got my heart beating again. Later, they told me it was only because I was in good physical condition that I didn't die. If I had been 40 years old, they said, I probably wouldn't have made it. I remember that when they said that, 40 seemed impossibly ancient. I also wondered whether, since I had been legally, although briefly, dead, I could get a life-insurance check from my insurance company.

They did the vein transplant and moved me back to intensive care. The two big problems with the leg were blood supply and infection that could turn to gangrene. If that happened, I could lose all or part of the leg. However, I never believed I would lose the leg. I figured maybe I'd lose a couple of toes at worst, and I could deal with that. It was upsetting in the abstract, but I was more concerned about losing my life, and when you look at it that way, a couple of toes aren't that big a deal. My mother was much more upset about that prospect than I. She and my father had been in Cherry Hill on vacation when I had the accident, so they had been able to get to the hospital quickly. They also took care of picking up my car and doing all the other things that have to be done when your life stops but the world goes on. My mother got upset about the toes. "What's going to happen?" she wanted to know. "You'll be on the beach and you'll have only two or three toes."

When they put me back in intensive care, they laid me on my stomach. The nature of the injury made it impossible for me to lie on my back. I had never been able to sleep on my stomach, and the position was extremely uncomfortable. On top of that, there was the pain from the gangrene that was starting to attack my leg. There's no way to describe that terrible, awful pain that the drugs they gave me could dull but not suppress.

My heart pounded at a frightful pace. Now, you can take a pounding pulse if you know it's because you brought it to that rate through exercise and it will subside. But this wouldn't slow down. It wouldn't stop. Hour after hour, my heart raced crazily in my chest. I was running a temperature of about 103 from the infection and was bathed in sweat. Because of the elevated heartbeat and the fever, I couldn't breath normally, but lay there panting like a sick puppy. And through the fog of the drugs, I imagined that I was hearing music that my heart was beating to. I imagined that the music—terrible music—was coming from a bar downstairs, below the intensive care unit. I told the nurses to call the bar and tell them to turn down the music, but it didn't do any good. Finally, because I was lying on my stomach with my head in a pillow, I couldn't see anything, I couldn't read, couldn't watch television, and had an awful time trying to sleep. It was like lying in bed with a terrible, terrible headache.

Under such conditions, your mind starts playing strange games. The only thing you can really do is think, and, because of the Demerol I was being given, I was also constantly stoned. The Demerol didn't make the pain disappear, but it made it tolerable. I became obsessed with the drug. I would get a shot and feel good and then, several hours later, I would start to feel bad again. I figured out that I was getting it every four hours, so, after three hours, I'd start asking the nurses if it was time for my next shot.

I don't think I was a very good patient, but they just ignored me or told me it would be soon. I couldn't get them to give it to me early. Sometimes I would wait until a new shift came on and tell them that the previous shift had forgotten to give me my medicine. That's when I first realized what drug addiction is.

Under those conditions, you start thinking things you've never thought before; stretching the limits of your imagination. Sometimes, it stretched into hallucinations.

For example, I thought that the way they air-conditioned the room was to move the bed back and forth. I really thought they were doing that. Another time, someone asked me if I knew where I was. I said, of course I did. I was in a museum exhibit in Montreal. I had tripped and fallen in the exhibit and I couldn't get out. As far as I was concerned, that was the absolute truth. Thinking about it later, I realized that if someone thinks he's Napoleon, to him, it's a fact, just as being trapped in that museum exhibit was a fact for me. It was so real that I pulled out my catheter trying to escape. Another time, I believed that the staff were occupying the patients by playing movies on the insides of our eyelids, so we could be entertained while our eyes were closed. I remember "watching" one movie in which people were strolling through the fields following Eddie Cantor. I requested that I be moved to another room where a different movie was reportedly being played. My parents wanted to have me checked for brain injury.

Because of the extreme discomfort—as the doctors liked to say instead of using the word "pain"—I suggested that the doctors put me in a coma until it was all over.

Lying there, I used to think of a quote that I had seen every day in high school. Horace Mann, after whom the school had been named, was an influential American educator whose career spanned the first half of the 19th century. During his final year of life—1859—he gave the commencement address at Antioch College and delivered the line for which he is best remembered. "Be ashamed to die," he told the graduates, "until you have won some victory for humanity." The quote was written under a huge portrait of Mann that hung in the hall outside the entrance to the school auditorium. We used to laugh about it, as students will.

Then, as I lay in bed, the words kept coming back to me. I can't die, I thought. I haven't won a victory for humanity yet.

Seven days after the accident, the doctors decided they would have to amputate my leg. It simply wasn't going to heal, and if the gangrene were allowed to advance, it would kill me. They told me what they wanted to do and asked me to sign the necessary releases to allow them to perform the amputation. I refused to sign. "I'd rather die than lose the leg," I insisted. They were just as insistent and kept telling me to sign. I knew that if I were going to sign anything, I had to read it first, but I couldn't see the writing on the papers because my vision was blurred from the drugs. Finally, I signed.

That's what they told me. I don't remember signing anything. I don't even remember being told that the leg might have to come off. After they took it off and I was more coherent, I asked them why they hadn't told me they were going to amputate. They said they had, and that I had signed for the operation. I have no reason to doubt it.

I was in such poor condition, they decided against giving me a general anesthetic, fearing that I might not wake up. Instead, they gave me a local anesthetic and a lot of other drugs. As they cut and sawed away at my leg above the knee, I dreamed that I was at a party of the sort I imagined they had in 16th-century England when Henry VIII was king. The doctors were the cooks and they were carving a roast for the guests—a rump roast that was me.

When I regained a portion of my senses in intensive care, I was lying on my back. My heart had stopped racing. The fever was going down, and someone had pulled the plug on that horrible music. Even if they had taken my leg off, I was grateful to be on my back.

But when I looked down, I saw I still had two legs. They told me they had taken it off, but I could feel the leg and see it. Actually, what I felt was the phantom sensation that most, if not all, amputees feel. And what I saw wasn't the leg, but a rope that they had attached to the end of the stump. The rope ran under the sheets and over a pulley at the end of the bed. This was to keep the stump straight. When the nurses removed the sheet to change the dressing on the stump, I could see that the leg really was gone. I thought of a scene in *All Quiet on the Western Front*, in which a soldier lost his leg. He screamed when it happened. In my case, loaded with drugs and finally relieved of the horrible pain, I was nonchalant.

I was out of the woods in the sense that I wasn't going to die. I didn't know that, though. In fact, now that I was in no danger of dying, I became convinced that I was headed for the Great Beyond. The reason I thought I was dying was the tremendous amount of drainage coming out of my stump. When they do an amputation like that, they leave the wound open. At least on my leg they did, because there wasn't enough skin to make a flap to cover the end. Later, they would do a graft and what's called a re-amputation to prepare the stump for a prosthetic leg. But for now it was open and draining a Niagara of fluids. I didn't think it was possible for me to get enough fluids to replace what was flowing out and so believed that I was bound to die.

Having just gotten engaged a month earlier, I wanted to be sure that when I died my fiancée got what money I had. My parents didn't approve of the engagement, and I knew that if I didn't have a will, Rosalie wouldn't get my inheritance. So I asked one of the nurses to write my will for me. She said they didn't have a secretary there right then, but they could do it the next day. She asked me to try to hold out until morning which was only 10 hours off. If I could do it, they would provide a secretary! It was like the joke about the cop who dragged a dead horse from Schemerhorn to Jay Street because he couldn't spell Schemerhorn for the report form. I guess this was my first encounter with bureaucracy. Of course, the next day I felt better, and I didn't bother to make out the will.

I was still in intensive care and would remain in Camden for another 11 days after the amputation. Although my right leg wouldn't be a problem again, my left leg was still in serious shape. It, too, had been severely broken at the thigh. When you have a break at that level, they put a cast onto the joint above the break and then one beyond that. So if you break your calf badly, you have a cast to your hip. I broke the thigh so I was in a cast up to my neck.

Now, although I was on my back, I still couldn't do much, and I started to learn what it means to be institutionalized. When you're in that situation, you can't do everything for yourself and have to rely on others who don't work on your schedule and who don't do things the way you do. You then have two choices: You can fight it, in which case you become a troublemaker and the nurses start ignoring you, or you can become docile like a herded animal. This is what happens to people who are institutionalized for long periods. I have seen men in veterans hospitals lined up quietly for hours waiting to get some medicine. The pills may have been some sort of sedative to keep everyone quiet, but it amazed me how patiently everyone stood in line and how no one complained. They had given up.

Most people will try to find a middle line where they don't become too much of a nuisance but still maintain some independence. You pick your battlegrounds. Mine turned out to be toilet paper. It may sound bizarre, but the way the nurse cleaned me after I used the bedpan became a very big thing to me. I couldn't wipe myself because of the cast. So this nurse—perhaps 22 years old—would do it for me. Only I was sure she wasn't being as thorough as I would have been. We would have scenes in which I'd demand to see the toilet paper to check the job she'd done and insist that she take another swipe. She would insist everything was fine and would get the heck out of there. It might have been funny to watch, but to me it was a major issue.

Another thing I became intrigued with was seeing my stump. They changed the dressing regularly and I would ask a nurse to hold up a mirror so I could see it. She resisted. She wasn't going to let me look. So I devised another way to check it out. The table on wheels that they rolled over the bed for meals had a mirror underneath for grooming. I managed to set the mirror in such a way that, when the nurse took off the old dressing, I could see the stump in the mirror. When I finally got to look, what I saw was the shank end of a beef round roast. The bone was in the middle and the red meat was around it. I didn't get sick or anything, but I never wanted to see it again. It was a long time after that before I could eat roast beef.

I was in the intensive care unit for 24 days. I couldn't leave the bed, even to see out of a window. I could see sky through the window, but nothing else. I imagined a lovely scene outside, with trees and flowers and fields. That became one of my entertainments. Another was to observe the other people in the unit. There was no television and I couldn't read, so that was all there was left. I think there were seven beds altogether, and most people were only in intensive care a couple of days, so dozens and dozens of people came through there during my stay. They were in for all sorts of injuries and illnesses. I remember one man who had been in a very bad auto accident. He had obviously been drunk, because he was still reeking of booze when he came in. I asked the doctor how he felt operating on someone who had put himself and others in a potentially fatal situation. The doctor didn't answer.

Many people come to intensive care and don't leave alive. There are heart attack victims who lie there hooked up to machines as families come in, crying. In my drugged state of mind, I watched these scenes as if they were movies and I would grade the performances of the sufferers and mourners as if they were actors and actresses. I'd think, "That was good, deserves an Academy Award." Or, "No, you're overacting now." And, "Why don't you try saying that line this way?" It sounds heartless, I know, but this was a different world, and, with the drugs I was getting, normal rules were suspended.

After a while, I was probably the healthiest sick person in the unit, and I wanted to talk more than anyone else. Even that was difficult. Most people were in no condition to talk and few could manage more than a couple of sentences. Besides, everyone else was just as goofy with medication as I was. There was one guy who came in who refused to eat some soup they were trying to feed him. He thought that the soup was water and from what he could see the water wasn't pure. There was something in it and he wasn't going to drink it. "Can I have it?" I asked. When he heard that, he decided he wanted it after all.

The doctors and nurses wouldn't tell you what happened to people who left the unit. I would see them wheel someone out and would ask what happened to him. "We took him to another room," they'd say, not finding it necessary to note that the "other room" was the morgue. Unless I asked specifically, "Did he die?" they wouldn't say. But a lot of the people who came through during my stay did die.

None of this made me think that much about fate or God. As I said before, I don't believe in fate. It's strictly a matter of probability that I got hit. I was raised a Jew, but I was never religious. It's not that I don't believe in God. I do. It's just that it always struck me as being somewhat dishonest or selfish to be saying all these prayers and going to synagogue so that God would see to it that I maybe got a better ticket to the big title fight. I know you pray to God to give thanks, but it never felt to me as though that's what I was doing. I had the feeling that I wasn't really giving thanks. I was hoping that, by giving thanks, I would persuade God to be nice to me next year. That seemed devious.

I think spending too much time in church can be terribly self-indulgent. It's as if you really enjoy the piano and play it for hours by yourself. It gives you a lot of pleasure, but helps no one. I feel it's the same with going to synagogue. If you go back to early Christianity and Christ, my feeling is he was more interested in our helping others and doing good deeds than he was in our spending a lot of time in church praying to God. My feeling is if it came down to spending two hours in church or two hours doing something for others—like taking care of people with AIDS—God would want you to help others. Think of it in terms of getting points. Some religious leaders want you to think that if you do certain things you earn points with God. Going to temple on the appropriate days is one of those things. If you don't do them, you lose points. Now one thing I believe is that, if there is a God, the last thing He wants people to do is get down on their knees and tell Him how great He is. I think He'd rather have you doing those good deeds, and if it comes down to going to temple on Saturday or helping people in an Achilles race that is taking place at the same time, He'd give you more points for helping people. And if you did go to temple, maybe it would be better if everyone spent the hour or two hours they were there doing something for the temple, even something as simple as stamping envelopes for a fund drive. In other words, if God does have an accounting system, as many believe, then He would give you more points for being active rather than passive. And helping others is more active—and less self-oriented—than praying.

Then there's the whole issue of which religion is the right one. I don't know how many religions there are in the world, but I know there are a lot. And they generally have two things in common. The first is that each thinks that theirs is the only true religion. So if you really think that the way to heaven is believing in the true religion, then you should be out there hedging your bets and spending extra time every day praying to several different Gods just to make sure you have the right one. Because what happens if you spend all your life praying to Christ and then die and find out that you should have been praying to the Buddha?

The other thing religions have in common is a Golden Rule—do unto others as you would have them do unto you—or some variation of that. So it would seem that it makes sense to worry more about that than about how many hours you spend in church.

But religion works different ways for different people. My mother-in-law was a very devout Catholic. As a girl, she wanted to be a nun, but when she asked to enter a convent, the Depression was going on and times were so tough that the religious order she applied to couldn't support new members. She was the oldest child in her family and the nuns told her that her mission wasn't to be a nun but to stay at home and take care of her younger sisters. That was what God wanted her to do. Like so many others who lived through the Depression, she went through a great many hardships in taking care of the family, but her belief that she was doing God's will made it possible for her to pull through. So, for her, religion was of great value and a source of much comfort. It works that way for many believers— maybe for most. It just doesn't work for me.

Even though I don't believe that God picks people to suffer broken backs and to lose legs, when something like that happens to you, the thought does occur to you that something other than probability is involved. You wonder whether this happened to you for a reason. I think it's natural. However, I don't think that God goes around punishing people who break His laws. One of our members, though, has considered the possibility that her accident was a punishment. She is Jewish and, instead of going to synagogue, she went to the beach one Saturday. As she was swimming, a wave caught her and threw her on her head, breaking her back and causing her to become a paraplegic. She has considered the possibility that God was punishing her for swimming on the Sabbath. I can't believe that. If God went around punishing people who break His laws, just about everyone in the world would be on crutches or in wheelchairs.

I recognize that there are things we don't understand. I

think it's somewhat like taking a dog on an elevator. The dog goes in and the doors close. When they open again, he's somewhere else. He has no idea how it happened because he can't understand the concept of an elevator. I'm sure there are many things that we humans also aren't wise enough to see. So even though I don't think there was any divine purpose in my losing my leg, I can't say for sure that there wasn't.

Whether there is or isn't divine purpose isn't relevant, though. What is important is what you do with your life afterwards. When I was in the hospital, I had that moment after the amputation when I felt that I was going to die and that it wasn't fair. I had looked at life as a franchise that you have for a certain number of years. During those years you can do whatever you want with the franchise. It's like being a president—you have four years to do your thing. Now, all of a sudden, someone was pulling in my franchise and I hadn't had a chance to do what I wanted. I hadn't accomplished anything meaningful. I had thought, like most young adults, that life would go on, if not forever, at least so long that the end wasn't remotely in sight. I thought that if I had known I had only 24 years, I would have done things differently. True, I had been a serious athlete; I had run my own business; I had nearly finished getting a doctorate. Considering my age, I had done a lot, but it was as if I had all this preparation—almost 20 years of school— and I hadn't yet done anything with it. It was like spending 12 years preparing for the Olympics and then not going. I wanted to see the world. I wanted to have children. I wanted to test my abilities. I felt as if I had been reading a biography only to find the pages in the last two-thirds of the book were not printed.

That's part of what I went through when I was preparing to die. The other part was thinking of the nice moments in life. In effect, I was writing a mental autobiography, assembling a mental photo album. I thought of my enjoyment of folk music and sang in my mind many of my favorite songs. I remembered the joy I had experienced in summer camp when throwing pots on a potters' wheel. I had had some success as a wrestler in high school and college, and I thought of a few favorite matches. I thought of the soft-drink delivery business I had run in college. It was ironic that, while I regretted I would never get to put my education to use, I also was relieved that I wouldn't have to go through the agony of getting that education again. No more tests, no more struggling to understand things. I was not what you'd call a good student. I had some sort of disability that made it very difficult for me to learn, so I didn't get good grades. And now at least I would be free of that frustration.

And then I found out I wasn't going to die, and it was like getting a second chance. I knew that I wouldn't waste it, because I now had an advantage many people my age didn't; I knew I was mortal and that life is finite. I estimated the life expectancy of a male my age was 73. At 24 1/2, I had used the first trimester of my life. If all went well, I had another two sections of the theoretical autobiography to complete. I would use the time wisely. I would grasp all the experiences possible. I would smell the roses. I wondered what I would be doing 24 years from now. I guessed that I would be running my own consulting business.

Although the crisis was past, I wasn't ready to go home and get on with life. Not by a long shot. I still had a long stay in intensive care ahead of me, and then months of healing and rehabilitation.

In late June, I was in good enough condition to be transferred to a hospital in New York. I was still in a body cast up to my neck and my stump had yet to be covered with a skin graft. As they prepared me for the trip, I asked to be wheeled over to the window so I could look outside. I had spent so much time imagining the lovely scene outside, I had to see it. You can guess the rest: instead of birds and trees and flowers, I saw a parking deck and some rooftops. Fantasies often surpass reality.

They drove me to New York in an ambulance, and it wasn't a relaxing ride. It would be some time before I could be comfortable in a car again. Every time another vehicle got close, I got very nervous. But what bothered me is that cars were passing us all the way up the Jersey Pike and here we were in the left lane in an emergency vehicle with the lights flashing! I thought they were incredibly stupid.

I should have gone straight to New York University Hospital, but an uncle encouraged my admission to the Rusk Institute. My uncle knew Dr. Howard Rusk, the founder of the institute and the man known as the father of rehabilitation medicine. I didn't really belong there yet. The institute is where you learn to walk again and get fitted with a prosthesis. I was still several months from getting out of the cast and still had to have my leg reamputated to fit an artificial leg. So I stayed at Rusk that time for only three days before being moved to New York University Hospital. Still, my brief stay at Rusk wasn't without its benefits. Dr. Rusk came to see me shortly after I arrived. He shook my hand and said, "Congratulations on being alive." The fact that he visited made me a VIP. I confess to taking advantage of that status to become a nuisance. All I had to do was ask for a glass of water or anything and someone would take care of it immediately. The other benefit of being in the institute was realizing just how lucky I was. Basically, I was the most fortunate person there. A leg was about the least you could lose and be there. Certainly, losing a leg is less of a problem than, say, losing four fingers. Fingers are much more useful and their function is more difficult to replace.

I also learned how much one can lose and still live. One man there had had a hemicorporectomy. He had had cancer, and to save his life the doctors had amputated his entire lower body from just below the rib cage. He got around in a prosthetic lower body sitting in a wheelchair. At night they'd take him out and put him in bed. The prosthetic body—chest and legs—would stay in the wheelchair, looking like a headless horseman. So when I got out and people would say to me, "Gee, it's terrible that you lost your leg," I could truthfully tell them it wasn't such a big deal.

It was a shock being in the Rusk Institute. I realized immediately that I wasn't just visiting; I was there because I belonged there. I was part of this group. Many years later I saw people have the same sort of reaction when they came to an Achilles workout for the first time. There's nothing like being in a group of people who are all disabled to drive home your own disability.

I had to stay in the New York University Hospital until my left leg healed enough for the body cast to be removed.

One of the problems with this leg was that it was broken so badly the doctors were concerned about its healing straight. To help it do this, they attached a rope with a weight on the end of it to the leg below the break. It's like having your teeth straightened by an orthodontal device. The tension is increased continually. The only problem was that the force had to be applied directly to the bone. To do that, they showed up in my room with a drill—your basic surgeon's model Black & Decker—with a stainless steel rod bit.

"What are you going to do with that?" I asked with some trepidation.

"Don't worry. It won't hurt," was the response.

They injected the area with a local anesthetic and drilled the bit right through my leg—skin, meat, bone, and everything—and out the other side. The doctors were right. It didn't hurt, but it looked awful. Then they attached ropes to either end, ran them over a pulley at the top of the bed and hung several pounds of weight from them. The principal discomfort with being rigged up in this manner was that the weights tended to pull me down toward the end of the bed and I kept having to haul myself back up. The only major problem it caused occurred one day when the rope broke. The sudden removal of tension was agony.

The hospital was a source of learning for me at many levels. I was on the plastic surgery floor because I had to have a reamputation of my stump. It's like a "nose job" for the leg. It involves reshaping the stump to fit a prosthetic leg. What it meant socially was that there were a lot of young women coming through the floor to have deviated septums corrected.

I also had a number of roommates. One that comes to mind was one of the "little people." He had fallen off a seat in a movie theater and broken his back. Now a quadriplegic, he also had a miserable personality. This, coupled with the fact that he couldn't move, made him a far from ideal roomie. He smoked huge cigars but since he was paralyzed, he kept demanding that people hold his cigar for him so he could smoke. For me, this was a lesson in power. While he essentially had no power, if he could get a volunteer to hold his cigar, then he could exercise some control because the person had to hold the cigar to his lips for him to puff, then take it away. He could thus make them cater to him. While he got several minutes of pleasure from the cigar and from the sense of power, he rarely saw a volunteer return. His power plays worked in the short run; but in the long run, they failed.

An artist who had gone blind taught me another lesson. He had come in for eye surgery and talked constantly about how many shows and exhibits he had had. Finally, I asked him how many paintings he had sold. He said none. After a while, he had someone bring in a few of his paintings. I realized that he hadn't sold any because he wasn't a very good artist. Yet he had this wonderful ability to think of himself as someone with great talent who just hadn't been discovered. From this experience, I learned about dealing with and avoiding failure.

One of the orderlies on the floor was an immigrant who had been a lieutenant in the Israeli army. He had served in wartime and during one of our conversations told me why Israel had the best small army in the world. One of the requirements for every soldier in that army, he told me, was to complete a 100-kilometer march in 24 hours. That's 62 miles, but more important, it's the width of Israel. The idea is that, even without motorized transportation, the army can get from one side of the country to the other in a day.

There I was, in a cast up to my neck with a metal pin through one leg and a stump where my other leg used to be, and I told him that some day I would like to do that. I don't know why I said it, but I believed it.

And that was years before I ever considered taking up running for any purpose other than catching a bus.

Some funny little episodes like this plant seeds and help set goals that can be important later. When Terry Fox was given my picture before his amputation, it planted a seed. I recently wrote a letter of recommendation for a friend from China who had helped us develop our Beijing Chapter and who wants to attend graduate school at an Ivy League college. I indicated in the letter that someone like him could one day be on the board of the institution. He wrote to thank me and tell me he is saving a copy of the letter and hopes someday to remind me of it when he is placed on the board.

After what seemed an eternity, they finally took the rod out of my leg and put me in a hip-high cast. It was the end of August, almost three months after the accident, and I was ready to go home. I'd be in a wheelchair, and I'd have to come back to Rusk for rehab. It would be months before I'd get an artificial leg, but the day I finally rolled out of those doors, it was as if I'd been released from prison. To this day, I love the outdoors, and part of that love has to be the result of my three months inside.

At the time of the accident, I had weighed about 165 pounds. Now I weighed only 135 pounds, and only about 10 pounds of the weight loss was from losing my leg. I had a lot of weight and strength to regain, but that wasn't a problem. Just moving myself around in a wheelchair provided the exercise I needed. I found that getting around New York City in a chair didn't require a big adjustment. Not on my part, anyway. For others, it was sometimes difficult. I considered that everything is relative: Losing a leg looks bad, but I'd rather have one leg than be an alcoholic. Similarly, if I had a choice between losing twenty IQ points and losing a leg, I'd lose the leg every time. I'd much rather have one leg than have my son become a drug addict. It's all relative, and in the grand scheme of things, my loss is really not that big a deal.

The biggest surprise for me about being in a wheelchair was that taxis often wouldn't stop to pick me up. Even now, cabbies don't want to deal with a wheelchair. They see themselves having to get out of the cab, maybe having to lift a disabled person out of his chair. They don't realize that the chair folds quickly and the person in the chair simply slides into the cab, pulling the chair in after himself. It takes about 15 seconds.

But I found I had to play games with the taxis if I wanted a ride, and sometimes nothing worked.

One day, for example, I came out of New York University Hospital and wheeled down to an oval where there's a drop-off zone. A cab pulled up and dropped someone off and I motioned to the driver that I wanted a ride. He didn't want to bother with me, though, and started to drive off. I saw what he was doing and zipped across the oval to cut him off. When I blocked his way, he tried to back up around the oval. I zipped around the other way and blocked him again. This went on for a while, back and forth as if the cab were in a rundown between second and third base. He finally stopped the cab and let me come around to the side to get in. Just as I reached for the door, he gunned the car and made his escape. I was livid and filed a complaint with the city's Taxi and Limousine Commission. This isn't an easy or quick process. It involves going downtown, filling out forms, and going back for hearings. I followed it all the way through, though, and finally the cabby admitted what he had done. What punishment, if any, he was given, I never found out.

But things like that happen frequently. One time on First Avenue, I rolled up to a cab and when the driver saw me, he moved ahead to pick up a woman who had arrived after I did. I followed and told the woman that I had been there first and it was my cab. She was very embarrassed about the situation and was apologizing when the driver saw his opening and simply took off, leaving us both on the curb.

These incidents convinced me I needed to be independent. I was living with my parents at 86th Street between Broadway and Amsterdam Avenue. The Rusk Institute is at 34th Street and First Avenue. It's about a mile and a half across town and two and a half miles downtown. My need for independence translated into deciding to wheel myself the four miles to Rusk.

I had a few accidents early on, including one time when I flipped the chair over backwards and had to right the chair and haul myself and my cast back into it. But after a while I could get up and down curbs at full speed. It was a little rough on the chair, but, what the heck, it was only a rental. I had been told not to buy a chair, primarily because if you buy a chair you don't have as much incentive to get out of it as you do if you're paying rent on it. Another benefit, I found, is that every week I could go to the rental place and get the chair repaired for free. And the way I ran around in that thing, it needed adjustment constantly. At first, the repair people would apologize profusely because they thought they had given me a bad chair. Then, after seeing me come in in a full sweat every week for a while, they started to wonder just what I was doing with the thing.

I got so I could make the run from home to Rusk with

ease. My best time was 57 minutes. Coming back was more difficult because it is almost all uphill, and that's no fun in a wheelchair. The best part of these excursions was wheeling through Central Park. Occasionally I would pass a biker. This was my first exposure as a disabled person to long-distance exercise.

In November the cast was taken off my left leg and I switched to crutches. Rehabilitation now included building up the strength in my leg and stump so that I could finally get a prosthesis and continue with my life. It was during this period that I broke off my engagement to Rosalie. The engagement had been all wrong from the beginning, but I hadn't realized it. I was 24 going on 20, and she was 27 going on 30. She had a serious professional career and had been on her own for a number of years while I was still going to school. As a result, she called the shots in the relationship. Ninety percent of the time, I'd simply back off and go along with her. I guess what I went through after the accident matured me, and I realized that if we got married, my disability would create even more problems. Rosalie thought she knew what was best for me. To see if this were indeed true, I put it to a test. I was on crutches at the time and we got into a debate over whether to watch a movie from the balcony or from downstairs. I wanted to go to the balcony so I could smoke my pipe, which was allowed in theaters in those days. She wanted to stay downstairs because she didn't think I should walk up a flight or two of stairs on crutches. I held out for the balcony and she wouldn't budge. So I watched from upstairs and she watched from downstairs and we met after the movie. That's when I realized that the marriage would not work. I broke off the engagement. Rosalie was upset and worried that people would think she dumped me because I was disabled.

But it was I who was different and unhappy in the relationship. Going through something like losing a leg changes you. It makes people tougher and more self-centered. They want more control over their lives because they've experienced the loss of control that comes with being institutionalized. I found I was much more serious about life than I had been before the accident, and I wanted to control that life, rather than let it be controlled by someone else.

Once I broke off the engagement, I faced the anxiety that most newly disabled people go through of wondering what effect my disability would have on my social life. This was a major concern, since I had the normal intentions of any 25-year-old. I talked with other amputees about it and my own experience later confirmed that it's really not a big deal. This was surprising, but also reassuring. I remember only one woman I dated whose parents were upset about our relationship because I was missing a leg. And for those who are wondering—yes, you do take your leg off before jumping into bed.

While I had lost my fiancée during my rehabilitation, I had also found the woman who would eventually become my wife. Betsy had come to New York from Michigan and was working as a private duty nurse at NYU Medical Center (of which Rusk is a part). The person she was taking care of had lost several fingers on both hands in an industrial accident. He was getting two new thumbs in a procedure that involved fashioning them from a piece of his own rib. He had visited me while I was in the hospital and when I came back as an outpatient, I visited him. One day Betsy was there and I started talking with her. It turned out we shared a mutual acquaintance—Tim Costello, a deputy mayor in New York at the time. She had worked with him on an election campaign and I had written my master's thesis with him as a professor. With that as a base, we got to know each other. Two years later we were married.

It took two months after my cast was removed before I received my artificial leg. When I finally started practicing with it in January 1966, it was absolutely unbelievable. I could walk around without crutches. The feeling of freedom and mobility was like the excitement I had experienced when I first got my driver's license. I felt I could go anywhere I wanted. In the middle of January I wore my leg in public at a family celebration. I even went out on the dance floor and danced with it. I didn't dance well, but then I hadn't danced well before I lost the leg.

I was free from hospitals and doctors and rehabilitation.

It had been eight months since the accident and I could finally get on with my life.

FINISH

Chapter 3

Failure is impossible.
—Susan Brownell Anthony

I was born November 18, 1940, on the West Side of
Manhattan in the city in which I have lived all my life. My
father, Aaron Traum, was an executive in the notions
business, which is to say his company sold sewing accessories.
It was a family business he had entered at the age of 15 with
his older brother.

My father had been born in New York on Christmas
Day, 1903, the seventh of eight children. My grandfather,
who died suddenly in 1914, when Dad was 11, was a tailor.
The other tailors with whom my grandfather had worked
contributed money to the family—five dollars a week—to
help keep everyone fed.

My father lived at home during the Depression, working
and taking care of his widowed mother. He had a secretary,
a young woman named Lilly Korn, of whom he was very
fond, but his duty to his mother came first, and he put off
marriage. Finally, in 1938, one of his older sisters divorced
and moved back in to take care of their mother, so my
father decided he could marry and move out on his own.
He and Lilly were married on Thanksgiving Day that year
and I was born two years later. In 1945, my sister Joanne
was born. The Traum family was complete.

My father continued to work until he passed 65. Two
weeks after he retired, he had a nosebleed. The loss of blood
was followed by a heart attack, and shortly after, he died
without ever having a chance to enjoy his retirement. That
was in 1969. It was another powerful reminder to me that
life is indeed finite and that every moment is precious.

When I was six, my parents enrolled me in Hunter College
Elementary School on 68th Street, between Park and

Lexington on the East Side. Hunter was an experimental school begun in the early 40s. Its mission was to see if gifted children would benefit from an enriched academic program. This was in keeping with the prevailing thought of that time, when more resources were diverted to the above-average students while below-average students were pretty much left to fend for themselves. Of course, those were the days when you didn't need a great education to get a decent job, even in New York City. Today, resources are allocated the other way around, with more emphasis on the below-average students.

An IQ of 140 or better was needed to enter Hunter. Considering the grades I earned in high school and college it's probably hard for people to figure how I qualified. But, as I said, I had a problem retaining information. I was smart enough. It just didn't show in conventional ways.

The school was in a typical Manhattan building, which is to say it went up instead of out. The facility had eight floors, and the 500 or so students had to get to their classrooms in the morning by way of two elevators. Since you couldn't get all those kids in the building at one time, in the morning we milled around outside until we could crowd onto the elevators. This is where I left my lasting mark on the school and learned an important lesson about human nature.

It happened in the fifth grade when I became a monitor, one of several students whose job it was to keep chaos from breaking out every morning at the elevators. Rather than have everyone aimlessly milling around outside, I decided the students should walk counterclockwise around the block until it was their turn to enter the building. That way, we'd have a steady stream of students and no unmanageable crowd out front. It was a totally arbitrary decision, but it worked. It was also the first time I got people to exercise.

(Four years after I left Hunter at the end of sixth grade, I came back to attend my sister's graduation. When I got to the building, the students were walking around it counterclockwise. I asked a teacher why everyone walked around the block in that direction. She didn't know; it was just the way it was done. Seeing that, I realized how customs can get started. You don't need much authority. Someone just says, "Let's do it this way," and it becomes the rule, even though no one knows why they're doing it. A lot of life works that way.)

I did the usual things that middle-class kids did growing up in New York. One of those was to spend eight weeks every summer at Buck's Rock Work Camp. That's where I learned and became skilled as a potter. The other kids would make little ashtrays, but I wasn't interested in art. I went for size and quantity. I'd make these huge creations, each one larger than the one before, with some over two feet high, lined up waiting to go into the kiln to be fired. After a while, the counselor started charging me for firing my pots because I was monopolizing the kiln. Instead of being rewarded for my enthusiasm and diligence, I was penalized. I was also the butt of jokes. Somebody found a cartoon about a potter making a vase so large he had fallen into it, and only his feet were sticking out of the top. They had written my name underneath the cartoon, and posted it on the bulletin board.

I also learned in camp that if you want to accomplish something, you have to start it. That sounds simple, but it's true. There was a long-distance swimming test which was the prerequisite for taking a canoe out by yourself. It involved swimming what looked like an enormous distance out to a rock in the lake and then swimming back. I didn't think I could swim that far, but I practiced. When the day for the test came, I still didn't think I could do it. It was probably four or five hundred yards each direction. But I figured I was good enough to swim out, so I signed up for the test. My strategy was to swim out and then figure out how to get back. After all, they wouldn't let me drown. I surprised myself when I passed and was declared an advanced swimmer.

I didn't understand it then, but I was taking a calculated risk, which is not necessarily a bad thing to do. When you attempt a long shot, the worst that can happen is you fail, and if that happens, so what? You were supposed to fail. You've lost nothing. But if, by chance, you pull it off, you've really done something. It's a no-lose situation.

In high school, I came to understand what I had intuitively learned in summer camp. Horace Mann High

School, located at the north end of the city, was one of the
top 10 prep schools in the country at the time. I am not a
great athlete, but I went out for football, wrestling, and
track in high school. I was a fullback in football, and,
although I could run fast enough in a straight line, I had no
football sense. If they told me to run between guard and
tackle, and every player on the other team was there waiting,
I didn't have the instinct to cut to daylight. I ran between
guard and tackle and got killed.

But I learned some valuable lessons. The coach, Bill Quinn,
impressed me with some of his methods. One thing he
would do was let one of the players lead exercises before
practice. He wouldn't choose the best players, but rather
those who had lots of spirit. One time, Coach Quinn picked
a second- or third-stringer, Eric Berger, to lead the calisthenics.
This kid wasn't a particularly strong or talented athlete, but
when he was put in the position of leader, he performed
with a strength and endurance he had never had when he
was a follower. (Personally, I would rather have had one of
the coaches lead the exercises, because the players always
were more aggressive than a coach would have been.) I
recognized that when you select a leader, that person
becomes empowered and does things he or she wouldn't
have been capable of as a follower. I believe that my
leadership of Achilles greatly facilitated my ability to
eventually complete a 62-mile (100K) race.

One of the things that spurs any competitor on to
extraordinary effort is the crowd. I encountered that in
wrestling and I remember two matches when it really kicked
in and from which I learned two lessons. The first time, I
was a freshman wrestling on the varsity team, which was
fairly rare. Wrestling is a sport in which the better man
usually wins. Anyway, we had a meet in which I wrestled a
senior who had placed third in a major eastern tournament
at Lehigh, and was much better than I. My coach, Ian
Theodore, didn't try to tell me how I could beat this guy.
Instead he tried to prepare me for the disappointment of
losing. But my opponent made the mistake of being
overconfident against a freshman. He bullied me around for
a while and I went along with it. Suddenly, I shot a move
on him and, just like that, I pinned him. He couldn't believe

what had happened, and neither could anyone else in the gym. They were all screaming for me, and I felt wonderful. I had done the impossible. I went on and finished second that year in the Ivy League Prep School Championships. I'm really proud of that. The lesson I learned here was never to underestimate your opponent.

As I got older and better at wrestling, it became more difficult to do the impossible and harder to be proud of finishing second. When I experienced a rare loss, everybody asked me what had gone wrong. Nothing had gone wrong. I had simply lost. I didn't enjoy losing, but sometimes it happened. But perceptions were different. Once, any win was great. Now, winning was expected. Instead, losing was now news, because it was different from the norm.

Those who suffer most from losing aren't the guys who finish last, but those who finish second repeatedly. Look at the Buffalo Bills. It's an enormous feat to get to the Super Bowl three straight years as the Bills did, yet the team is the object of ridicule because it never won the big game.

Some people understand the snags of finishing second and so manage not to do it. The Brooklyn Dodgers once had a player named Billy Loes. Loes always had a winning record, but never won more than 12 or 14 games a year. Sports writers couldn't understand why a man with his ability didn't win 20 games a year. When they asked him about it, he said, "If I win 20 one year, they'll expect me to do it every year." This was the same man who once booted a ground ball and explained afterwards, "I lost it in the sun." Billy Loes understood the two-edged sword of high expectations. As long as he avoided great success, he also avoided great failure.

To regain that feeling of triumph from the ninth grade, I actually had to lose. The defeat came when I was 17 in a match against a national-class wrestler from St. Paul Prep. This kid was going to school on a wrestling scholarship and had actually finished fourth the year before in the U.S. Olympic Trials. He was much too good to be wrestling at the high school level. But he was in the league, and when tournament time came around, I had to wrestle him. When the ref blew his whistle, my opponent came out and, within a minute, had put me on my back. I spent several seconds doing a bridge, which is when you hold your shoulders off the ground by arching your neck and supporting your weight on your head. I had never been pinned and all I could think of was that this shouldn't be happening and how unfair it was for a wrestler that good to be competing in a league like ours. I became outraged about the situation and something snapped inside. I felt like the comic-book character who, in times of great stress, turned into the Incredible Hulk. With an effort that was beyond my ability, I flipped the guy over and put him on his back. There were almost a thousand people in the gym watching the match and when Dick Traum put this Olympic-caliber wrestler on his back, they made more noise than I've ever heard in my life. That gave me even more strength. The kid I was wrestling was so shocked he didn't know what to do. He was a poor wrestler on his back—probably hadn't had much experience in that position,

The ref didn't know what to do either, because this was the last thing he had expected. As a result, he was slow getting into position and didn't call the pin, even though I'm willing to swear even after all these years that I had my opponent's shoulders down for the two seconds. The period ended. My opponent returned to form and subsequently pinned me. I lost, but no one asked me what had gone wrong. I had returned to the safe ground of having tried to do the impossible. The mere fact that I almost pulled it off was enough to make me a hero.

Horace Mann was a great school, and one of the best things about it was that the faculty had been consciously assembled from a broad range of personality types. We had everything from do-what-feels-good liberals to authoritarian conservatives. I didn't see the wisdom of this at the time. As a New Yorker, I was quite shocked to be exposed to authoritarian figures. But it taught me to work with all kinds of people, and I'll always be grateful for that.

During high school, I got the ultimate kid's job, better even than a paper route. I sold food at Yankee Stadium. That was my first experience with unions. Whether you worked depended on how big a crowd they expected for the game that day. The order in which they gave out the jobs was determined by colored work cards. The best color card for non-professionals was white. Those were the first guys called and, if you were old enough, you got to sell beer—a big money-maker—instead of being relegated to peanuts. I asked around and found out that the way you got a white card wasn't through some sort of merit system but by paying the union guy $9, a substantial sum of money. But first you had to corner the guy, which wasn't easy. I finally got to him, gave him the $9, and from then on I had work every day I wanted it.

(Years later, when I completed my doctorate, I was amused to realize that it was the professional equivalent of that white card. It didn't necessarily make me a better worker, but it got me in the door.)

The concession job soured me on Mickey Mantle for life. Before the games we used to shape up for work by the players' entrance. Kids would wait there for autographs, and the prime catch in those days was Mantle, who typically refused autographs. One day, there was a kid in a wheelchair who wanted his signature, and Mantle stopped and signed for him. That offended me then, and it still does. What he was saying was that he couldn't be bothered with a bunch of kids, but he didn't have the guts to pass up a kid in a wheelchair. I guess he thought that that would have looked really bad, so he signed. After I became disabled, my feelings didn't change. I thought, and still think, the rule should be either sign for everybody, or don't sign for anyone.

In my senior year, I was accepted by Cornell University, partly on the basis of my having scored 790 out of 800 on the math portion of the College Boards. This score caused quite a bit of consternation and one of my teachers didn't believe I could have gotten that score honestly because my grades were poor—I had a learning problem with math. But my ability with tests was a different matter. I used to practice taking tests, and I had set out to get a perfect 800 in the math boards. I did that by figuring out what the examiners were looking for. One thing I kept in mind was that the questions usually get progressively harder. So if, late in the test I came to a question that was easy, I knew I'd made a mistake and should try again. By looking at the answers, I could often tell what the question was testing. If most of the answers were the same, but the decimal point was in different positions, it was apparent that the placement of the decimal was the issue. Of course, there was more to it than that, but I had a knack for it.

During the summer, I worked for 7-Up and Coca-Cola at different times. I loved the jobs in a simplistic way, because I'm a simplistic guy. At 7-Up, I was probably the most productive man they had out of 50 delivery men. It was so unlike school or life in the white-collar world. When you deliver soda, you work really hard, and the harder you work, the more you're rewarded. It was the same effort-equals-results situation I've since rediscovered in running. No matter which company you worked for, the Soft Drink Workers Union had a daily limit of 149 cases of soda. You could sell fewer than that, but you couldn't sell more. As a part-timer, I'd get lousy routes, so it wasn't easy to sell that much. So I'd play a game in which the goal was to sell my 149 cases a day and, in addition, pick up one new account. A perfect week involved moving 745 cases and getting five new accounts.

I stayed only one year at Cornell as a mechanical engineer major before transferring to New York University, where I received three degrees. Although my parents would have paid for my education, I put myself through school. It was better than having to keep explaining my poor grades— about which they gave me a lot of grief—to my parents. This way I could say, "Look, this is my business. I'm paying for it. You can't tell me how much it's costing, how hard you worked. I'm paying for it myself."

Getting through college was frustrating. I was trying hard, but I'm a slow learner. I would push and push in class and come home with a C or D. But then I'd go out on the soda truck and I could do better than anyone else. I appreciated the success on the truck more because I was not effective at school. For me, school was like eating spinach. I did it because it was good for me. Delivering soda was dessert— my reward for eating the spinach.

This was in 1959, and I could make $500 a week with commissions and the automatic two hours overtime that everyone got. That was a fortune, more than triple what a college graduate might expect to get coming out of school. I was only 19, and my parents were worried that I would be so taken with the money I was making that I'd give up school. They didn't have to worry. I was determined to get a doctorate, because I believed even then that you only get one shot at life and you'd better be as well-armed as possible when you take it. Having a doctorate opens doors that delivering soda doesn't.

I had so much success working for the company that when they started a program allowing employees to buy their own truck and route and work as a contractor, I was among the first to take them up on it. The cost of a route was $5,000, and I bought two. On top of that, I had to buy trucks to work them. Since I was still a teenager, I had to talk my parents into cosigning for the loan. They didn't want to because of their fear I'd take it up as a career. But I promised that I would continue to attend school full time. They knew they couldn't talk me out of it, so they went along. I didn't do a lot of research to see if it was a good move. I've never been one to do marketing studies. I'm basically a counter-puncher, a guy who waits until he sees what looks like an opening and then reacts. This looked like that sort of opening, so I took it. In a way, I was again taking a calculated risk. A kid wasn't supposed to be able to go out and buy some trucks and run his own soda delivery business. If I failed, it was expected and it wouldn't be a failure. Again, I couldn't lose.

I hired three men to work for me. I would drive one of the trucks from the warehouse to the first stop, then I'd turn the truck over to an employee and take the subway to school. After school, I'd take the subway back and check out the trucks. Management had no idea I was going to college full time. I didn't look particularly intelligent, and I've never been one to dress any fancier than I have to. Eventually, the managers found out that I wasn't on the routes full-time. This wasn't the way they had envisioned the business. They sold the routes so the drivers would be more aggressive. What I was doing was not in their bailiwick—making money from the efforts of others. They disapproved so eventually I sold my trucks and routes. But I continued to deliver soda. Beyond that, it was my first experience with being in business for myself and I found that I was comfortable working that way.

I'll always remember those days as fun. I learned not only about business and the sheer, dumb joy of putting in a hard day's physical labor, but also about a segment of society I never would have gotten to know if I'd stayed in my middle-class world. There were regular guys, working stiffs, and it was exciting to hang around with them. After work on Fridays, we'd have a craps game and, of course, I learned how to play. Floating craps games are always ready to welcome new money. One night I got lucky and won over $150, all in ones and fives, which made a huge bankroll. We went to a bar to have a few beers, and I was enjoying myself when one of my friends who was older and wiser finally said, "Dick, pick up a round." I was neither street-wise nor sensitive enough to realize that, as the big winner, that was my obligation.

Despite my difficulties in learning—or maybe because of them—I got my undergraduate degree in 1962 and entered grad school. I thought it would be like being a priest admitted to the Vatican and allowed to see all the books that the general public isn't allowed to view. Here is where I was going to learn the secrets of the world. Gradually I learned that the secret of the world is that there is no secret. The Holy Grail is in your head. I completed my masters in business administration in 1963, and began working on my academic union card, my doctorate.

By the end of the spring semester in 1965, I had finished my written tests for a doctorate in management, industrial psychology, and human resources. I was almost 25 years old and all I had left to go through were my orals and dissertation. I was engaged. I still had a great job delivering soda. Summer was at hand.

And then I lost my leg.

The worst thing about losing the leg was that I lost half a year. Instead of doing my orals in the fall of '65, I had to complete them in the spring of '66. My career as a delivery man was over, and this underlined the value of an education. If I had quit school and gone into the business full time, I would have been out of luck with one leg. But I didn't need two good legs for the work I was going to do.

The winter after I got my new leg I spent working for a professor and studying for my orals, which I passed in the spring. Although I still had to finish my dissertation, I had so many job offers that I don't remember the number. (The job market was a lot different then, and graduate degrees hadn't yet reached the dime-a-dozen stage.) One that I did check out came from a college on Long Island. I hadn't considered becoming a teacher, but one of my professors had recommended me. We never got as far as discussing employment. The building I would have been working in had three stories and no elevator, and when they heard I had only one leg, they turned me down because they were afraid I couldn't walk the stairs. That was relayed to me later, and I was annoyed because I could walk up steps as well as anyone.

That was the only time I can remember being discriminated against in the workplace because of my disability. But what I found more interesting about the whole experience was the college's initial interest in me, even though I knew a lot more about delivering soft drinks than about teaching. Colleges were judged then—and still are—by the number of PhDs they have on their faculties. So no one really cares if you can teach or not. They just care if you have that degree—the academic union card. It's kind of funny when you think about it. You have to take education courses and have a teaching certificate to teach five-year-olds how to hold a crayon, but to teach graduate students how to run the world, you don't need any certification at all. It's only in the past few years that colleges have begun to question the emphasis on advanced degrees and to ask whether the first requirement of a college-level instructor ought not to be an ability to instruct.

I began to work with Celanese Corporation in August 1966 at a salary of $11,500. I was corporate now, and it was fun. The position I was hired to fill—personnel research analyst—had just been created, so I was free to develop it without having to deal with what had been done before. Celanese had recently developed a human resource information system, and I was given the job of finding ways to use the data it generated. My first major product was a budget projection matrix. It was part of a "Pay-for-Performance" program. It gave managers a tool to use in awarding merit pay increases by pinpointing an employee's performance potential and place in a salary range and associating it with salary increases. The process was used for budgeting. It was also used to provide feedback on manager rating skills. For example, based on previous salary actions, ratings could be calculated and compared with what was actually done.

My second major area of emphasis was to develop ways in which the human resource function could contribute cents per share impact on profitability. Within this framework my interest was in reducing the number of levels of management, reducing the proportion of people at higher levels of management, and reducing turnover of valuable people while increasing turnover of below-average incumbents. I was also interested in improving the performance rating process and insuring that an appropriate number of people were ready to be promoted in each major level and function. The process was called EMM for Effective Manpower Management indices.

I was excited about being on the cutting edge in corporate America, working to develop these great methods of saving money for all of the major corporations of the United States. Of course, what I was really doing was figuring out for them ways to get more work out of people without their knowing it.

While I worked there, I was also supposed to be writing my doctoral dissertation. I thought that's what I was doing, but my doctoral committee gave me a hard time because they felt I wasn't serious about it. And I really wasn't. I'd come in to work on it one day a week, on Sunday, and it would take me three hours to get back to where I had been the previous Sunday. It's no way to write anything, and I was turning out garbage.

I didn't really care. I had until 1973 to get the dissertation done, and meantime, there was too much else going on. In 1968, after two years on the job, I married Betsy, the woman I had met at Rusk. We had dated after we met in 1965, but a year later she felt I wasn't serious about getting married. Little else was going well for her. She was working 12-hour days and not saving money. Then, when her apartment was burglarized, she didn't feel safe. So she returned to Detroit, where she had grown up. But I was in love with her, so I kept in touch, traveling frequently to Detroit to see her.

Then, on July 4, 1968, I asked her to be my bride and she accepted. It took me two years to catch her, and I don't intend to let her go.

In 1970, after four years at Celanese, I saw the first clouds on the horizon of my sunny existence. The economy was taking a downswing. Before that, I had always assumed that you were hired by a corporation, you did a good job, they rewarded you with regular raises and promotions, and you lived happily ever after. Now I saw it wasn't that way. Worse, since this was my field of expertise, I realized that when a company starts to terminate people, the first ones to go are those who aren't adding immediate value to the company. My department was one of those areas. A further blow to my job security was the fact that when you start laying off employees, you need fewer people in personnel management. It was a double jeopardy situation. I wasn't in immediate danger, but I could see that I might be. I had always thought of going into business for myself, and now I decided to do it. I didn't have a marketing plan or a brochure or even an office. I started in my apartment and put the word out that I was available to do consulting. I remained at Celanese and let them know what I was doing. They didn't object. They were good people who realized that the employees they hired—the best available—would stay for a while and then move on to better opportunities.

My first client—Glenn Smyth—was a former employee of Celanese, with whom I had worked. He had left to take a job as head of international personnel for General Electric. At Celanese, he had been a very good friend of my boss' boss, so when he called me to consult for him, I had everyone's blessing.

Looking back now, I had developed some of the freshest concepts in human resources, which explains why I had no trouble picking up clients. I worked that way for two years, charging $200 a day, while still holding down the Celanese position. Then I received an offer from a consulting firm who invited me to lunch to offer me a job. During the discussion the partner who came to talk to me kind of mumbled something that I thought was, "If you join us, you'll never become a millionaire."

"What did you say?" I asked, not believing I had heard him correctly. He repeated it quite clearly. It was his way of telling me I'd be paid well enough, but I wasn't going to get an extraordinary package. My response was, "Well, I guess it's not for me." It wasn't that I was thinking about becoming a millionaire. I had been ready to join them as a partner and start developing new areas of business, yet they were inferring that if these ventures were successful I would keep my job. If not, I would be out. I decided right there that I may as well take the risks myself. If it worked, I would have equity. If it looked like it wasn't working, I would be in the same position as if I had joined the consulting firm.

In late 1972 I left Celanese, which subsequently became a client and eventually my landlord, inasmuch as I leased office space from them.

The deadline for my dissertation was finally looming, and I still hadn't made any headway. I'd start going one way and the committee would push me in another direction. I'd pursue that route and then they'd push me back. Finally, I realized that I had to get the thing done or I wasn't going to get my union card. I settled down and seriously poured my efforts into it. As if by magic, the committee became encouraging. Magic, of course, had nothing to do with it. As long as I was playing around with the dissertation, they played around with me. When I got serious, so did they.

Anything I learned by doing the work was outweighed by what I learned about the process. The objective wasn't to develop a Nobel Prize–winning theory. I was really learning how to get people with varying viewpoints to agree. They were teaching me how to manage a project. This is the valuable part of the process, because when you go out into the world, you're going to be working with different people with different objectives, time frames, and interests. My real job in doing the dissertation was to corral them together and get them to agree. They never tell you this. It's like the process of becoming an adult. You have to learn to communicate, to push, back off, cooperate, and compromise. When I understood that, they approved.

After I completed everything, I had to pay some $45 to have the dissertation reproduced and another $25 for my diploma. I considered not paying the $25 and becoming the only person whose status was "All but Diploma," meaning that I had met all the requirements except paying for my diploma.

Getting that doctorate was difficult, and that's part of the value of it. It's a badge that says you put in a lot of time and effort and study. I don't believe you have to have a doctorate to know what you're doing. A surgeon, for example, doesn't really need a doctorate to remove an appendix or even a limb. Surgeons may argue with this, but you can learn how to do it the same way a master craftsman learns cabinet making, by becoming an apprentice and learning by watching and doing until you have demonstrated the skills needed to be a full-fledged surgeon. Getting a doctorate is like pledging a fraternity. You go through a lot of tests that don't really mean anything to become a member. But it's not necessarily bad, because what it does is prove that you have the desire necessary to succeed.

With a doctorate, you don't necessarily know more than someone who has done the same sort of work but doesn't have the piece of paper. But having the diploma proves you have done the work. Getting it requires intelligence, but more than that, perseverance. Probably half the people who get to the dissertation stage don't get a doctorate. They get frustrated and quit. That could easily have happened to me, except that I need a bit of grit to irritate me enough to produce a pearl. My difficulty in learning was the grit. When I was going to school, they hadn't yet "invented" learning disabilities and so I was accused of being lazy. That made me work harder. I didn't have the grades, but I got the job done. And I really believe that C students like myself are the ones who make it. Often, the guys who sail through with straight A's have not had the frustrations in school that prepare one for the real world. The C students have had plenty of frustration, so when they meet up with it in their working lives, it's an old friend. Just the same, I don't want to go through the experience of getting an education again. To this day I have nightmares about forgetting to go to a class or not having bought a textbook that I'm being tested on in the morning or having a final exam that I haven't studied for.

Once you have a doctorate, the trick is learning how to

use it. Some people use their degree like a club to let lesser mortals know that they have a doctorate and others do not. That alienates people. In everyday life, I don't use mine. But if I'm having a problem with the phone company or some other bureaucratic outfit, then I introduce myself not as regular, everyday guy Dick Traum, but as Dr. Traum. I'm no different, but perceptions change, and in many real ways, you are what others perceive you to be. It's one of the wonderful things I see every day with Achilles runners. When they first arrive, they're just another unfortunate in a wheelchair or on crutches or whatever. Then they do a marathon and they're no longer looked at as someone to pity, but rather as someone to admire. They're official heroes. They have earned the diploma.

So having a doctorate is sort of like having the keys to the executive washroom of life. If you have a speaking engagement, simply being introduced as Doctor So-and-So makes the audience listen a bit more closely than they would if you took the lectern as Joe Blow. It's funny when you think about it, because it attributes more to people who have an education than is appropriate. What's even funnier is that people who do have the credentials are less willing to admit to an outsider that they don't know something. It's like being a talk-show host. You'll never hear Rush Limbaugh admit he doesn't have an answer to each of life's problems.

Basically, whatever the title or distinction you hold works in large, ad hoc groups, particularly if no one knows you, but not in small groups of your peers. Being a two-star general does you no good in a meeting of two-star generals, but it may get you a good table in a nightclub. The difference is that there are group norms that keep individuals in check within the group. But outside the group, the norms don't apply. This is how Communism was able to take hold and why it eventually failed. In the beginning, Lenin and his small group of comrades kept each other in check because they all knew the rules. But when they went to larger groups, the norms didn't work anymore because the peer pressure of the small group didn't work in a large group. In the original cells, if you broke the norms, everyone knew about it immediately. But in a big city like Moscow, where few people knew you, you could break the norms without fear of reprisal by the group. Stalin understood this better than any of them, which is why he was able to take over Russia when Lenin died.

To put it in more immediate terms, if you visit a village in Maine, everyone drives considerately because everyone knows everyone else. But if you try driving considerately in New York City, you'll never get out of your parking space—provided, of course, that you had a space to start with.

I don't advertise the fact I've only got one leg. It's like the doctorate in that regard. You shouldn't advertise it unless it will do you some good, and if you overdo it, you just turn people off. As a result, most of the people I dealt with in my business never knew I had an artificial leg. If they noticed me walking with a limp, they might ask if I hurt my leg, and I'd tell them the truth—yes, I had. I just didn't tell them how much hurt. I still do this today. Sometimes, it leads to situations that are pretty funny. One embarrassing but amusing situation arises now and then when I'm mixing with a group of people and I step on someone's foot with my prosthetic leg. When that happens, I can't feel it, so I keep standing on the person's foot until he says something. But he's too embarrassed to say anything about it, figuring either I'm doing this on purpose or I'm just too dense to notice. When I finally realize what I'm doing, I apologize profusely and explain about the leg. Then the other person is the one who's apologizing to me for having his foot in the way.

Another fun situation is when we go to the beach. I'll wear a running suit to the beach. When I want to swim, I walk up to the water's edge, and take the pants off with the leg inside them, then hop into the water. That way, when I get out, the leg is right there. Once, when we were vacationing in the Caribbean, I was in the water and watched as a group of Japanese tourists walking down the beach came across my pants with the leg sticking out. They thought it was a real leg that had washed up on shore, probably from some unfortunate who had been eaten by a shark. They were running around trying to find someone who knew what to do about such matters when I came out and reclaimed my leg. They probably still tell their friends about that. I do.

On a different vacation in St. Thomas, I was scuba diving and swimming away from a shark. Another diver noticed my missing leg and came over to help me. He thought the shark had eaten my leg and I was swimming away in shock, unaware of it!

A little-known idiosyncrasy of prosthetic legs like mine is that they are held on by suction. When you're standing and rocking back and forth—as when you're giving a speech— you start to lose suction now and then. To remedy that, there's a valve on the leg by the knee that allows you to release the air pocket that's formed. You have to do that or the leg will fall off. So when I give speeches I have to reach down every now and then as unobtrusively as possible and push the valve. But when the air comes out, it sounds as if I'm passing gas. One day I explained this to a colleague and it was as if I had revealed one of life's great mysteries. Until that moment, he said, he had thought that somehow I was farting through my knee.

Of course, it's impossible to pass gas through your knee, but hey, doing the impossible is what I try to specialize in. And if I can't do it, at least I haven't failed.

FINISH

Chapter 4

If the Lord had meant for man to run,
He'd have given him four legs or at least
made him late for a bus.
                    —Red Smith

I used to think as much of running as Red Smith did, except I was usually late for a plane. I'd play tennis, baseball, and golf, snow ski, do pretty much everything. But I didn't do anything physical regularly, and by 1975, at the age of 34, I fit the classic Type A personality. I was too busy tending my growing business to worry about staying in shape. Hustling with an overnight bag down the concourses of LaGuardia Airport was my main form of exercise. That and lifting a fork to my mouth. Truth is, if I have a vice, it's eating. I love eating the way my wife loves flowers—and it didn't take a detective to know it. One look at my waistline was all the evidence needed. Not that I would have done anything about it, even if I were so inclined. I had been too busy getting my business, Personnelmetrics, Inc., rolling. I'd start working at 8:30 in the morning and, after the regular working day was over, I was buying inexpensive computer time to work on my projects. I wasn't getting finished until 11 p.m. I'd been working like this for a few years. By 1975, the business was doing nicely and I was trying to keep it that way.

Then one day a business colleague who was the same age as I had a heart attack that subsequently caused his death. It happened after an American Management Association program. My colleague was a program director for the association, and lived in terror of how his program would be graded. Apparently, he, too, had been a Type A personality waiting for disaster to strike.

Another colleague, Mike Richards, took a good look at

me and saw a pudgy man who looked to be so out of shape he walked with a limp. Worried that I was headed for a coronary, too, he suggested that maybe I should get into an exercise program that the West Side YMCA ran. My colleague's heart attack had jolted me. I was already intimately aware of my mortality and the limited time I had in life, but I hadn't thought it would be quite that limited. I had just gotten rolling, and I wanted to keep it rolling. I didn't need much convincing to sign up for the course. At the beginning of my first class, Peter Roth, the instructor, asked each new member to identify himself. As we did, he asked us if we could run. Anyone who said no was told he couldn't participate, because too many people had been doing the 30 minutes of calisthenics, then cutting out when the running began. Peter wanted everyone to get the full benefit of the 45-minute class, and the 10 minutes of running at the end, while the least popular part, was also one of the most important. When he got to me, I thought about the $250 I had already paid, and realized if I didn't run, I'd have paid the money for nothing. I was stuck. The only answer I could make was, "Yes, I can run."

The class was 30 minutes of stretching and calisthenics, which is what we used to call exercise before aerobics, followed by 10 minutes of running. With my leg amputated above the knee, I can't run like someone with two legs. The prosthesis I wear has a hydraulic system in the knee joint that controls its gait. I run with a kind of hopping action. It's very similar to a two-legged person running with a cast on one leg. I work just as hard as someone with two good legs, I just can't go as fast. A below-the-knee amputee can run considerably faster because he can pull his lower leg with his thigh muscles. He can't push off on his foot, but if he's a good athlete and in good condition, he can outrun the average weekend jock. These are things we know now, but in 1975, I was breaking new ground.

That wasn't my purpose. I just wanted to get in shape, and when I found I could run, I also found I enjoyed it. In a lot of ways, I had come to the right place at the right time. Just three years earlier the idea of running for fun and exercise had been a contradiction in terms for most Americans. In New York, Fred Lebow, a reformed fashion knock-off artist, had caught the bug and, in 1970, had been responsible for the first New York City Marathon. He organized the race through the New York Road Runners Club (NYRRC), a small outfit that had been founded by the city's running enthusiasts in 1958. That first marathon had been held entirely in Central Park and had drawn 127 runners, all of them male, of whom 55 made it to the finish line. Fred was among the finishers, the last time he ran the race until 1992.

Then Frank Shorter won the 1972 Olympic Marathon and started the running fad.

By then, Fred had been elected club president. He wasn't president of much, there being only 270 members, less than one percent of the current membership. An organization that small didn't need a lot of space, but they did need some, and they found it at the West Side Y, where one of the most influential men in the sport ran the adult exercise program. That man was Bob Glover—runner, trainer, writer, team manager, and all-around running guru. This is the mix I walked into in 1975, and, given my personality, I was soon involved in the club and the Y. In less than a year, I was on the Y's Sports Fitness Committee. The head of the committee was the late Dr. Milton Brothers, husband of Dr. Joyce Brothers. Years later, after we had become friends and he had become my physician, I asked him if he had been worried about my injuring myself when I first started to run seriously. He said that, after sifting through his considerable store of medical knowledge, he decided to let me try it and see what happened. Milt had a wonderful sense of humor, and you never knew when it would come out. Once, when he was giving me a physical, he stopped while he was checking me for a hernia, and said, "This is when I like to talk about the bill."

The running was a progressive sort of thing. At first I could only run three minutes without stopping, but gradually progressed. After three months, I had built up to running comfortably for 15 minutes. At that point, I took a fitness test that involved riding a stationary bicycle. When I showed up for the test, the technician running it took one look at me and went for help. "How do you test a man on a bicycle ergometer who only has one leg?" (Actually I can ride a bike, although not well.)

I set my sights on entering a race, not to break ground or make history, but because I now considered myself to be a runner and that's what runners did. By May of 1976, I could run three miles in reasonable comfort and ready for my first race. The Road Runners and the Y jointly sponsored the race, grandly named the Second Annual New York Road Runners YMCA of Greater New York 5-Mile Championship. In 1975, the inaugural race had drawn 43 runners to Central Park. One year later, I was among 147 who lined up along the starting line. My uniform was a plain, white T-shirt, white "Y" shorts with red piping, matching white crew socks on each leg, and a tag with my entry number—38—pinned to my shirt. The tag alone is a giveaway to the different eras. It contained a number and nothing else. Today, entrant tags have advertising logos and bar codes on them, but those were simpler times.

I didn't exactly burn up the course; finished dead last, in fact, in a time of 72:49, just 46:09 behind David Murray, the winner. But I finished and I got a red ribbon as well as a special award to prove it. A CBS camera crew caught sight of me and ran a story. The Associated Press wrote, "Dick Traum of West Side also received a special award for finishing the race despite being slowed down by an artificial leg."

The stories didn't stop with AP. The *Syracuse Herald American* ran a story noting, "Dick Traum took last place in a YMCA-sponsored five-mile run in New York's Central Park yesterday but received the largest ovation. He has one leg and runs with a prosthesis. It was the first time the 35-year-old behavioral scientist had entered competition."

The quote that ran in most stories pretty much stands today. "I'm not trying to prove anything," I told the writers. "I run for relaxation. It relieves tension that sometimes builds up. I don't really run, but sort of hop and swing my leg through."

My favorite story about the race, though, wasn't in a newspaper or magazine. It was the reaction of a woman who was watching the race and saw me go by with my hop-swing action. Apparently, she didn't notice the artificial leg, and someone overheard her ask a friend, "Is that a new kind of running?"

For me, it was the only kind of running, but it was,

indeed, a new kind of running that would make me the focus of feature stories whenever I showed up for a race. As far as I was concerned, I had just run my first race and wasn't any different than any other first-time runner. In fact, I told Bob Glover that I felt a little guilty because I was getting all this attention, when I didn't think I had worked as hard as the other runners.

In August, when I showed up for my first half-marathon, a new wave of stories hit. As far as I was concerned, I was just taking the next logical step when I entered the Puerto Rican Hispanic Half Marathon. The goal then, and now, of most runners was to do a 26.2-mile marathon, and before you could go that far, it's best to try a half-marathon. I had worked my way up to nine-mile workouts around the short track at the Y. That's 207 laps, and the trick is to do that many laps without getting bored. My technique, I think, is fairly common among runners. Since women run along with men, I just pick out a nice bottom and follow it, and when she outdistances me, I pick another one. I suspect women do the same with men, so you have all these runners going around in circles contemplating each other's backsides and forgetting about how far they still have to go.

The half-marathon was run on a hot day, and I was doing fine until about 2.5 hours into the race, when I hit the proverbial wall. From then on it was a matter of gutting it out. Again, I came in dead last—363rd—in about 3.5 hours, nearly an hour behind the next-to-last runner and almost 2.5 hours behind the winner, Puerto Rican Olympic Team member Tony Colon. Bob Glover had run with me last, and to help combat the heat, he had kept pouring water over my head. As we ran together, my leg felt heavier and heavier. When I finally got across the line, I sat down and took it off, and discovered that it really was heavier than normal. I turned it upside down, and a quart of water poured out—the runoff from Bob's efforts to keep me cool.

The writers were again waiting for me. This time, I made *El Diario la Prensa*, a Spanish-language newspaper in New York. They identified me in a photo as "Richard Trawber, quien finalizo la prueba con una pierna postiza... who finished the race with a prosthetic leg."

Most of the story lines were the same—I was the official

inspirational presence wherever I ran. Even the West Side YMCA Running Club newsletter picked up the theme by putting an item in about me and adding: "Dick, you're truly an inspiration. Keep on truckin'!"

Every disabled person who does anything more difficult than getting out of bed and brushing their teeth gets a large amount of support. Everybody keeps telling us how inspirational we are. That's nice, I suppose, but it's also too much, because we're not trying to be inspirational. Disabled golfers are trying to play golf, skiers are trying to ski, runners are trying to run, just the same as able-bodied people who undertake the same activities. It doesn't matter on what level you're competing. Jim Abbott, the New York Yankee pitcher who was born without a right hand, has been in the league since 1989 and has established himself as a top pitcher, but he still gets people who want to portray him as an inspiration for overcoming something that, to him, is truly not a handicap. Anyone who doubts that should just talk to the batters who have tried to hit his 94-mile-an-hour fastball.

Being the official inspiration is an uncomfortable role; the role of the stranger in literature. It makes you an outsider. And I wasn't an outsider. I thought of myself then and do now as a runner, a peer among the other runners with whom I associate. If another runner is inspired to greater effort by seeing me hop-swinging my way around the park, that's fine because it's helping a fellow athlete to perform better. People within a group use one another for inspiration all the time, which is why so many people tend to perform better when they're a member of a group than when they go it alone. And that's what it's all about, because I can draw inspiration from an able-bodied runner who cramps up a mile from the finish line but keeps going through the pain.

The next step was a 30K run in Central Park. That's 18.7 miles, just eight miles short of the marathon distance that I planned to run in October. I was now doing two two-hour runs, and one three-hour run a week on the Y track. I had lost five pounds, and this time, when I ran the 30K, I didn't hit a wall. I did, however, hit a bicyclist, or, more accurately, the cyclist hit me. This is an occupational hazard for anyone who runs regularly in Central Park, where bicycles, runners, roller skaters, and these days, wheelchairs, all compete for the same roadways and all fairly thoroughly hate each other. Bicyclists are particularly hazardous and also the most disdainful to those of us who go by foot. It's particularly bad during a race. The New York City police can't spare the manpower to clear the running course of bicycles, so this big gang of runners will be charging down the roadway and they'll have to dodge bicycles coming against the traffic. The bicycles don't recognize that a race is going on and they don't accept the park rule that gives the right-of-way to the slower-moving person or vehicle. They just curse us for making them move and we curse them for being such fatheads. The bottom line on all of this is that I figure if you run regularly in the park, you'll get hit by a bike once every 5,000 miles or so. I don't know how often bicycles collide with each other, but whenever I see it happen, I think, *That's two fewer bikes*.

Anyway, in this race, I got whacked by my first bike. He hit me, and my prosthesis—which, remember, is held on only by suction—was knocked off, and sent skittering across the pavement. His first reaction was to scream at me for getting in his way, and he was having a good time doing this when he realized I no longer had two legs. For a horrified moment, he thought he had somehow severed my leg. I assured him it was artificial, and I was not hurt, but he remained very apologetic as he collected his bike and got the heck out of there.

After the 30K, I was ready for the 1976 New York City Marathon. My mother, who wasn't excited about my new-found athletic obsession, wasn't so sure. She suggested that since I had only one leg, I should stick to a half-marathon. My new-found hobby was starting to wear on Betsy, as well. I was finding that for every hour I spent running, I needed an extra hour's sleep. I'd go out on Saturday and put in a three-hour session, come home, get something to eat, soak in the tub, and then fall asleep for three hours. If I went out at 10 a.m., it meant that I wasn't ready to do anything until 5 p.m., which meant that Saturday was pretty much ruined as far as the two of us getting out and doing anything was concerned. She went along for this marathon, but she told me I shouldn't plan on doing another.

My sister, however, was delighted with my new avocation and felt, as I did, that it was too bad my father wasn't still alive to see me run. Joanne—now an administrator in the computer science section of a large company and living in Delaware with her husband, Jeff, and three children, Allison, Lori, and Kenny—was a fine tennis player, and we sometimes played against each other. Right around the time I was training for the marathon, we had played tennis and she had beaten me. But at first, she didn't enjoy the victory because she felt that perhaps the reason she had beaten me was because I had only one leg. I had to assure her that my leg had nothing to do with it. She was simply better than I. Only then could she appreciate her triumph. As a college athlete, I was embarrassed to play with her because she was just a high school kid.

One happy coincidence about my running that year was it would be the first time that the race would be run through the five boroughs of Manhattan, starting at the Verrazano Narrows Bridge and ending in Central Park. This had been Fred Lebow's idea, and it turned the race into the greatest spectacle in running and the largest single spectator sporting event anywhere. In 1975, the last year the race was run in Central Park, it had attracted 534 starters. When Fred announced the change to a five-borough course, he said, "This could be the start of a new era in running for the city, and we want to make it the best." He was right on all counts. This year, 2,090 showed up at the starting line. That was twice as many as the Road Runners had expected when the new course had been announced earlier in the year. The running boom was in full flower. Frank Shorter, who had helped start it all, was entered in the race along with Bill Rodgers, the 1975 champion of Boston and one of the greatest runners ever produced by this country. The total number of women entrants was 104, which doesn't sound like a lot, but was double the total of the prior year. The runners ranged in age from 10-year-old Jerry Pierce of Muncie, Indiana, who ran with his parents, to 71-year-old Robert Earl Jones, the father of actor James Earl Jones. One blind runner, Joseph Pardo, entered, along with marathon swimmer Diana Nyad, Newark Mayor Kenneth Gibson, and George Hirsch, publisher of *New Times* magazine, who would become publisher of *Runner's World* magazine and a great supporter of Achilles.

Doctors, lawyers, and scientists accounted for the biggest block of entries, numbering 317. Close behind were 300 runners who identified themselves as students. And, as one newspaper put it, "Dick Traum will try to complete the course in eight hours wearing an artificial leg."

I knew I was attempting to be the first amputee to run a marathon. I had met Ted Corbett, a legendary runner who had run something like 200 marathons. Ted was on the board of directors of the New York Road Runners and someone asked him if he knew of any amputees who had run a marathon, and he said that he didn't. (Earlier in my training, I had asked Ted Corbett if he had ever seen another amputee run. He thought about it for while and said that he hadn't.)

After I had run the half-marathon in August, Ron Englehardt, a class leader at the West Side Y, introduced me to someone as, "Dick Traum, who's an amputee marathoner." I hadn't actually run a marathon yet, but back then not everyone knew what one was, and it was Ron's way of saying that I ran long distances. That's when it really struck me, as I suddenly realized that this was probably the first time those two words—amputee and marathoner—had ever been used together. I loved the sound of it and the idea of it.

We all knew at Road Runners that it would take me considerably longer to finish the race than the pack of runners, and Fred was worried that if I started with everyone else I would be running through Harlem by myself in the dark. So we finally decided it was best if I started early. Besides safety issues, that way I wouldn't finish alone in the dark at a deserted finish line. We planned a 7 a.m. start, but I really got off at 6:49. I couldn't wait to start. By then I had spent so much time preparing and anticipating the event that it was no longer fun. It was nerve-wracking, and I just wanted to get the tension over with.

These days, we have a sizable early start, but back then, I would be running alone for almost four hours. But I wasn't crazy. I had a support group with me. My wife, Betsy, and my brother-in-law, Jerry Chmielak, followed me in the car.

They had a pair of crutches with them. If I was anywhere within several miles of the end, I figured I could finish on the crutches. I also had Brian Smith, the son of a friend, riding alongside me on a bike.

Once I got going, I was fine. Running is for me, above all, fun. Bob Glover wrote about me, "Perhaps he has an advantage over us all in that he sees and enjoys a certain inherent beauty in running that many of us miss in our quest for speed. It takes Dick about 30 minutes to warm up, and then he reaches a high that can't be topped by any of us mere mortals."

I don't know about the "mere mortals" part, but Bob had a good point about my approach to the sport. Even if I had two good legs, I wouldn't have been a great long-distance runner. I was okay in a sprint, and ran on the freshman relay team in high school. But I was too stocky to be a competitive long-distance runner. Top marathoners tend to look anorexic, all bones and angles. Even at the 165 pounds I carried as a younger man, I was 30 pounds heavier than most top male runners. With one leg, of course, there was no way I could think of finishing even in the top 90 percent of the race.

The downside of lacking the talent to compete at the top level is, you never win the New York City Marathon. The upside is that you're free to enjoy the sport. Top runners are like elite golfers. They enjoy the competition and the winning, but if they had to compete on a mortal level, most would give it up because they don't enjoy just going out and finishing. Running is particularly insidious in this regard, because you have such a short time at the top. Marathons do a lot of damage to a body, particularly when you're going so close to your maximum output for so long. Very few people spend more than a few years at the very top level. That's what made Grete Waitz, the great Norwegian runner, so unusual. She remained at or near the top for more than a decade.

The training needed to stay at the top is torturous and continual. Even though you put in a vast amount of work, you can realistically run only two or three marathons a year at that level. So, when you actually get in a race, you're telling yourself you have to go harder than 100 percent, which is, of course, impossible. In a sprint, the fastest man in the world will win almost every time, even if he's only a hundredth of a second faster than the number-two guy. In a marathon, it doesn't work that way because there are so many more things that can go wrong over 26.2 miles. Most top runners, then, are usually failing. Consider the Olympics. Maybe 120 runners—the best from each country—start the marathon. Maybe half of them hope to finish in the top ten, and most of them aren't capable of that. They end up viewing themselves as failures not because they really did fail, but because they didn't meet their unreasonable expectation. They're beating themselves half to death for something they're not successful at. This isn't fun, and when they finally finish their careers, they frequently don't go near the sport.

Middle-of-the-pack runners have many more opportunities to be successful. A triumph can consist of running a new personal record, or a PR as it's known in the business. It can be beating some other runner. It can be finishing under a given time. It can even be simply finishing. If you don't feel well, you don't have to go at 100 percent. And even if you fail to meet any of those goals, you know it's not your profession. You don't lose money and it doesn't impact your life as it would if it were your job. So, any recreational runner can enjoy a race, whereas the professionals never really get to enjoy the sport. It shows most of all in the workouts. For a guy like myself, a workout is a chance to get out in the park and enjoy the scenery and the air, and to spend three hours chatting with dozens of other runners. If I were doing it professionally, I couldn't do that; I wouldn't be out there for fun.

In that first marathon, I had the added benefit of not being able to fail. No amputee had ever run a marathon. Amputees did not attempt such things because they couldn't be done. I was lucky in that no one told me that. I had fallen in with runners and they all said to go for it. But the fact remained I was attempting the impossible again. Even if I failed, I would succeed merely by having made the attempt.

That's how people looked at it. But the big secret was that it wasn't impossible at all. I knew from my workouts that I could run the distance. It was only the norms—the customs—of society and sport that said it was impossible. I had the advantage of understanding how customs arise, thanks to having set the counter-clockwork in motion back at Hunter College Elementary School. Even though the original decision had been totally arbitrary, it would have been very difficult to change it a few years later, because it had become a custom, a norm. Basically, to break a norm you have to be either really dumb or you have to be brave enough to do what feels right for you. Not so long ago, it was supposed to be impossible for women to run marathons. As recently as 1975, when I joined the Y, a big debate was going on about whether women could even exercise with men. As for marathoning, the first woman to post an official time was Dale Greig of Great Britain, who in 1964 ran a marathon in Ryde, England, in 3:27:45. In 1966, Roberta Gibb ran uninvited in the Boston Marathon. The organizers, who did everything they could to keep women out of the race because it was a macho event, refused to recognize her or any other woman until 1972, when they finally opened a women's division. Nina Kuscsik, a great pioneer and a board member of New York Road Runners today, won that race in 3:10:36. In less than three decades, women have cut more than an hour off Greig's first race. In the same time, men have reduced their world record by only six minutes.

Nina Kuscsik is an exceptional woman with a great deal of courage. Entering Boston was a big enough step in itself, but when she was running the race, she did something truly extraordinary by ignoring the rules of etiquette that would indicate that she should stop to go to the bathroom when her bowels rebelled. She ignored the norms and won the race!

You run into norms everywhere in sports. In golf, going past parallel on your backswing was thought to create a swing that's impossible to control, so you were taught not to do it. Then John Daly came along and swung his club so far past horizontal it was nearly perpendicular to the ground. And he won that way.

In baseball, hitting more than 60 home runs in a season was thought to be impossible, an opinion that kept anyone from hitting that many for 34 years until Roger Maris finally pulled it off.

In running, the norm from the beginning of modern track and field was that you couldn't run a mile in under four minutes. This opinion was so widely held that it became an actual barrier, and Roger Bannister had to use every ounce of energy he had to finally break through it in 1954. Now, four minutes isn't a barrier, but a floor. If you can't run a mile that fast, you might as well find another event.

I wrote my master's thesis on group influence. My study illustrated the fact that, when you are a member of a group, you don't break the group norms. The people who break norms are outsiders, which is why, when corporations want to make a fundamental change in the way they do things, they bring in an outsider. Thus, when Lee Iaccoca came as an outsider to Chrysler, he was able to do things that an executive who had come up through the company couldn't have done.

Creative people in general are people who break norms, whether in business, sports, or the arts. As a disabled person, I was breaking a norm. As a runner, I was acting as a group member. Members of this group run marathons and the group supports members who run marathons.

(By the way, this is why your teenager dresses and acts in ways you, as an adult, might find incredible. Teenagers are members of a smaller group with different norms. When they finally join the adult world, they're stuck with your norms. We call it growing up, but it's really just changing groups.)

So there I was, all by myself with my little convoy, working hard but enjoying the run, when I got to around the 10-mile point, somewhere near the Brooklyn Navy Yard. Today, a blue line painted on the pavement marks every step. But back then, there were large gaps across major intersections, and, since the real start of the race was more than an hour away, the course hadn't yet been closed off. We came to an intersection where I could go one of three ways and I picked the wrong one. I must have run about a half-mile before I realized this wasn't right. I thought about getting in the car and driving back to where I had taken the wrong turn and then finding the right way, but I realized it would be just my luck for someone to see me in the car, and how would I explain that? I could almost see the headline: "Amputee Runner Caught Cheating." So I put in an extra mile running back, sent Brian Smith ahead on the bike to find the right way, and got on with the race.

I had gone about 18 miles and was running to the left of the East River, when the leaders finally caught up to me and whizzed past as if I were going backwards. As Bill Rodgers, who would win the race, shot past, he yelled, "Attaboy, Dick!" That had to be one of the most exciting moments of my life.

Now I had other runners catching up, and now I had the crowd on the sidewalks. The last time I had heard the roar of the crowd had been as a wrestler in college, but I had never experienced anything like this before. I was hurting from sheer physical exertion, but when I heard that cheering, it just carried me along. No way was I going to stop. The last quarter-mile of the race, when the course was packed with spectators on each side, they roared as if I were running down the football field with the ball, headed for the winning touchdown. The difference is this didn't stop after 15 seconds, but went on and on for what seemed like forever.

I had aimed at finishing in eight hours and I actually finished in 7:24. I was more tired than happy when I finally got across the line, but the excitement wasn't over. Several hours after the race, the Road Runners held an awards ceremony at Avery Fisher Hall. They gave out the awards to the top finishers and then they called me up. The place erupted in a prolonged, standing ovation as they hung a medal around my neck. To this day, people will stop to tell me, "I was at Avery Fisher Hall in 1976 and the air was electric." It was the same for me, just unbelievable. It was something I had never felt before and never expect to feel again. I remember waving and putting my hands up in the air as the clapping continued and continued.

The *New York Daily News* did a story about me two days later. Written by Harry Stathos, it read:

1 Leg, 26 Miles of Heart.
Marathoner's remarkable race
A considerable amount of rubbing alcohol and wintergreen ointment was used yesterday morning to soothe the aching muscles of the

4,179 legs that took part in the New York/ Bicentennial Marathon.

The reason for the odd number of legs is that one of the runners was Richard Traum, a 35-year-old behavioral scientist from Manhattan who lost his right leg above the knee in an auto accident 11 years ago.

Wearing an artificial leg made of steel, plastic, and plywood, and with a rubber foot, Traum finished the 26-mile, 385-yard trek through the five boroughs in seven hours and 24 minutes...

"I was very satisfied with my performance," Traum said. "This morning, my leg was stiff. Surprisingly, my arms were stiff, too. I assume it was because I kept them parallel to the ground for more than seven hours..."

"I was amazed to see a man running with a wooden leg in the race," said one spectator. "I couldn't believe a person with a handicap could work up the nerve and strength to compete. It said something to all of us. It says our troubles aren't so great. If he has enough stamina to do that, we have enough stamina to do what we have to do."

The New York Times also ran a story that got picked up by *The International Tribune*: "The biggest applause always went to Richard Traum... who lost his right leg in a freak auto accident 10 years ago. He wore an artificial leg and finished 1869th."

Despite the pain and the tension, that day remains very special to me. If I had one day in my life to live all over again, it would be my first marathon.

At the same time, I'm the first to admit that I didn't deserve all the publicity. There's a big difference between quantity and quality. Quantity is finishing. Quality is finishing third, yet I got more publicity than anyone except the winner, Bill Rodgers, and the second-place finisher, Frank Shorter. If anyone other than Shorter had finished second, I would have had more publicity than him, too. That's unfair. I was a recreational runner and the guys near the top had spent their lives doing this and yet went totally unrecognized.

But people want to read about underdogs. It's the Rocky Syndrome and I was Rocky. If the definition of news is that which is different, then I certainly was different. And in successive years, in fact, papers wrote less and less about me as they pursued other, newer stories. Even so, I was still the one-legged runner. In 1977, I ran the marathon again and knocked a minute and a half per mile off my pace, which is an excellent improvement. No one wanted to know about the time, though. They just wanted to know about the leg.

The fallout from that race was far-ranging, although it took some time for it to show up. One of the first things that happened was that Jim Fixx, a writer, ran in that marathon with me. Jim had been planning to write a book about fitness but then he ran the race and got turned on to running. He changed the focus of the book, and *The Complete Book of Running* became a bestseller and a bible to runners in those early days of the boom. He included me in the book as an example of what you can do when you put your mind to it and how anyone can run. Bob Glover also wrote about me in his own bestseller, *The Runners Handbook*. Stories and pictures of me ran in just about every running publication.

When the marathon was done, I returned to my real life, which was changing at warp speed. The biggest change came in December, when Betsy and I became parents. The arrival of our son, Joey, precipitated a string of moves.

At the time, we were living at West End Avenue and 87th Street in a one-bedroom apartment. I was also running my business out of the apartment. But it became apparent almost immediately that a baby consumes space at a rate entirely disproportionate to its size. We started looking for a new apartment with two bedrooms, and found one early in 1977 on Fifth Avenue overlooking Central Park. New York City was on the verge of bankruptcy at the time, and property values were depressed. Friends told us we shouldn't be buying in that climate, but the apartment, which had 1,500 square feet, seemed too good to pass up. We paid $55,000 cash for it, figuring that if it lost its value over the 30 years we expected to live there, it would have been worth it. Ten years later, when real estate prices were going through the ozone layer, it was clear it was the best purchase we ever made. The value had increased by a factor of 10.

Betsy had been working as an industrial nurse at IBM's New York headquarters. She quit that job when she became a mother, so now both she and the baby were home all day. At the same time, my business was growing rapidly and just after we moved, I went shopping for permanent office space.

I ended up back at the Celanese Corporation, this time as a tenant. That worked out well, since Celanese was a client. Up until then, I had been renting computer time to run my programs, but now I was in a position to buy my own computer. It cost me $160,000 and I used to impress potential clients by pointing out that it had a RAM capacity of 256K and a 96-megabyte disc drive—about what you can get for less than a thousand bucks in a laptop machine today. We were really proud of that computer, and even gave it a name: Emm. I named it that because it was the first sound that Joey made, "mmm."

I had been hiring college students to write programs for me. When I got my own machine, I hired one of the students, Ken Anderson, Jr., on a full-time basis, as head of computer operations. Ken had just graduated from Rensselaer Polytechnic Institute. In my two decades in business, I have never met a more skillful computer professional. I also found I needed a full-time secretary, and Betsy told me about a woman she had become friends with. Like Betsy, Karen Gale was a new mother who took her child to Central Park during the day to play. While they were watching the children, Betsy and Karen talked, and one day Karen mentioned she was looking for part-time work as a secretary. Betsy suggested I hire her, which I did, on a full-time basis, and for the next 13 years, Karen Gale was the best secretary anyone could ever have. Karen got to know me and the business so well that frequently, when I was giving her dictation, she'd have written down what I was going to say before I said it.

Those were good years. I did continue to run, but not as much as I had while getting ready for the 1976 marathon. Eventually, Joey joined me on the runs on his bicycle, which he taught himself to ride at age four. I'd be chugging along and he'd be riding circles around me, up and down hills, down flights of steps, through every puddle in the park. He and that bike were almost one.

I also joined a running team that Bob Glover had put together. The team was eventually called "Atalanta," and became an elite female running club. Bob liked classical images, and Atalanta was a beautiful maiden in Greek mythology who could run faster than anyone. She offered to marry any man who could beat her in a footrace. Hippomenes accepted her challenge but took with him three golden apples. Each time Atalanta would begin to pass him, he would drop one of the apples and Atalanta would stop to pick it up. In this way Hippomenes won the race.

I don't think Glover's team had more than one runner leave and then set a new PR. During the early years, after a team workout, we'd stop at a working-class Irish bar in the 60s on Broadway and start ordering pitchers of beer. The women runners couldn't have averaged more than 110 pounds each and they'd be outdrinking truck drivers. How they could drink so much beer without seeming to get drunk was a running discussion at the bar. It's the running that does it. Of course, my excuse was that I had a hollow leg to put the beer in.

I was a full-fledged member of the New York Road Runners inner circle. We had a room at the West Side Y so small that to make space to move around in it we had to move a pile of boxes out into the hall. When we closed up for the day, we would move the boxes back inside. The organization was starting to grow, but it was still small enough that if you hung out there regularly, you soon discovered that you were on the board of directors, which is what happened to me. The position sounded more impressive than it was. Most of the time, when Fred called a meeting of the board of directors, it meant he needed help stuffing envelopes.

I did have one important job. For a few years, I was one of the New York Road Runners' bag men. In those days of alleged amateur purity, races did not offer prize money— officially. But if you wanted the best runners, you had to pay them. They were devoting their lives to their sport and most marathoners in those days were the embodiment of the starving artist. Yet, if they accepted official prize money, they would be ineligible for amateur competitions, which meant all official races, including the Olympics. So they had to be paid as athletes had been paid for decades—under the table. That first year I ran, the prize was modest. Bill Rodgers, who won, was flat broke and living on food stamps. He had driven down from Boston for the race and parked on the street. When he left his room Monday morning, his car was gone. It had been towed. So his prize was the $50 it took to redeem the car from the pound. In future races and as his fame grew, he began requesting appearance money just to run. He wasn't alone in that. All the top runners wanted to be paid to attend and any marathon organizers who wanted an elite field had to pay them.

Most of the runners, once they had their money guaranteed up front, stopped running as well as they had been running. One notable exception was Grete Waitz, who won no matter what. Grete was also the most civilized negotiator I ran into. Some runners would make demands and become confrontational. Grete was a real lady—sort of the Helen Hayes of running.

As appearance fees climbed, so did the unofficial prize money. During the week after the race, I'd take the winners down to Manufacturers Hanover Trust (currently Chemical Bank and a sponsor of the Achilles Track Club) and make some withdrawals. The public thought that the awards ceremony had taken place after the race when the runners were crowned with laurel and took delivery of their trophies, but the real ceremony was at the bank, when I delivered the cash. This went on until the mid-80s, when Fred admitted that we were paying prize money and even appearance money. At about the same time, the Olympic rules were changed to allow runners to earn a living through their sport, and the money changed hands in the open.

After running New York in 1976, I was now a runner, and I decided I wanted to run the granddaddy of marathons—the Boston Marathon. When I made some inquiries, however, I was told I wasn't welcome. Boston was a serious race for serious runners, not a three-ring circus, I was told. Obviously, they considered me a clown at best and a freak show at worst. I was upset by their reaction, not as much by the implied insult as by the fact that I was being excluded. If you're a runner, you want to run Boston, just as if you're a golfer, you want to play the Old Course at St. Andrews.

The vast majority of runners are terrific people, but there

is an elitist element in the sport. In the United States, Boston holds down that position. They do it by setting time requirements for runners. As a male in my mid-30s, I would have had to have run under a 3:30 marathon somewhere else to qualify for Boston. That's something more than an hour slower than the best runners, and considerably faster than the four or five hours a typical recreational runner needs to run a marathon. But it was twice as fast as I could run. Boston does this to limit the entries to a manageable level and to keep its reputation as a serious race intact. To run Boston's qualifying time, you have to be a serious runner—and have all your limbs. So it didn't matter how serious I was, I wasn't going to run there.

It's an unusual attitude for the United States, where we tend to be inclusive rather than exclusive. But it's not uncommon elsewhere in the world. Fred Lebow discovered this a few years ago when he was invited to run in the Beijing Marathon in China. The Chinese had heard about Fred, as all runners have, and decided they would invite this great American runner to their big race. Since he has such a monumental reputation, they assumed he was an accomplished runner. Nothing could be farther from the truth. Fred is as serious about running as anyone. He puts in the miles and the work. He's just flat-out slow. No one's ever held that against him, and he's never held it against anyone else. Over the years his biggest problem with the New York City Marathon has been finding ways to increase the size of the field without the race becoming a logistical nightmare.

Anyway, Fred accepted the invitation to run in Beijing, thinking that he was going to run in a typical, big-city race with a horde of runners of every conceivable ability. When the race was about to start, he lined up at the front, where they insisted he be, and at the gun, set out at his customary lope. But the runners behind him weren't loping. They thundered across the line at a gallop and ran right over Fred. He hit the pavement hard and felt something go in his shoulder. The shoulder was separated, but Fred continued the race. In New York, the crowds would pick up on something like that and cheer mightily for someone showing such courage. But the Chinese looked at sports differently.

They felt that if you didn't have a chance to win, you shouldn't be in the race. The concept of recreational running hadn't occurred to them. So when Fred ran by at his slow and balanced pace, the crowds looked, gawked, and broke out laughing. Fred heard the laughter and couldn't understand what was so funny. He thought maybe his pants were torn, but that wasn't it. Finally, he figured it out. And he finished anyway.

That's sort of the way the Boston Marathon directors looked at me in 1977. As a joke. Since then, I have gotten Achilles runners into the Boston Marathon. They still haven't taken me, but we have blind runners, others with multiple sclerosis, and below-the-knee amputees who get around in 4.5 hours or less, and they've decided they can live with that without debasing their race.

None of this discouraged me. I could run in New York any time I wanted, and no one laughed. They cheered. As far as I knew, I was still the only amputee runner. But that was about to change.

Early in 1977, a young Canadian who had been a good high school athlete, was lying in a hospital waiting to go into surgery. During his senior year basketball season, his right knee had begun to hurt. He had gotten through the season and then gone into a hospital for tests. The doctors found bone cancer of the same type that Ted Kennedy, Jr., had. The only treatment was amputation. The young man's name was Terry Fox.

The day before the surgery, Fox's high school basketball coach, Terri Fleming, came to see him. Thinking that Fox needed something to boost his spirits, Fleming brought with him a recent copy of *Runner's World* magazine, which included a photo of me finishing the New York City Marathon and a story about my race. As Leslie Scrivener wrote in her book, *Terry Fox: His Story*:

> That night a dream started germinating in Terry's brain. It wouldn't reach full flower for another three years, but the seed had been planted. That night an 18-year-old athlete who wasn't sure he'd be able to walk again decided he wanted to run across Canada.

Fox himself put it this way in a letter he wrote to potential sponsors for his run, which would be dedicated to defeating cancer:

> ...I decided to meet this new challenge head on and not only overcome my disability, but conquer it in such a way that I could never look back and say it disabled me... By April next year I will be ready to achieve something that for me was once only a distant dream reserved for the world of miracles; to run across Canada to raise money for the fight against cancer...

Fox was doing exactly what I set out to do. Like me, he was willing to take a calculated risk in an effort to be successful. Some psychologists would call it denial. You are denying your disability by doing something that most able-bodied people wouldn't—and couldn't—do. You can call it neurotic, but a little neurosis is good, and I don't think you have to dig down very deep below the surface of most successful or creative people before you unearth the neurotic within.

I knew nothing about Fox and what he was planning to do. He never wrote to me or called me. I was, in his mind, this heroic and unapproachable figure. Just knowing I had done it was enough to let him know it was possible to run. If he had asked me, I would have advised him that the pace he intended to maintain was too grueling. His idea was to take my marathon and run that distance every day until he had crossed Canada—the second largest country in the world—from the Atlantic to the Pacific. I would have told him either to run fewer miles each day or to schedule some breaks. The problem with running long distances with a prosthetic leg is that, eventually, the stump starts to bleed. No matter how much you train, there are some places on the stump that simply won't callus over, particularly on the back of the leg. It's like wearing a woman's shoe held on by a strap across the heel. It's going to chafe and eventually it will bleed. The bleeding itself isn't a big deal, even though it can look gruesome when the blood starts running out of the air valve at the knee. The real danger is of infection setting in if you don't give the wound time to heal.

This did, in fact, happen. Fox had gone a considerable

distance when it did, and his support crew, I learned, attempted to contact me but was unsuccessful. I would have told him to run for two or three days and then take a day off. I didn't think he was being foolish because I thought he would get the message soon enough without my help. But he just kept on going. As he did, he generated considerable press coverage in Canada. Not all of it was favorable. Several newspaper columnists criticized him harshly. It was the sideshow mentality at work. But most people recognized his fundamental sincerity. He was doing it with a minimum of sponsorship and support. He wasn't trying to turn himself into a hero, but was genuinely interested in raising money to fight cancer. That's why he called his run "A Marathon of Hope."

The first I learned of Terry Fox was when I saw a piece about him on a television show called "That's Incredible." I found it interesting, but didn't really give it a lot of thought. It crossed my mind that perhaps I had inspired him, but this was up in Canada, and I had my hands full in New York, running my business and just plain running. I didn't hear anything else about Fox, and gave him no further thought until several months later when I got a phone call from a Jonathan Rosen, who was very enthusiastic about the Marathon of Hope and called me asking for a donation. I sent along something and later, I heard that Terry had had to call off the run after finishing more than 3,000 miles of his 5,000-mile journey. The cancer had recurred, this time in his lungs, and he was in a hospital undergoing chemotherapy. I dug out a photo of myself from the 1976 marathon and sent it to him along with a letter wishing him well and a donation. I never heard back from him, but Fox was getting thousands of letters a day and he probably never saw my letter. Besides, his condition was getting worse. Late in June, around the 25th, a Canadian radio station called me and told me that Terry Fox was near death. We talked about his run and what he had accomplished. A few days later, on June 28, Terry Fox died.

When he died, my life was in the process of changing profoundly under the force of two pressures. One was my business, which quadrupled in size between 1977 and 1981. The other was the New York Road Runners Club, in which I was becoming increasingly involved. And the bigger the business got, the more I was drawn to running. By 1980, the club had not only outgrown its tiny offices in the West Side Y, it had also worn out its welcome. There was a guy who worked for the Y who must have weighed 350 pounds. He hated us for no better reason, it seemed, than that we had to move all these boxes out into the hall every morning to have room to use the offices, and that made it difficult for him to navigate the corridor. "Make the skinny twerps put the boxes back inside," he'd grouse. "It's a fire violation to have them in the hall." On top of that, I managed to alienate Hans Lindner, the executive director of the Y. I didn't think that Lindner was doing a good job running the place, and I tried to get him moved to a corporate position. So when several of us suggested that Road Runners and the Y run a joint aerobic testing facility, he turned us down. The idea had been for us to rent the fifth floor and turn it into a testing center. Both the Y and Road Runners could make money. When Lindner turned us down, I started to become less active in the Y, for which I was also a board member, and turned my attention to the running club.

I still attended board meetings at the Y, and I learned that the YMCA was, indeed, moving to terminate the Y's relationship with the New York Road Runners. This put me in a delicate position because of my status as a board member of Road Runners. I couldn't come straight out and tell my fellow runners that they were on the verge of eviction. At the same time, I couldn't sit back, do nothing, and watch the Road Runners get pitched out into the street with nowhere to go. While I was trying to figure out what to do, I had lunch with Richard Mardus, a public relations man, and Vince Chiapetta, a fellow Road Runners board member. Mardus was pitching an idea to bring in a lot of money to the club, and felt we could raise money by fund-raising. While we were talking, the idea of buying our own building came up. For me, it was the perfect idea. Without violating my trust with the Y board, I could steer the club toward a solution to everyone's problems. And even if we had been on perfect terms with the Y, it was a good idea. With running booming and new memberships pouring in, we needed a home of our own. With it, we would move beyond being merely a club and become an institution. No one would tell us to get the boxes out of the hall.

When I suggested finding a building, Fred said what he always says when someone has an idea: "See what you can do." Fred's management style is to never say no. If you have an idea and are willing to follow it up, he lets you develop it. There's plenty of time to make a final decision once he sees where it's going. During 1980, I put in probably 300 hours working on the project. Finally, I found just what I thought we needed. It was a brownstone on East 89th Street, just half a block off the park and a block away from the 90th Street park entrance, where most of the club's races started. The building had been used for psychologists' offices. The tenants were moving and the owners put it up for sale. It was a gorgeous place, six stories tall with 14,500 square feet of space in 30 or 40 rooms. Sure, it was twice as big as we thought we needed and, at $1.4 million, cost twice as much as we thought we could afford, but it was ideal for our purposes. I swore the minute I saw it that if we could buy that building, I'd jump up and down on one leg.

Most people said it was impossible at worst and foolhardy at best, but the opportunist in me took over. The building was there, we needed it, and so what if our net worth was a negative $50,000, and the prime rate was around 20 percent? We could figure out how to pay for it after we bought it.

I gathered some fellow board members, went to Manufacturers Hanover Bank (Chemical Bank), which was our major sponsor in those days, and asked for a loan, offering $100,000 as a down payment. The executive we talked to said we didn't have the resources. I asked if we could twist his arm. He said we'd have to break it off. The next day we got the loan.

I got it by convincing 10 other fools to cosign notes for over a million dollars' worth of owner financing. I was the 11th fool. I know that because when I asked someone I knew whether I should get advice from a lawyer about cosigning, he replied, "You don't need an attorney. You need a psychiatrist."

Once Fred found out we were actually going to go through with the purchase, he got very nervous. He simply hadn't thought we could pull it off so he hadn't objected. When we got to the closing, though, he had second thoughts. If it fell apart, the club he had worked so hard to build would implode. But he didn't have the heart to tell me this. So he simply didn't show up at the closing. I signed for it without him, and suddenly, the NYRRC had a home.

The building changed everything. When we were kicking cartons around at the Y, we were just a bunch of guys who hung out together and ran now and then. We didn't budget our money well because we didn't have the big nut of a mortgage to pay. When we got our own headquarters, we became respected members of the corporate community to whom we looked for sponsorship of our programs. It became much easier to raise funds now that we had a mortgage to pay, and at the same time, we became much more professional and less wasteful in the way we managed our money. In effect, the mortgage forced us to save, because we didn't know how long the running boom and the income would last. We ended up paying the building off in five years and it peaked in value during the late 1980s at around $6 million. In 1993, in a weak economy, it was still worth $4 million, a tidy bit of equity to fall back on.

As if to prove the value of the building, shortly after we signed for it in January 1981, a developer approached us about buying it. He wanted to put up a high-rise on the site and offered us $2 million, a $600,000 profit virtually overnight. I didn't think we could pass up that kind of profit, and suddenly I was going around to all the people I had talked into buying the building and trying to talk them into selling it. The deal never did go through, and we kept the place, but I figured right there I had made more than half a million dollars for the NYRRC.

The high from pulling off the deal was incredible. It was, I felt, the best thing I had ever done, if only because I hadn't done it for myself or for my business, but for the good of a group. I got my share of congratulations, too, but the voices I heard at first, with disbelief, were the ones who came out of the woodwork to criticize the deal. We had paid too much, they said. Yes, we had, I countered, but we needed it and if we had held out for a lower price, we would have lost it. Then some members complained that it wasn't right that their running club had nicer quarters than they had at home. Others groused that it was too far from the subway, which stopped several blocks to the east on Lexington. Here they were, runners, complaining about having to walk a couple blocks from the subway to go run.

The criticism I found the most biting was that I had only bought the building because it was close to my own home. It was true that I live just a few blocks south on Fifth Avenue and that the Y was all the way across the park and another 20 blocks south, but the charge was ludicrous. The building was a block from where we started our races and gathered for workouts. It was in a terrific neighborhood.

The episode taught me that no matter what you do in life, you'll always have critics. Terry Fox had had critics. One of them had even taken the time to write to me to blame me for his getting cancer and to tell us Americans to quit trying to get the rest of the world to do crazy things. All you can do with critics is ignore them, because if you refuse to act until you find a situation in which you get no criticism, you'll never get anything done. If you're going to be successful, you have to understand that.

The other set of events that was conspiring to change my life involved my business. In 1981, Personnelmetrics had 25 employees and had outgrown its offices. As a temporary measure, I split my staff between two buildings while I looked for quarters that would accommodate an operation that I anticipated would shortly double in size again. When I had started the business, I had dreamed of the day I would be the CEO of a real corporation. But now that I was heading in that direction, it turned out that it wasn't as much fun as I had thought it would be. It had been a grand adventure in the beginning, when everything was new and I was personally involved with everything that went on, directly supervising every employee.

But when you pass a certain size, you can't be as involved anymore. For me, it happened when I got to 20 employees. Suddenly, I had to hire a personnel manager, and the employees reported to others. If there were problems with accounts, I didn't hear about them. Everything was fine. And if there were problems with employees, it was my fault. Beyond that, it became impossible to maintain the quality of which I was so proud. It's like a small restaurant that serves excellent food and then gets discovered. All of a sudden, lots of people are coming in and the restaurant expands. Now, the person who made the small bistro so good can no longer be personally involved in every meal and the quality falls off. Mama Leone's fell prey to that syndrome. Once, it had been a delightful place to eat. Then it got discovered, got big, and ended up as a place that lived on its reputation and off tourists. It was still packed, and everyone talked about it as a landmark, but the old crowd which had so admired the food and atmosphere stopped going there. As Yogi Berra once put it: "Nobody goes there anymore. It's too crowded."

But I wasn't thinking in those terms then. I was just concerned with keeping the growth curve going. I finally tracked down nearly 5,000 square feet of space—twice the size of my former quarters—in a building managed by the Helmsley Spear Corporation. This was another mistake, because the way Harry and Leona Helmsley made out was to offer the space for a price that looked very reasonable but to fill the lease with little gems that quickly made it very expensive. One of the items they hit you on was electricity. The lease said I paid for my own power, and I had no problem with that. But when I got the bill, it was for around $3,000 a month. That was much more than I should have been paying, and I eventually caught them.

That's a Helmsley operation for you.

My business had been so easy until then. It had been like having an apple tree behind the house that was always bearing fruit. Anytime I needed to, I could just walk outside and pick another apple. My "tree" was the Celanese Corporation and its network of former employees. Wherever they went, they hired me to handle their personnel data systems. I didn't have a brochure, a mailing list, or a salesman; not even an ad. Yet I had all the business I wanted. I even had a contract to come up with a way to establish a pay scale for baseball players based on performance—not just batting statistics, but position-by-position fielding statistics, as well. We even had a factor for guys who did things like bunt and steal bases and who maybe didn't have the big numbers, but brought a lot of people into the park. Obviously, it was an idea whose time had not yet come.

Prospects knew I was providing the best service available anywhere. I truly believed that. I still do. It was all custom work, which is one reason that I never considered trying to become an ADP-type operation, providing a standardized kind of service. So I was expanding, but the nature of my business was that I couldn't expand. Unfortunately, you don't find out these things until you've already crossed your business Rubicon.

Another thing you don't find out is that, when you expand rapidly, your cash flow is terrible. You're paying more taxes, buying more equipment. You're also bringing in new accounts, which just makes matters worse. What happens then is that you have your first meeting with the client in July and bill them, say, $5,000, the first of August. They put it in their stack of bills payable and by the time the bureaucracy finishes grinding the necessary gears, it's October and they're just paying for July. Meanwhile, the bills for August, September, and October are pending and the net result is you've got $20,000 in accounts receivable. The money isn't doing you any good, since where you really need the money is in your payroll account.

I had to start pinching pennies, which meant that I couldn't take risks and try new things. And all the while I was trying to maintain the one thing that all my business was based on—quality. In this kind of climate, borrowing money was very difficult. I was out there on my own.

We moved into the new building June 28, 1981, the day Terry Fox died. Then, within three months of the move, I lost my biggest account, Norwest Bank, which was probably bringing in 20 percent of my gross. I had known they intended to set up their own personnel data system; they had been talking about it for five years. I knew it wasn't going to be as easy as they thought, and the process stretched out forever. But finally, they got it up and running, and the loss of their account was a big hit to take. When I said that none of this was fun, that wasn't the half of it. Distress and pressure were coming from every direction and I really thought that it was my fault. It was the first time I had ever failed at something.

Failure is good in the abstract. It makes you stronger, it gives you perspective. It makes success that much better. In

the concrete, it's a misery that worms way down deep in
your subconscious mind. I guess it came out one night
when I had an incredibly vivid dream. The dream was that
I was the CEO of a mighty corporation, just as I had thought
I would be when I went off on my own. I had spent most of
my life developing the business into this great institution
and now they were holding a dinner for me. Somebody
made a speech, called me up to the podium, and handed
me a plaque. The audience stood and applauded for 15
seconds or so and that was it.

I went home with the plaque thinking, "Is this what I
was doing this for all these years? A handshake, 'Thank you
very much,' and a plaque? And then, 'See ya'?" That was
the dream. It was also becoming the reality. And it was ludicrous.
When I woke up that morning, I asked myself, "Am I doing this
to become Mr. Computer of New York City?"

I was spending my whole life trying to build something
that really didn't mean anything. It wasn't as if I were
building a business for my son to take over. I didn't need a
bigger car or a bigger apartment. I guess the child who had
only thought of making the biggest pots and who had
wanted to create the biggest business had grown up. I realized
I didn't want big anymore. I was in business solely for the
opportunity to do something exceptionally well. I had done
that. The rest of the package—titles, perks, money,
whatever—was as shallow as a network sitcom.

The thought that I had had in the hospital when I lost
my leg began to come back to me. Life is short and you
don't get to repeat it. I was closing in on 41 years of age,
and I probably had 25 good years left. It was time to think
about doing other things. Getting the headquarters building
for the Road Runners was the beginning of that. Now, in
September, 1981, just as Personnelmetrics began to bleed,
Terry Fox returned to my life.

Jonathan Rosen, the man who had first called me a year
earlier to tell me about the recurrence of Terry Fox's cancer,
called again. Although Fox had died, his drive to raise funds
to combat cancer hadn't. His friends and supporters decided
to memorialize him and continue to raise money by holding
a series of 10K Terry Fox Runs throughout Canada in
September. Rosen talked to the organizers and convinced

them that it would be good publicity to invite me to Toronto to help promote the events.

I didn't handle the initial phone call with a great deal of grace. When the organizers called me, I was still busy raising funds to pay for the Road Runners headquarters. So I told them I'd love to come, and if I did, maybe they could donate some money to the mortgage fund. Okay, it was an inappropriate thing to ask, not to mention rude and maybe even classless. But I really wanted to get that building paid for, especially in view of the heat I was taking for buying it. They told me they couldn't make a donation. They were trying to raise funds themselves. They were nice about it, though, probably figuring that I was just a typical American, always looking for what was in it for me. I said something about having a busy schedule and needing a vacation and they offered to bring me, my wife, and our son, who was four years old, up to Canada and pay our expenses. So that's how we did it.

For the first time in my life, I was a celebrity. In Canada, they set up a schedule and got a limo to take me around. We had one day to get settled and the next morning the car picked me up at the hotel at 6 a.m. to take me to my first television appearance. At first, I thought, "This is really neat." I was being driven around, being taken to makeup, and sitting on a TV set talking about how great Terry Fox was and how important it was that people contribute money to the cause. Then I was whisked off to another studio to do it again.

After the first three or four stops, the novelty had worn off. After a few more, it was not too neat anymore. But it just kept going on, from seven in the morning until midnight, and I was expected to be just as bright-eyed and bushy-tailed at the end of the day as I had been at dawn. Stardom, it turns out, is hard, hard work. It's like a conveyor belt in a factory that never stops and never lets you relax. Or, maybe a better analogy, it's like spending a day tasting ice cream where you have to eat a bowl of it at every stop. At first, it's great. At the end, it's all you can do to force it down.

Today, during election seasons, I watch politicians making the rounds of the networks and radio talk shows and I realize that they're going at a similar, if not faster, pace than I had gone. They can't possibly enjoy it.

I ended that second day in Toronto by taking part in a 24-hour relay race being run around a track in the city to kick off the Terry Fox event. I ran a lap in that race and finally called it a day. Later, I found out that, after one of my television appeals, $17,000 was pledged by listeners. I found that to be astonishing, particularly since, when I was sitting in a TV studio, it was only me, the host and crew, and a couple of cameras. I didn't really think about the hundreds of thousands of people watching because I couldn't see them.

The next day was race day, and I got up early again and went to one of the events to run a few miles. There were some more radio spots and print interviews, and then I ran in another 10K that was held in the afternoon in another location. They were small races; just a couple of hundred people running, and no crowds to speak of. I signed some autographs, which was another interesting experience and another revelation, because nobody tells you that after a while your hand gets tired from signing. I was supposed to run in three races that day, but we didn't get to the third one. (Earlier in the day, a reporter asked me about running three races in one day, and I said, "I'm delighted to run in three races. I'm sure if Terry were here, he would have run six.")

We took another day to see a bit of Toronto, and then that was it. When we got home, I didn't think much more about it. At the same time, I was intrigued by having seen more disabled people as spectators at the runs than I remembered seeing in the States, never realizing that since the runs were in memory of Terry Fox, that was to be expected. Instead, I simply thought that Canadians were more accepting of people with disabilities than Americans were.

I suppose that's when the idea of doing something more than just running in races began to germinate. But it hadn't taken root yet. I still had too much to worry about with Personnelmetrics.

Looking back, I see that the business peaked in 1980. That's when I was doing things that big companies like IBM are just starting to understand now. But when you're the best, there's nowhere else to go. Meanwhile, the industry is catching up to you. In personnel data systems, programs that a company could buy and run on their own computers were then being developed. Remember, this was also the time when computers were getting smaller and enormously more powerful, so that you no longer needed a huge mainframe to do what we think of today as relatively simple things. Since a lot of my business had been the rental of computer time and the use of my programs, there was a natural contraction there. Basically, the kind of personalized services I offered was becoming obsolete.

As I continued to wrestle with a contracting business, I continued to run, and, for the first time, I began to have company. A friend, Diane Israel, introduced me to a friend of hers, a fine athlete who had lost a leg in a mountain-climbing accident out west. She came back to New York with her new prosthesis and asked me to run with her and give her some advice. So we did some laps together around the reservoir in Central Park. She went back home and a little while later Jack Terry, an amputee from Pennsylvania, called me up and came to the city to run a five-mile race with me. At the same time as this was going on, I was getting phone calls from other amputees who wanted running advice, and I found myself coaching them by phone. I began to think there might be more that I could do in this area.

September rolled around again and I got another call from Canada to participate in the second annual Terry Fox Day runs. I went up again and found that the novelty that makes you a celebrity wears off quickly. If Charles Lindbergh had tried soloing across the Atlantic a second time, he'd have discovered the same thing. It's old news. I did some television and a few interviews, but it was nothing like it had been in 1981. It also was no longer exciting for me. As far as I'm concerned, being on television once is enough. Now it was all work. I did run in two more 10K races, though, and the interesting part about that was that a film company was on hand shooting scenes for a movie about Terry Fox's life. It also seemed that I saw more disabled people both watching the races and participating in them.

By the time I got back to New York, I knew what I was going to do. If I was seeing so many disabled people around the running scene in Canada and hearing from them in the States, there must be a lot more out there who would like to get involved in running. All they needed was some help getting started.

FINISH

Chapter 5

It may be we shall touch the Happy Isles,
And see the great Achilles...
—Alfred, Lord Tennyson

The financial obligation of the Road Runners Club building was under control and I wanted another project. Helping disabled people get involved in running seemed perfect. I had no intention of forming a club or starting anything permanent. My original idea was merely to set up an eight-week series of running classes. I took it to Fred Lebow, and Fred gave me his usual response: "See what you can do." I told him it was possible that only a few people would show up for it. "Even if three people show up, it will be worth it," he said.

With funding that Fred authorized, I made up a letter introducing the course and mailed it to all 1,100 doctors and other medical professionals who were on the Road Runners' mailing list, figuring that even though these were able-bodied people, they might have disabled patients who might want to get involved in running. We set a $40 fee for the course, which I described as being for amputees and people in wheelchairs. Those were the only "disabilities" I thought existed, since I had no disabled associates or friends and knew absolutely nothing about the range of disabilities or the disabled community.

Bob Glover agreed to teach the course. Everything was set. All I had to do then was wait for the applications to come pouring in.

Only the applications didn't exactly pour in. They didn't even trickle. Fact is, I didn't get a single response! Now my fears of no one coming were real. The first session was set for Wednesday evening, November 10, 1982. At the appointed hour, Fred, Bob, and myself gathered at the

NYRRC, waiting to see if anyone would show up.

Fred had said if three people came, it would be a success.

We got two people.

"It's a success anyway," Fred said.

I was so concerned with getting things started and doing a good job of teaching that I honestly can't remember who the first runners were. But I know that among the first were Linda Down, John Paul Cruz, Pedro Hernandez, Jim Rosenberg, Marty Ball, and Fred Trinkel.

Linda Down was probably at the first meeting and has been with us ever since. She is now on the Achilles board of directors. We never did collect the $40 fee for the class from anyone, and I never asked for it. In the 11 years since then, no one has ever had to pay to join Achilles.

Linda was already an accomplished runner and a media star when she joined. She was born with cerebral palsy, and about a year before she joined us had gotten her master's degree in social work. But in 1982 the economy was in a down phase and, despite months of searching, she couldn't get a job. So, early in 1982, she decided that, if she couldn't find work, she could at least get in shape. She had gotten the idea of running when she and her twin sister, Laura, who also has cerebral palsy, watched the New York City Marathon on television in 1981 and Laura remarked, "Maybe we ought to try that." Linda decided that she actually would.

When she started working out, she couldn't do 10 sit-ups, but by the time the marathon rolled around, she was running the crowded streets of Manhattan for six and seven hours at a time. Running for her was slow and painful. She had a pin in one hip and needed crutches to navigate. Her left side is her strong side, and she'd lead with her left leg and then follow it by swinging her right leg in a big, awkward arc. With each stride, her toes scraped along the pavement, and with each footfall, her toes were mashed inside her running shoes. She started with the pack in the 1982 marathon and finished at 9:30 at night, more than 11 hours after she started.

Her gutsy performance attracted a lot of television and print exposure and when President Reagan invited the race winners, Alberto Salazar and Grete Waitz, to the White House, he also invited Linda. So here she was on top of the world at the White House, when just six months earlier she had been despairing of finding a job and just starting to run to lose a few pounds and get in better shape.

I had seen Linda in the race, and afterwards I called her up and invited her to come to the workouts.

Marty Ball was another racer I had seen in the marathon. He was a top-notch wheelchair athlete, and had entered the race—even though Fred didn't allow wheelchairs in it—and done quite well. I approached him at the finish line and invited him and his friend, Jim Beckford, a volunteer, to come to the classes I was starting and to help coach. After a while, he brought his girlfriend, Natalie Bacon, another top wheelchair racer, who became our first female wheelchair marathoner. Marty stayed with us and was a great coach until he moved to California, where he sells racing wheelchairs. Sadly, Natalie died a couple of years ago of cancer.

When Jim Rosenberg was just 13 years old, his mother somehow heard about the classes and brought him down to Achilles. He stayed with us for a while and then dropped out. Fred Trinkel had severe arthritis and came out from Long Island to run with us. Pedro Hernandez was a double-amputee who used a wheelchair and was legally blind, although he had a slight amount of vision. He came from 116th Street and First Avenue for the workouts, but his problem was that he didn't want to go home to Harlem in the dark. No problem, I said, and offered to drive him home.

Someone else might have given up on the club before it even started. There were so few people at those early meetings that it probably didn't make sense to go on. But one of my personality flaws is that I tend to hang on to things too long. I was doing that with my business, trying to maintain its volume when the changing computer market was making that impossible. I had also hung on too long years earlier when I was trying to learn how to water-ski on my one leg. Skiing on one leg is very difficult to learn, and I couldn't do it. I'd put the ski on in the water, signal for the boat to start, and hang on. Invariably, just as I'd start to get up, I'd lose balance and go down. When that happens, you're supposed to let go of the rope and wait for the boat to come around to try it again. But I'd hang on to the rope and be dragged through the water, as if I thought there was some way the ski would magically come back up if I just held on long enough.

So if only two or three people were showing up at the sessions, I would hang on, sure that somehow I would get more. Since mailings hadn't done anything, I went to the method employed by the British Navy three centuries earlier. Anywhere I saw someone who was disabled, I'd do everything short of dragging them down to Road Runners to get them to join. That's how John Paul Cruz—another of the earliest members—was found. We called it "street recruiting."

I didn't find John personally. One of my employees at Personnelmetrics, Dr. Joe Cody, did. He would stroll through Bryant Park during lunch time. One day he saw a young man with one leg selling marijuana. The seller was a good-looking young man and had an athletic bearing, so Joe told him about a running group his boss had going, and asked him to check it out. The young man took him up on it, and that's how John Cruz came to join Achilles.

The classes built slowly. By the end of the eight weeks, we had eight people coming more or less regularly. We hadn't originally planned on doing anything after the classes were over, but at some point Bob Glover suggested that we form a running team instead of offering another set of classes. Because Bob was fond of Greek mythology, he suggested the name "Achilles," after the Greek hero whose mother had dipped him in the river Styx at his birth, making his entire body invulnerable except for the small spot on his heel where his mother had held him. And so the Achilles Track Club was born.

Those first weeks were sometimes awkward for me. Although I was and am considered disabled, I really didn't know anything about disabled people, and in my business, lacking one leg wasn't a disability at all. As a child, I had known a couple of kids who had disabilities. In those days— the 40s—every kid had a classmate who was partially crippled by polio. Basically, we didn't think anything about it. Once I grew up, I had very few dealings with disabled people. One I had known was my first fiancée's father. He had lost both his legs to diabetes, but he could still climb up a flight of stairs to get to his office above the movie theater he owned in Montreal. I felt awkward around him, but I was impressed by the way he got around. I first met him a few months before my accident. Looking back, it was as if I were being prepared for a new journey and experience.

I could deal with an amputee, but I knew nothing about other disabilities. I didn't know if it was proper to ask people how they had become disabled, or even if I should mention the disability. Personally, I don't care if people ask about my leg. When I started running, "The Six Million Dollar Man" was a hit television show, and kids would see me running and ask me if I were that man. I'd tell them I was, but one of my computer chips was broken and that's why I limped. Others with disabilities feel differently.

I found that one question you should cautiously ask blind people is how they lost their sight. I asked Tom O'Connor, an early member, that, and he said, "When I was 12 my mom caught me masturbating and told me I'd go blind if I kept doing that."

Then there were the wheelchairs. When people in wheelchairs showed up for workouts, I didn't know whether it was appropriate to help them over a curb or not. When I had been in a wheelchair people had tended to be overly helpful, and I didn't want to make that same mistake. Some people don't want you to touch their chairs without being asked. If you help someone in a wheelchair, you're doing him or her a favor that's not easy to repay. On top of that is a psychological question of roles. Some men who are helped over a curb resent the role that puts them in.

My son, Joey, who was eight at the time, would sometimes join me at workouts and amuse himself by borrowing a wheelchair and practicing maneuvering in it. One night, he was running the chair up and down the curb at 89th Street and Fifth Avenue when a passing limousine came to a sudden stop next to him. A dignified gentleman, having seen Joey in the chair, had ordered his driver to stop. The gentleman got out and went over to help Joey. Not knowing how to react, Joey got out of the wheelchair, pushed it up the curb himself, and got back in. I've always wondered whether that good Samaritan ever stopped to help another kid in a wheelchair.

One of our early members, Janet, would become hysterical if anyone touched her wheelchair. The chair was an extension of herself, she felt, and touching it was like touching her. Because of this attitude, I kept losing volunteers who came out to help disabled people run. I'd assign one to Janet and forget to tell them about Janet's sensitivities. Inevitably, they'd touch Janet's chair and Janet would start screaming at them, "How dare you touch my wheelchair!" The volunteers, often young women, would come back to the club in tears, unable to figure out what they'd done wrong.

Janet strongly encouraged me to get a wheelchair ramp for the entrance of the Road Runners building. There are three sets of steps going into the building, and it would require taking out part of the outside wall and building a new door. We got some estimates on the work, and discovered that it would cost $250,000 to put in a ramp. For the small number of wheelchairs we had, it didn't make sense to spend that kind of money. Janet, herself, was able to walk beside her chair and climb the few stairs while somebody else pushed her chair, but she didn't think that was appropriate. Our total Achilles budget was less than the interest required to be paid on a $250,000 loan to cover the ramp. Janet insisted that this was an appropriate use of funds. My own feelings were that we should make the environment as friendly for the disabled as possible, but also that there was a point beyond which it just didn't make financial sense.

You have to pick your spots. The law is such that, when a New York hostel recently looked at the possibility of upgrading its accommodations by installing bathrooms in each guest room, they were told every bathroom had to be wheelchair-friendly, which would effectively eliminate at least one-third of each guest room, because wheelchair bathrooms are so big. It makes a great deal of sense to have bathrooms that the disabled can use. It makes no sense to require every bathroom in every room to have that kind of facility. But that's what you run into. Because of such laws, construction which could be done to help people, simply isn't.

In the early days of the club I discovered there were many disabilities of which I hadn't been aware. Linda Down has cerebral palsy. How do you react to that, if at all? Another early member, Paula Schillo, had suffered a stroke that had partially paralyzed one side of her body. When she first came to a workout, I didn't even know she was disabled, because just walking, she looked fine. I found out about her paralysis when I asked her to help me move the big table in the Road Runners library where we held our pre-workout meetings. She told me she couldn't lift it because she had had a stroke.

Then there were blind runners, a class I hadn't considered at all. Blind people can often navigate so well you can't tell they can't see. One night a new blind runner came and I thought he was a volunteer, there to run with a disabled runner. So I told him to go out with someone in a wheelchair.

"Should I hold on to the chair?" he asked.

"That's not necessary," I said. "You can just run along next to it."

"But I can't see it," he said. "I'm blind."

I made that mistake—among many others—with some frequency at first. Somebody would be disabled and I wouldn't realize it and would assign them to work as a volunteer until they straightened me out. Once I realized that you can't always tell that someone's disabled by looking at him, I had fewer problems.

I also learned that there was a whole world of disabilities I had never imagined. Jeff Dutton, for example, came to us with something called small bowel syndrome, which left him incapable of digesting food. Instead, he took specially prepared nutrients in through a catheter fixed to a surgically implanted valve in his abdomen. Before a race, he would increase the nutrients and the amount of water, since he didn't get any benefit from drinking water normally. He could, however, absorb alcohol if he had a drink.

I got to know Jeff pretty well and invited him over to my place for dinner. First, I asked him if he ate, and he said, "I only eat socially."

I never felt a desperate need to get enough people to get the club to a self-sustaining level, although that first winter I carried a constant low-grade fear that one night I'd face the embarrassing situation of having no one show up for practice. One gray night I thought that had happened. Then I realized that I had gotten one runner, after all—me. But that's what it was like. At first, I was just trying to get enough people to have a practice. Then it was enough to have a presence. Finally, it was enough to have the critical mass at which point the group would become self-sustaining. I figured I needed at least eight regulars to pass that point. But I didn't look at it as a do-or-die kind of thing. If I seemed overly eager to get new members, it was only because I loved running and thought it would be nice to have new people to run with.

It doesn't matter to me how fast or slow a runner is. Some outfits want only the best and sleekest. This is just as true of disabled groups as it is of groups for the able-bodied. It's especially true of wheelchair groups, where the difference between athlete and fun-runner is most pronounced. The best wheelchair athletes can turn a marathon in about an hour and 20 minutes—almost an hour faster than someone on foot. These guys are built like Hercules from the waist up, and they can just fly. In Boston, the top wheelchair athletes have been timed by police using radar as hitting 62 miles per hour going downhill. I guess they could be ticketed for speeding. They're every bit as talented as the finest athletes in any sport. So, just as professional golfers don't want 30-handicap duffers playing in tour events, the elite wheelchair athletes don't want regular Joes and Janes competing with them. As much as anything, it makes them look bad by implying that they're the same as a guy who does a marathon in six hours. It's discrimination and it's elitism, but that's the way it is.

I don't care about any of that. I don't promise new recruits that they'll break records or do anything other than finish a marathon. I promised that to the original group and I promise that now. Just as long as you stay with the program, we'll get you to the finish line. Other than that, my only rule is: have fun.

I really think that's important. I don't tell people to run because it's good for their hearts or because it will lower their cholesterol and help them lose weight. It will do all that, but a lot of people don't like hearing, "Do it. It's good for you." They've heard enough of that from parents and teachers and clergymen when they were growing up. The other thing that people get when they're young—at least when I was growing up, they did—was the concept of running as punishment. That was always happening in team sports. If you screwed up, the coach made you run laps for punishment. Perhaps that's why you used to see so many former top athletes get big guts when they retired. They view running as punishment and so they don't do it. They've also had as much competition as they want, so they don't need to take up running to fulfill any competitive urges. So I don't talk about competition or how good it is for you. I just talk about how enjoyable it is.

But for it to be fun, we had to have enough runners of varying abilities to give everyone a partner they could comfortably run with. That's where a lot of the fun is, in the interaction between two runners. Runners talk a lot when they run, and they don't have to worry about finding an appropriate subject. They talk about running, the conditions, technique. And for some of the Achilles runners who haven't had the variety of social experiences of others, this is a wonderful thing. But we needed that critical mass to have the social interaction. And once we had it and had an official group, we could have group norms and shared motivation. That's why so many Achilles runners wind up running a marathon—it's the group norm. And belonging to a group helps you over low periods because you have so many people carrying one another along toward the common goal. It's a cliché when an actor receives an Oscar and makes a speech in which he thanks his agent, the director, his co-stars, the cameramen, and everyone down to the key grippe and gaffer. But it's also true. He's acknowledging that he's part of a team, and without the team, he wouldn't have gone as far as he did.

Another place I went in my constant first-year search for critical mass was to the Ronald McDonald House on 86th Street and York Avenue on the East Side, where children who were undergoing prolonged treatments for illnesses—frequently cancer—stayed between outpatient visits to hospitals for chemotherapy. I needed runners to keep the club going and this seemed like an ideal population. They were stuck in the city for the duration of their treatment without a lot to do. By my standards, they were disabled in the sense that they had cancer.

The kids had no easy way of getting to the workouts, so I'd drive to Ronald McDonald House and pick them up myself. Bob Glover had worked out a program where they'd go up to 97th Street in Central Park—where there's a running oval—run two laps, and then go back down to the park entrance at 90th Street. But these kids were pretty wrung out from the chemo, and they didn't really have enough energy to get back to 90th Street after they ran the laps. Bob wasn't at the workouts to see them, but was basically coaching by telephone. He'd call and give me a program and then I'd supervise it along with Patti Parmalee. I wasn't satisfied with the arrangement. Bob wasn't interested in coming to the Wednesday night workouts. He had become a father and wished to spend more time with his son."

Not long after that, Bob Glover and I decided to part ways as far as the coaching arrangement was concerned. Patti Parmalee stayed on and has been a wonderful coach over the years.

I never had more than two or three kids from Ronald McDonald House at any one time, and eventually, we gave it up. It just wasn't working. The kids weren't permanent residents of the area, so there was no continuity. It was also a hassle for the staff there, which truly had enough to do already, to get them ready. So they weren't terribly excited about keeping it going.

Although our program with the Ronald McDonald House hadn't worked, it didn't end our involvement with kids. Later, Barrie Slatis, a teacher in the Adapted Physical Education Department of the New York Public Schools, set up a chapter for disabled school children. Irv Bader directs and Howie Futterman runs the program now. Through Irv, Howie, and Barrie, we have come to know some of the most inspiring people I have ever met.

One is Andre Donegon, who had been born without legs and with only short stumps for arms. His parents, who were immigrants from Trinidad, couldn't care for him and put him into foster care. He landed with an Irish Catholic family who had 13 other kids in Queens. The Donegons loved Andre so much they adopted him. When he got into high school, he was recruited for Achilles and did a couple of marathons, propelling his wheelchair laboriously with the stumps of his arms. Like so many others, he didn't think it was possible, but when he finished and they hung the medal around his neck, he was perhaps happier than he'd ever been in his life. Lacking arms, he also couldn't take the medal off— but I don't think he wanted to.

Another chapter for youth was set up by Tim Erson, a physical therapist at the A. Harry Moore School in Jersey City, New Jersey. One year, one of his volunteer runners was Mariel Hemingway. Tim has since moved to Corpus Christi, Texas, where he has established another Achilles children's running program. We have others—from one coached by Max Rhodes, an 80-year-old paraplegic in Miami, to some as far away as China. Norman Brickell, who started the American Suicide Foundation, is working with me on developing a running program for children who have attempted suicide.

Other chapters sprouted through the same sort of dissemination. One of our early runners, Peter Roth, had a twin brother, Alan, living in Washington, D.C. When Alan saw the good things Achilles was doing, he founded a chapter in the capital. The Los Angeles chapter began when Jon Ross, an early volunteer, moved from the East Coast to the West and took Achilles with him. Other chapters were started by disabled people who came from various locations to run in New York and took club franchises back home with them. Among them were Dan Coster, a blind runner who runs Achilles of Westchester County, New York, and Stan Levine, a stroke victim who started the Summit, New Jersey, chapter.

The Ronald McDonald experience also gave me another idea. The McDonald people, who wanted to start a second facility, could set up a West Side facility at the Y. There was some initial interest, but it turned out that kids undergoing chemotherapy are particularly vulnerable to chicken pox, a disease that, to them, could be fatal. And in a mixed facility like the Y, there was no way to adequately shield them from exposure. Then I got the idea of setting up a facility like Ronald McDonald House for adults who have to come to New York for chemotherapy and radiation. I knew the Y's motto was "Mind, Body, Spirit," and this project was perfect to further that objective.

My idea was to take one floor at the Y and upgrade the

rooms by adding a private bath and a kitchenette-dining room and living room, and then renting them out through the hospitals to people in town taking special treatments. It would be inexpensive and, since the Y had close to 550 rooms and was nowhere near full occupancy, it would be putting under-utilized space to better use. Besides, it could be a step toward taking a bit out of the negative cash flow the Y was experiencing.

I took my idea to Grace Christ, who was a senior-level official at Memorial Sloan-Kettering Hospital, which estimated it provided 80,000 outpatient treatments to people who lived too far away to return home immediately after treatment. She liked the idea, so I started to look into fund-raising. I determined it would take $400,000 to do the renovations on the floor. The Y did up a couple of rooms as a demonstration while I went ahead and got its permission to look into bigger funding.

One of my clients, Washington National, had a computer they were replacing and asked me how to go about selling it. I suggested they donate it to the Y, and then I sold it for $5,000, which was a good start. Then Grace Christ introduced me to Joe Cruikshank of the Clark Foundation. I told Joe about my plan and sent him a brief proposal for a grant. As proposals go, it wasn't much—a couple of pages with an attached newspaper article. But Cruikshank liked it. The Clark Foundation donated $60,000 to the project.

Getting the check was reward enough, but last year I was flattered again when The Foundation Center, a group that provides information on fund-raising, asked me if they could include my proposal in *The Foundation Center's Guide to Proposal Writing*, being published this year. It is being used to show that a proposal can be brief.

The project dragged on for years, from my original idea for a Ronald McDonald–type house, through to the idea of providing rooms for adults in a facility that would be called Y-House. I got enough additional funding to provide $200,000 to start renovating rooms, but the Y kept finding problems. I kept solving, but they were still reluctant to push it. Besides, the new rooms with private baths and kitchens were so much better than the standard Y cell that Y employees who had to stay overnight in Manhattan took to staying in them. Then one day, I had lunch with Joe Cruikshank and he asked me how the project was going. I told him it was not going well. Joe is one of the sweetest people I've ever met, but when I told him that, he was furious. He called the Y, got hold of the top executive, and demanded to know what was going on. They said they needed a medical committee, so I found a doctor to set that up. Then they said they needed a brochure, so I got the Greater New York Hospital Association involved and they said they'd be delighted to make up a glossy brochure. Finally, just this year, the project got rolling. The whole, lengthy episode taught me that to get something accomplished, you have to be able to come at it from two sides. I wasn't strong enough to break the West Side Y's institutional inertia, but when Joe Cruikshank came in from another angle, the gears finally started to grind and creak and the wheels started to move.

The Y program was a typical project for me, not very different from the beginning of Achilles. None of my projects involve lengthy research or studies. An opportunity presented itself, and, like a counter-punching boxer, I took a swipe at it. Some punches landed and others didn't. I didn't have any grand plans for Achilles. Indeed, at the time, I saw it only as a New York City running club program operating under the aegis of the Road Runners. As for a group goal, it was the same as every runner's goal in New York—to run the marathon.

Toward that end, as soon as I had my little core group of runners, I got them into races. Our first run as a team was in January 1983—a five-miler Road Runners race in bitter cold in Central Park. Our little group continued to show up at other races and I kept looking for new members wherever I could. Not all of them worked out perfectly. We had one blind man join who was also gay. I had no problem with that, and no one else did, either, until he started touching the volunteers. It turned out that he couldn't keep his hands to himself. One volunteer, a 62-year-old runner, told me, "Dick, I don't know how to explain this, but for the first time in 30 years, I've been goosed!"

We found out that the blind man was so forward that even a gay runners' group had kicked him out, and we, too, had to ask him not to come back.

Then there was the lost runner. We had a program at Coler Hospital. In addition to going to Ronald McDonald House, I had gone to Coler Hospital, where there were many people with disabilities. We'd load up a van with patients and take them to the park to run. One of the patients—I'll call him Chris—was a schizophrenic. He had had one leg amputated and used a wheelchair. What we didn't know is that sometimes he'd go into a catatonic state, where he became utterly motionless and didn't hear or see anything. One night, we were all doing laps on the running oval in Central Park. When we were finished, we all jogged back down to 90th Street, and when we got there, we discovered Chris was missing. This was definitely not good. All I had to do was lose a runner and Achilles was history.

I got in my car and drove all around the park, but I couldn't find him. I went home and finally, the next morning, I got a call from the hospital telling me that he had been found and everything was fine. He had been going around the oval when someone on his way to a "Shakespeare in the Park" production asked him if he was going to the play. That was good enough for Chris, and he wheeled off to the play. They put him in the first row and I guess he remained there, watching Shakespeare. After the play, when he didn't leave, the security people found him. They quickly realized that he matched the missing-person report we had filed and they got him back to Coler without further incident.

Another problem runner we had was a man who had arthritis and was also mildly retarded. A race-walker, he got around with a cane. He had a competitive personality and hated anyone passing him. Occasionally when someone did start to pass, he'd stick out his cane and attempt to trip the unsuspecting runner. It was pretty funny, but also dangerous, and we had to threaten to take his cane away if he did it again. That solved that problem.

Of course, anytime you have a club, you're going to have some people who aren't as easy to get along with as others. You're going to have guys who hit on all the women. You're going to have women who think all the guys are hitting on them. You're going to have people with lousy personalities. We even had one guy once who was homeless. He'd come to workouts from a shelter or wherever he was staying at the time, and then he'd hit the members and volunteers up for donations. He saw the group as a potential gold mine. After all, who could spend an hour or two running with a guy and then not dig into his or her pocket when he told you, "I haven't eaten for 24 hours. Could I have a dollar?" You just can't say no, even when he does it every time you see him. And what happens is that you can't look at him anymore and see a person. You just see dollar signs flashing back at you from his eyes. I talked to him and told him he just couldn't do that, and he promised not to. Then the next week, he did it again. So I had to take the volunteers aside and tell them that this person was going to do this and they didn't have to give him any money. Eventually, he stopped coming and that was the end of it.

But the bottom line for us was running. If you did that, we could try to deal with the rest. Usually, the really bad apples took themselves out, and in the 10 years the club has been in business, we've only asked one person—the gay, blind man who couldn't keep his hands to himself—not to come back.

All that's getting a little ahead of myself. In 1983, we were just doing everything we could to keep going. By the middle of the summer, we were enough of a presence at Road Runners races that one of New York's newspapers, *Newsday*, discovered us, and ran a major story on the club. In the article, writer Dave Rosner had asked Bob Glover, who was still coaching the team, about the beginnings of Achilles. Bob said:

"We've treated them as athletes, not as fitness objects. At the beginning, the idea was to just get them out there and get them moving. We were afraid to push them and take a chance of hurting them; it was radical enough just having them out there running. Now, we give them speed workouts and hill workouts. The training is based on the same exact principles that I would use for anybody else. Now, they feel more like athletes."

I added my two cents worth:

"These people are typically very sedate. You don't know what sedate is until you're disabled. I mean, it's an imposition to go to the bathroom, let alone to go running in Central

Park. This is my way of saying, 'You don't have to rely on others; you can do whatever the heck you want on your own.'"

I told Rosner a story I tell to new members about being able to do anything you set your mind to. The story's not true, but it could be, which is just as good. I tell them that when I was in the hospital recuperating from my accident, a psychologist gave me a pep talk in which he told me that line about being able to do anything.

I said, "No I can't."

The psychologist, as upbeat as an Up With People concert, replied, "Sure you can. Name it."

"I'd like to beat Frank Shorter in a marathon," I said.

Then I give them the punch line.

In 1977, in my second New York City Marathon, I set a new amputee record of 6:44. Frank Shorter also entered that race, and he dropped out around the 16-mile mark. So I beat Frank Shorter in the marathon.

Linda Down explained the value of Achilles to Rosner as well as anyone ever has: "I discovered I can stress my worst aspects—my legs and my body—and still be successful. And if I can take my worst aspects and be a success, then imagine what I can do with my best aspects. The focus now is on what I'm able to do rather than what I can't do."

This is what the psychologists call empowerment. When you've all but convinced yourself you can't do anything and then go out and find you can finish a race, it gives you this big shot of confidence. And if you can do something like that, you start thinking of other things you can do if you apply yourself as vigorously as you applied yourself to running. It's like getting that doctorate. You put in the time and you get the medal at the end. We've had many people over the years who have expanded their horizons through Achilles.

Down herself, who had considered herself unemployed a year earlier, had gained the confidence that resulted in two great job offers. She selected Manufacturers Hanover Bank (Chemical Bank) and worked with them for several years in the marketing department. Occasionally, Chemical loaned her to the United Way. Eventually, she left Chemical Bank to work full time for the United Way.

At the time the article was written, we had about 25 members, among whom was Pat Griskus. Griskus was a young man from Connecticut who had lost his lower leg in a motorcycle accident and, after many wasted years, had come back to running and was the top below-the-knee amputee runner in the world. Griskus was also a writer.

In the article, Rosner also mentioned a contradiction that continues to affect both Achilles and NYRRC to this day. We had Marty Ball and Jane Zirinsky and others who raced in wheelchairs, yet the New York City Marathon did not allow wheelchairs in its race. A disabled athlete had even taken the NYRRC to court over this, and I found myself in the peculiar position of testifying as a board member of NYRRC against the disabled. Fred Lebow's concern has been that elite wheelchairs, which can go over 60 miles per hour downhill, are just too dangerous in a race with over 29,000 other runners.

The Boston Marathon has solved the wheelchair problem as many other marathons have. They've established an elite wheelchair division and they send them off ahead of the main pack of runners, so that they finish more than an hour ahead of the winning male. But Fred wants his race to be for runners, a footrace. Wheelchairs, he feels, are more akin to bikes. The other problem with elite wheelchairs is that if you set up a division for them in the race, they're going to want prize money commensurate with that given the winners in other divisions. So, if the men's and women's winners get a new Mercedes, does the winner of the wheelchair division get one, too? Where does the money come from? And then if the wheelchairs have an elite division, are the blind runners going to want one, too? You can keep going along those lines until you have an elite division for runners with hemorrhoids. My own sympathies lie with the wheelchairs, but as a board member of the Road Runners, I've taken the club's position, which is that the elite chairs should remain banned.

In the fall of 1983, we ran our first marathon as a club. We had T-shirts that said, "Achilles Track Club" above the logo of the New York Road Runners Club—a pictogram of a runner superimposed on an apple. There were six of us in that race: Linda Down, Pat Griskus, John Paul Cruz, Marty

Ball, Tom O'Connor, and myself. Linda, John, and myself left early and I ran with Linda the whole way. She finished in 8:45, knocking almost three hours off her time of the previous year, when she had had to train alone. John, running on crutches, finished in 7:30 and became the official Achilles personality of 1983. That year, when President Reagan invited Fred Lebow and the marathon winners to the White House, he asked for Rod Dixon, the men's winner, Grete Waitz, the women's winner, and John, who had started the year selling nickel bags of grass in Bryant Park and ended it in the White House.

We got a lot of publicity back then and still do. Every year, there are new members with new stories that grab the press. The stories have helped us to grow around the world, but I still don't believe you should do things just to get in the newspapers. Some people tried to cash in on the publicity themselves with various stunt runs. Terry Fox was probably the original inspiration for many of these, and the thinking was that if Fox could move a nation with his quest, then someone else could do the same. It just doesn't work that way, though, and it doesn't matter whether the charity you're doing something for is worthy. The media have a very short attention span on these things. If it sounds like something that's already been done, they don't want to hear about it. They also have a pretty good sense of when somebody's doing something just to get publicity. The main reason Achilles gets attention year after year is because every year there's a new story. The people who run with Achilles aren't out after the publicity, and the media knows that. They're regular people who don't get paid to run. Their reward is in the accomplishment. I'm grateful for the coverage we get, but it still surprises me.

One of the early imitators of Terry Fox was a runner I will call Jack. Jack is an amputee and extremely competitive. He's also very publicity-conscious. He called me one year asking to get into the marathon. I told him I wanted to see him run before I'd give him a late entry. This is standard procedure. If someone doesn't train with an Achilles group, I want to be satisfied that he or she is in good enough shape to run a marathon. It's not much to ask. We want the Achilles runners to be in shape and have a safe run.

So far, at Achilles, we've only had one serious accident. That was a wheelchair racer who was flying down the downslope of the Verrazano Narrows Bridge when his wheel got caught in an expansion strip. He got thrown out, landed on his face, and was cut up pretty badly, but wasn't permanently injured.

Anyway, Jack felt he didn't have to perform for me to get into the marathon. He was young and a good athlete, and I guess it bruised his ego to have to prove his competence. I didn't care about his ego. I just didn't let him in the race. He wouldn't let it rest there, but went to the newspapers, saying the New York City Marathon was discriminating against him. The reporters called Fred Lebow and Fred let him in the race, figuring there wasn't any sense in getting a black eye over it. There was nothing we could say that would make us look good in that situation. So we sent him an entry and then he never showed up for the race. Later, I found out he didn't run because he was suffering from a hemorrhoid flare-up. When I heard that, it started a series of stories and jokes about hemorrhoids, disabilities, and the physically challenged.

After our first marathon, Achilles was still new, and the new track club got wide exposure. With the exposure came more members, and by the middle of 1984, we could count about 65 members, of whom 35 were regulars. Eleven ran in the marathon that fall, nearly doubling our first-year's participation. In the first year, we had got new members in some cases literally off the streets. Now, people were calling us. Al Reyes, for example, who lived in South Burlington, Vermont, called me during the summer. The 68-year-old veteran of three previous New York City Marathons, including 1983, had had quadruple bypass surgery in June and wanted to run another marathon. He ran with us, finishing in 5:58, and in the process founded an early Achilles chapter outside of New York.

Then there was Bob Greene, of Middletown, New York. Bob had been in a horrible traffic accident in 1981 in which both legs were shattered and his lungs and kidneys punctured. The accident had nearly killed him, and when he recovered, he had to get around with a set of Canadian crutches. (Those are the abbreviated ones that have cuffs that fit around the forearms.) Within two years of the accident, he entered a 10K race in Middletown and finished in just under three hours. The next year, 1984, he entered again and finished in just under two hours. He also ran in the Helen Hayes 10K in upstate New York, and that's where I saw him and invited him to join Achilles. It took him another year, but he ran the New York City Marathon and then graduated to triathlons. He also met his wife, Maria, one of the top local runners in Orange County, New York, on the race course.

Tom O'Connor came to us in 1983. Tom, who was 19 at the time, had lost his sight when he was 15 after being stricken by a mysterious illness that caused a fluid buildup in his head that somehow took his sight. Tom commuted 90 minutes each way from his home in the Bensonhurst section of Brooklyn to the workouts in Central Park. When he joined, he explained that he wanted to run the marathon. "It will give me more self-esteem and show I'm not a quitter," he said. Tom eventually set up an Achilles chapter in Memphis, Tennessee.

Slowly, horizons were expanding. In 1985, John Cruz, who had moved to Florida, started an Achilles chapter in Miami, and Andrea Morris, who had had polio as a child, founded a chapter in Amherst, Massachusetts. Ron Schaefer, who had lost a leg to bone cancer, called me from Jenison, Michigan, for coaching advice, and I invited him to join us in the marathon that fall, when we would again double our participation. Then, out of the blue, we suddenly leaped the Pacific Ocean.

I took the phone call from Brian Froggatt in the winter of 1985. To my amazement, he was calling from New Zealand, and he wanted advice. Froggatt, like me, was an above-the-knee amputee. Unlike me, the 27-year-old was a superb athlete. He told me that he sometimes trained by hopping two miles on his good leg around a track. That practice served him well in a bow-hunting club he belonged to in New Zealand. Once, at a shooting competition in which contestants had to run from station to station to shoot at targets, his artificial leg broke, so he took it off and hopped around the rest of the course and took second place. After seeing a piece about Achilles on television, he called me for training advice. That started a year-long correspondence during which I coached him by mail. He knew that I was the first amputee to run a marathon and had founded this track club for disabled runners, and in his mind, I was a super-athlete and a guru of sorts.

It was obvious even through the mail that Brian was an extraordinary athlete and I decided to invite him to the New York City Marathon. I got a grant to pay part of his expenses from Ted Rogers, CEO of NL Industries (and currently a board member of Achilles), and he raised the rest back in New Zealand, but I wasn't sure he was coming until I got a letter from him just hours before his plane was to land at Kennedy Airport. I hurried to the airport to greet my first international participant, and waited at the gate for him to come off the plane. He came off, looking for someone who would be somewhat stronger than himself. Instead, he saw this chubby 44-year-old waiting for him. He was kind enough not to laugh. He, on the other hand, was an amazing physical specimen, with muscles on top of muscles. His right leg—his good leg—had enormous strength, and his thigh was thicker than his waist.

Brian went out and finished the marathon in 5:10, knocking 1:34 off the record for above-the-knee amputees which I had set in 1977. What was more impressive was that he did it on a clanky old-fashioned leg that weighed around 13 pounds.

We also had another record that year, set by Paddy Rossbach, a 47-year-old amputee who had joined Achilles. Paddy was the first female amputee to run the marathon that year, and her time of 5:24 was also extraordinary. Giving 20 years away to Brian, she finished just 14 minutes behind him. Even when you factor in that Paddy's a below-the-knee amputee and Brian's an above-the-knee, it was a remarkable performance.

When Brian returned to his little home town of Dargaville, New Zealand, he received a hero's welcome from more than a thousand of the townsfolk, which was something like half the town. Local businesses shut down early, the town band came out, and the mayor showed up to give Brian an award.

We were doubling in size every year, and practically everything we did involved a record of one kind or another. Scott Wagner came up with John Cruz from Florida and became the first person with Down's syndrome to finish a marathon. Linda Down had been the first person with cerebral palsy to finish, and Bill Reilly was the first person to finish by kicking backwards in a wheelchair. John Cruz was the first amputee on crutches. Sandy Davidson was the first person who had had a stroke and then come back and run a marathon.

Dan Winchester, who also kicks backwards in a wheelchair, is one of my best friends. He's probably exploded as many stereotypes as anyone in the club. Dan's cerebral palsy is so severe he can't use his arms to move his wheelchair. He's hard of hearing and has difficulty speaking. Because of this, many people make the assumption that Dan is also retarded. Nothing could be less true. Dan has a PhD and he's not shy about letting people know it, which changes their perception 180 degrees. Getting the doctorate might be impressive enough, but Dan is a real achiever, and he came to Achilles determined to do a marathon, as well. To watch him run, you'd have a hard time believing he can do it, because he has to push his wheelchair backwards with his feet to move. But in the course of about 18 months, Dan went from not being able to go a quarter-mile to doing a marathon, and he's done many since.

Dan's ability to read lips to compensate for his hearing loss makes for some interesting times. We can be in a meeting together and I can mouth a joke to him across the room and he'll break out laughing, leaving everyone scratching their heads trying to figure out what's so funny. I like to run with him because the pace is leisurely and he's good company. When you run with Dan, you have to run behind him to keep an eye on where he's going, while he watches where he's been. I mentioned before how many runners keep going by watching the backsides of other runners of the opposite sex. Well, Dan happens to be a breast man, which is perfect because he watches the women coming toward him. Being a bottom man myself, I watch them going away.

He had been with us only a short time before I realized that Dan was watching the women. When that dawned on me, I also realized that we tend to think of people who are disabled as being asexual, which is not correct. Anyway, Dan, like more men than are willing to admit in these days of political correctness, likes to rate the women runners he sees. He does this by holding up fingers on his hands indicating a number. Now Dan's hands are bent from his disability and when he extends them, it's hard for him to hold them out and they tremble. To someone running by, it looks like he's waving. So a woman will be running toward him and he'll hold up, say, four fingers, which means the woman's a "four." She'll see his fingers trembling and think he's waving at her, and she'll think, "Isn't that nice. The poor guy is waving at me." And she'll wave back. But what he's really doing is saying she's only a four on a scale of ten.

This was all a learning experience for me. Like so many others, I never thought of the disabled as having normal human desires. But when I saw people like Dan and other Achilles members admiring the women volunteers, I realized that being in a wheelchair and having cerebral palsy or spina bifida or anything else doesn't have anything to do with it. People are people. I should have realized that. After all, having one leg didn't change my libido. Why should it be different with anyone else?

FINISH

Chapter 6

*Such attention as I have received is nice,
but the finish lines are fleeting, whereas the hard work
it takes to reach them is part of my life.*
—Pat Griskus

Pat Griskus didn't need the Achilles Track Club; not to run faster than any amputee had ever run before. But I'm glad he found us, and glad he stayed around. People like Pat don't come by often, not in any walk of life. I just wish he could have stayed around longer. If he had, he'd be the president of the Achilles Track Club now. At least that was my plan.

I've already mentioned Pat, because you can't tell the story of Achilles without him. But Pat was a lot more than a couple of paragraphs. He was a dear friend, for one thing. He was also the best of what I had hoped that Achilles could be.

Pat came to the club in its first year, 1983. Like Terry Fox and Brian Froggatt, he was a superb athlete. Unlike Fox and Froggatt, he hadn't made a smooth transition from the personal tragedy of losing a limb to the triumph of athletic achievement.

Pat had been an outstanding athlete in high school. He could sprint 100 yards in 9.8 seconds and run a mile in 4:28, a rare combination of speed and endurance. He joined the Marines right out of high school, and was stationed in Kansas City. Like so many of us, he was young and felt immortal. All that ended one day in 1967 when he was riding his motorcycle and a drunken idiot in a '59 Rambler plowed into him head-on. The doctors saved his life, but they couldn't save his lower left leg, which had to be amputated below the knee. It was a clean operation with no complications and when it was done, Pat spent one day in a wheelchair, and then got on crutches until he could graduate to a prosthesis. He moved back to Wolcott, Connecticut, near his home town of Waterbury and tried to get on with his life.

The adjustment wasn't easy. He gave up his athletic pursuits.

"I kind of filed that part of my life away," he once told *Newsday's* Dave Rosner. "Sometimes, especially when I had a few in me, I would talk about how I used to run the mile. But you accept that those things aren't going to happen anymore. You come a long way from what you were. I started drinking too much. I let myself go and felt sorry for myself. I didn't even see what I had become. You can't see how big the lake is when you're in the lake and under water."

I don't know how much Pat was drinking in those days, but I have a feeling it was a lot. He called himself an investment counselor, but I think most of his investments were made with local bookies on sporting events. He was actually a pretty good gambler, though. Just the same, it's not much to build a life on, not when the foundation is floating on booze.

Like Fox and Froggatt, he saw an article about me running the 1976 New York City Marathon. It didn't take right away, though. He told me that at first he didn't think about running himself. He thought it was something other amputees did. But around 1981, he started to understand that he, too, could be active. He started by lifting weights and swimming and went on to running. He started playing basketball, climbing mountains, and even tried sky diving; feasting on his newly reawakened appetite for physical challenge. And he gave up drinking. By the time he joined us, he had put in two years of training and had already run a marathon in 4:11. Shortly after, running with Achilles, he entered an eight-mile race up Mt. Washington, New England's highest mountain.

He liked to tell about how, near the beginning of the Mt. Washington race, a couple of runners passed him and as they went by, they applauded this poor guy on one leg and said, "God bless you." Then they were gone. Now Pat was a very fine athlete in top condition. And a well-conditioned amputee can make better time uphill relative to able-bodied runners, than on the flat. Going uphill puts more of an emphasis on power, and Pat had that. Personally, if I pass anyone in a race, it's going to be on the upslope. Going downhill is another matter, especially for an above-the-knee amputee like myself. If the slope is steep, you can't run straight down it like an able-bodied runner. Instead, you have to tack downhill, from one side of the road to the other. It's like traversing in skiing.

The Mt. Washington race has no downslope. And as the race went on, Pat started passing people. Finally, he passed the same two guys who had spoken to him earlier. As he charged past them, he turned around and said, "Hi." He nearly added, "God bless you," but he figured they were suffering enough as it was. Besides, it sounded just a little too cute.

You can bet he relished the moment, though. Pat was as competitive as they come. He hated finishing behind anyone. "It was like he refused to admit he had a disability," Patti Parmalee, our coach, once said of him. "He trained harder for endurance sports than anyone I have ever seen." He freely admitted he especially hated to be beaten by women.

"I'll compete against time and against as many people as I can beat," he said. "Competition is not charitable. No one gives me a break, and I won't give anyone else a break. It helps keep me motivated. I could find a lot of excuses for not doing anything at all."

He ran the New York City Marathon with us in 1983, lowering his time to 3:44. He eventually got it down to 3:31, which is just phenomenal. No one, myself included, thought an amputee could run that fast—fast enough to finish in the top half of the field. He credited Richard Press, a prosthetist in Stratford, Connecticut, for designing a high-performance leg that allowed him to run at that pace. He was so fond of that leg he named it Fred.

Always looking for new challenges, in March 1984, Pat entered the Empire State Building Run-Up. The race is exactly what it sounds like. A bunch of merrily insane people line up in the lobby of the Empire State Building and, at the gun, stampede down a hall and into the building's stairwell. First one to the Observation Deck wins. Pat didn't win. He finished 18th out of 26 runners and did it in less than 14 minutes.

This is where you start to get into trouble calling people

disabled just because they're missing a limb. Ninety-nine percent of the population couldn't beat Pat Griskus up the stairs of the Empire State Building, yet he was supposedly disabled. This actually became an issue about that same time when Gary Muhrcke, a former New York City fireman, ran the Empire State Building Run-up and won it. Gary had been a runner since way back before it was popular and had won the first New York City Marathon in 1970. Some years later, he had hurt his back in the line of duty and had been put on long-term disability, which meant he had a nice income and didn't have to work anymore. This would have been fine, but when he won the race, one of the newspapers found out that he was on disability from the fire department. Then they found out that he was still running marathons—rather quickly, too. New York tabloids love the headlines that sort of situation can generate, much to the embarrassment of the fire department. One editorial, for example, suggested that Gary could train the dogs in the firehouse to run faster, or perhaps even run in front of the fire trucks to clear traffic when they were racing to a fire. To save face, the department moved to take away his payments.

The department had a problem, though. Their doctors had put Gary on disability. He had wanted to return to work, but they felt that he could hurt his back worse, and they wouldn't authorize a return to active duty. But with the newspapers having a wonderful time with the story, they tried to take away the payments on the theory that anyone who could run a marathon could work as a firefighter. Muhrcke came to ask me to testify at a hearing that this wasn't necessarily true. He felt that since I was disabled and had run a marathon but did not think I would qualify as a firefighter, I would be a good witness. Being a fireman, he said, requires more than just climbing a ladder. You also have to be able to carry a 225-pound person down the ladder with you.

I told him I didn't want to testify, because if I went on the stand and they asked me if I could pass the fireman's test I would have to answer that I felt I could. Gary went to the hearing without me and kept his disability. He also continued to run sub-2:30 marathons. Several years ago, he started a chain of running stores called The Super Runner,

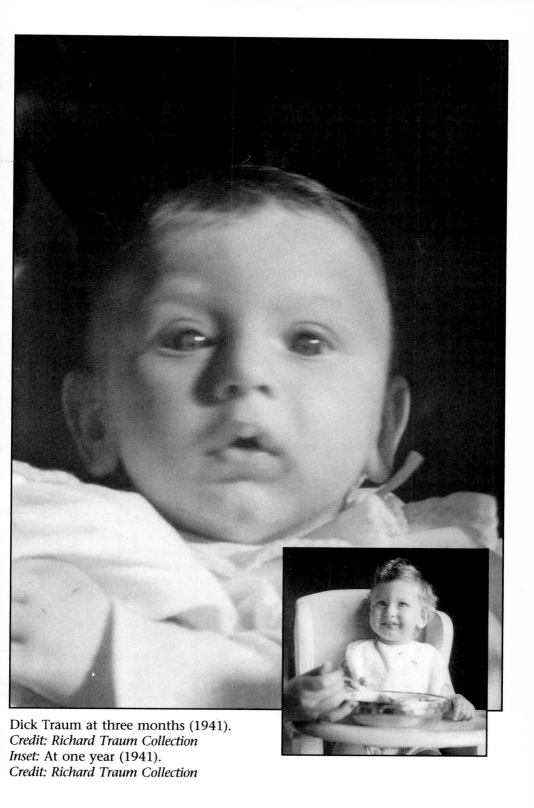

Dick Traum at three months (1941).
Credit: Richard Traum Collection
Inset: At one year (1941).
Credit: Richard Traum Collection

With maternal grandmother, Jennie Korn, in 1941.
Credit: Richard Traum Collection

With mother, Lilly Traum, Rockaway Beach in 1944.
Credit: Richard Traum Collection

Cousin, Sherry Sekler; sister, Joanne Traum-Raffel, and Dick in the summer of 1945. *Credit: Richard Traum Collection*

With sister, Joanne (January 1946). *Credit: Richard Traum Collection*

Aaron (father), Lilly (mother),
Joanne and Dick Traum at
age 9 in the winter of 1950.
Credit: Richard Traum Collection

Camp Takajo, (Dick at bottom left) Mohawk Bunk (1950).
Credit: Richard Traum Collection

Wrestling at Horace Mann at 15 (winter 1956).
Credit: Richard Traum Collection
Inset: High school graduation picture (spring 1958).
Credit: Richard Traum Collection

While at Celanese Corporation (1970). *Credit: Richard Traum Collection*
Inset: In Central Park (spring 1966). *Credit: Richard Traum Collection*

Wedding picture
(August 1968).
*Credit: Richard
Traum Collection*

Betsy and Dick in
Detroit (spring 1970).
*Credit: Richard Traum
Collection*

With son, Joey, in
his favorite position
in Maine (1977).
Credit: W. S. Goodwin

Dick and Joey in Florida
(December 1978).
Credit: Richard Traum
Collection

Dick holding his Man of the Year Award, West Side YMCA, 1987. *Credit: Richard Traum Collection*
Inset: Dick Traum presenting the Achilles Track Club Humanitarian Award to Albert H. Gordon, October 1992. *Credit: Richard Traum Collection*

Showing Joey how to center clay on the potter's wheel at Camp Androscoggin in 1989. *Credit: Richard Traum Collection*

With Joey and Betsy at Camp Androscoggin in 1989.
Credit: Richard Traum Collection

Dick running the 1976 New York City Marathon with volunteer-guide, Brian Smith, on bicycle at the 17-mile mark. *Credit: Steven Sutton, Duomo*
Inset: Completing his first race (YMCA five-miler) in Central Park, May 1976. *Credit: Richard Traum Collection*

At the 18-mile mark of the New York City Marathon, being passed by the winner, Bill Rodgers in October 1976. (Bill's autograph is at the top.) *Credit: Richard Traum Collection*

Richard,
You've got a slight edge on me in this photo; however we both had good runs at New York.
Good luck, Bill Rodgers

NEW YORK CITY BICENTENNIAL MARATHON
OCTOBER 24, 1976
RICHARD TRAUM   BILL RODGERS
7:24   2:10:10

After the first Achilles Track Club race in January 1983, seated left to right: Marty Ball, Natalie Bacon, Jim Rosenberg, and Fred Trinkle. Right to left: Dick Traum, Linda Down, John Cruz, and Bob Glover. *Credit: Richard Traum Collection*

Running in Central Park (spring 1986). *Credit: Richard Traum Collection*
Inset: First Annual Achilles Awards and Marathon Kick-off party: Standing: Betsy
Barlow-Rogers, Al Reyes, Linda Down, Sandy Davidson, Paddy Rosbach, Mayor
Edward Koch, Yvonne Myvette, Brian Froggatt, Pat Griskus, and Dick Traum,
and seated, Ann Applewhite. *Credit: Richard Traum Collection*

Completing his ninth marathon (fall 1987) with Bill Phillips, former CEO of Ogilvy and Mather and Achilles volunteer. *Credit: Tom Madine, TSC Graphics*
Inset: With Ted Rogers, partner, American Industrial Partners, at the Warsaw Marathon after establishing the Achilles Track Club of Poland (1987).
Credit: Leszek Sibilski

Dick Traum, running at the 70-kilometer mark of the 62-mile race in Kalish, Poland, October 15, 1988. He is accompanied by a young volunteer from Kalish. *Credit: Leszek Sibilski*

Dressed in appropriate garb and second from right, in the northern part of the Tumen area of Siberia about 100 miles inside the Arctic Circle with the Nantsia Indians (February 1989). *Credit: Richard Traum Collection*

Left to right: Jack Rudin, Dick Traum, Mayor David H. Dinkins, Fred Lebow, Andrew Tisch, Allan Steinfeld, and Bill Rudin. Seated: Anne Emmerman, director of the Mayor's Office for People with Disabilities. Taken at City Hall when Mayor Dinkins honored the Achilles Marathon runners (January 1990). *Credit: Joan Vitale Strong—Photographer to the Mayor*

Magdalena Ramirez, Director, Helen Hayes Hospital, with the Helen Hayes Award honorees: Former governor of New York, Hugh Carey, Dick Traum and Arthur Ashe (November 1992). *Credit: Richard Traum Collection*

and has supplied hundreds of pairs of running shoes to Achilles athletes at cost.

Gary was really no different than professional athletes who got deferments from military service because of injuries. The medical requirements of the two pastimes are so different that somebody can be qualified to play professional football but not be fit to be an infantry soldier. So it didn't bother me that Gary got to keep his benefits. What does bother me is what the system does to the people on the bottom of the economic food chain. We have a lot of these people in Achilles—people who are on supplementary social security or welfare because they can't get a decent job. The system gets them by punishing them for trying to work. If they are lucky enough to land a job paying minimum wage or even a bit more, they lose their welfare benefits and the health-care that goes along with it. They end up with less money than they were making on public assistance. It's an awful situation and it affects everyone on welfare. Believe me, a lot of people on welfare would love to work, but they can't afford to. You can't talk about welfare reform without addressing this problem.

Pat Griskus wasn't making a lot of money when he joined us. Still, he would drive three hours round trip every week to come to our workouts in Central Park. I make a point of telling every new Achilles member that we don't take attendance. You're not going to get a silver star if you come to 10 straight workouts, and we won't cancel the workout if you don't come. It's not a religion, and Tuesdays, when we work out, are not Holy Days of Obligation. I tell them I'd like them to come as often as they can, but not to become obsessive about it. We're there to enjoy ourselves.

Pat didn't need to come at all, but he was always there, even though it cost him $15 in gas and tolls just to get there, and he didn't have all that much money. I was surprised he was so conscientious, and I was also delighted. I can only guess why he did it, but I suspect it may have been because he was the best athlete in the club and the other members really appreciated what he was able to do. As far as I was concerned, I had gained more than a member, I had gained an extra coach. As such, he was a tremendous asset to the group.

Just running wasn't enough for him, though. He became interested in doing triathlons, which are races that involve swimming, riding a bike, and running. Most triathlons are run over modest distances—maybe a half-mile swim, 20 or 30 miles on a bike, and a 6.2-mile (10K) run. After doing a few of those, Pat decided he needed a bigger challenge, and he set his sights on the granddaddy of all triathlons, the Ironman, which was begun in Hawaii in 1978. The race is well-named. It starts with a 2.4-mile swim, switches to bikes for a leisurely 112 miles, and finishes off with a full, 26.2-mile marathon.

Pat applied to run in the 1984 Ironman and was accepted. Then, for no given reason, his invitation was withdrawn. Maybe the organizers found out he only had a leg and a half and didn't want to deal with him. I had been turned down by the Boston Marathon years earlier on that basis and Pat himself had also been rejected by Boston in 1983. But in the spring of 1984, after his ability had been proven, the Boston Marathon allowed him to run, and he responded with a 3:41 performance. The Ironman would be brought to heel the same way.

On September 8, 1984, Pat Griskus found himself at the starting line of a race that didn't care how many legs he had—the Cape Cod Endurance Triathlon. It was the same distance as the Ironman, with the biggest difference being that the water temperature off Cape Cod was a hypothermic 61 degrees. The other differences were more subtle. As Pat put it in a first-person article he wrote about his race in the *Waterbury Republican-American*, "So here I was, without major TV network coverage, no tanned wahinis, and not a single Hawaiian shirt in the crowd."

As he waited in the early morning chill for the race to start, Pat confessed, "I was scared. The Cape event was still an 'ironman' in distance and there was so much I had to prove. I knew how hard I had trained and even though I had 17 hours to finish, I figured I should be able to make it in 14.5 hours or less. I had even gone public with that prediction. I wish I had kept my mouth shut."

The weakest part of Pat's game was swimming. He kept dropping his times in running and bicycling, but his swimming times remained stuck at between 100 and 105 minutes for the 2.4-mile swim. In the cold water, that presented an immediate problem as he rapidly chilled to the bone. "I had passed up a chance to wear a wet vest," he wrote, "because most of the other swimmers weren't wearing them. I didn't want to look like a sissy. But that little touch of bravado came expensive; after about a quarter-mile of swimming, I was already becoming numb."

He had hoped that the thunderstorm of adrenaline that his first ironman was sure to unleash in his body would push him through the swimming portion of the race in a little over an hour and a half. Instead, it took his slow training time of an hour and three-quarters. He came out of the ocean blue and shivering and was immediately grabbed by a race official whose duty it was to save freezing runners from themselves. The official, Pat said, "grabbed me as if I weighed nothing and told me I had to warm up in an ambulance. I told him I didn't have time and that I was okay. He said that I did have time and I wasn't okay."

Pat went into the ambulance, but only long enough to get into his biking shorts and shirt and to buckle on his prosthesis. Then he was off and pedaling. He shivered for the first few miles, but soon warmed to the task—so to speak. He had anticipated 7.5 hours for the 112 miles of biking under optimum conditions, but his slow start and an equipment problem about 50 miles into the course convinced him he should stop thinking about time goals and start concentrating on doing the best he could. The course went 56 miles out to Provincetown, where he picked up a banana, cookies, and a jelly donut, then swung around to ride the route in reverse back to the transition area. On the second half of the bike leg, he started passing other competitors.

"It gave me a lift and made me ride just that much harder," he wrote. "In all of my races, I've always tried to... beat as many people as I could. This may seem like the obvious thing to do, but because I am an amputee, many people think it's enough that I just show up and complete a race. I'm not about to say that there's anything wrong with such thinking. But, speaking for myself, I can't see that there's anything right in it, either."

That was vintage Pat Griskus, ornery in the heat of battle and not willing to give in to anyone. The man was a competitor before he was an amputee. I was a jogger. He was a world-class athlete and he had the arrogance that goes with it. That quality sometimes made other competitors forget that he had just one leg and they were supposed to feel sorry for him. This is a phenomenon that the best disabled athletes are familiar with. If you're just plugging along, starting early and finishing late, you're inspirational, courageous, and even cute. But start messing with the good runners who build their identities on their performance, and you're a damned nuisance.

Elite wheelchair athletes know about this syndrome. Many elite runners don't like them because they're faster. Pat ran into it once at the finish of the New York City Marathon. As a runner who came in around 3:30, he was among the better recreational runners. The way a recreational runner gets to be that fast is through sheer, cussed competitiveness, because the closer you get to three hours, the more serious work it takes to get there. Anyway, Pat had finished this particular race with his normal kick and had just edged out at the tape a guy with two complete legs. Novice runners figure that once they've crossed the finish line, their place in the race is carved in stone, but experienced runners know it doesn't work that way. In a big race, the order of finish is a two-stage process. As the runners cross the line, a race official punches a hand-held switch that records the time. The runners are then herded into chutes, where other officials record their bib numbers. Then a computer puts the first finishing time together with the first bib number in the chute, the hundredth time with the hundredth bib and so on. If somebody passes you in the chute, they get your finishing time and vice versa. Often at the marathon you'll see novice runners labor across the line and then come to a screeching halt as they double over and try to collect their breath and what's left of their strength. While they're standing there with hands on knees, any number of runners finishing behind them will keep going into the chutes and the poor novice will never figure out how the 4:30:10 he saw on the clock when he finished turned into a 4:30:50 in the official results.

Anyway, the guy Pat edged out knew how the results work, so he knew that it didn't matter who crossed the finish line first. The order of finish would be determined by who got into the chute first. As Pat slowed to a walk after finishing, the beaten runner tried to shove past him, shouting, "No cripple is going to beat me!" But Pat knew the rules, too, and he informed the man that this cripple had, indeed, beaten him, and to please get behind him. And he didn't particularly care that the guy didn't find him the least bit cute or inspirational.

We've had other similar cases with Achilles runners. We have a female runner, Daniella Zahner, in Switzerland who does ultra-marathons on crutches and beats able-bodied runners, who have complained that her crutches give her an advantage. I once joked to an official of the Amateur Athletic Union that one day a prosthesis could be developed that would actually make you faster than running on a real leg. The official didn't get the joke and some time after that the AAU outlawed prosthetic limbs in races they sanction.

Then there was a July Fourth race in San Bernardino, California, to which some Achilles members from Poland had been invited. One of the Polish athletes, Tomasz Chmurzynski, was a man who was legally blind but could see enough to run by himself. He had to run by himself because nobody was fast enough to run with him as a guide. When he won the race, the race committee refused to give him the first-place trophy on the grounds that it had been unfair of us to bring in a world-class athlete to take a trophy away from the locals. We were entered as "honorary runners." The man who finished second, who was from the area, was given the winner's trophy, and he promptly turned around and gave it to the Polish runner, proving that it's only a few runners who are jerks about these things.

Finally, some guys just can't stand being beaten by women. Pat was like that. Another person who has the same attitude—we'll call him Jake—is a popular New York City television news anchor who is a fine athlete. Jake used to run at the West Side Y when I did laps there. As more women got into running and Jake got older, the inevitable day arrived when the best women were passing him on the track. This drove Jake crazy, but there wasn't anything he could do about it. They were too fast for him. Rather than admit it, he went out and got a set of hand and ankle weights and put them on when he ran. Now he could say that the reason the women were passing him wasn't because they were faster than he, but because he was running with these weights. And they say 'vanity, thy name is woman'?

Pat never ran into that attitude in the ironman. When you're going that distance, most athletes know what a supreme effort it takes, no matter what your abilities or disabilities. One of his fellow contestants, Walt Tajmajer, an Achilles runner with an artificial hip, had even given him a sweatshirt that morning to keep him warm while waiting for the race to begin.

Pat finished the 112-mile bike leg in six and one-half hours, an hour faster than he had planned. He parked his bike, readjusted his prosthesis, and set off running the final marathon leg. "I was surprised at how good I felt and the cheers and encouragement from the crowd made me feel even better," he reported. He had anticipated walking considerable distances during the marathon and running when he could, but he found he could not only maintain a steady run, but even pass a few more competitors. Like the bike portion, the marathon was a loop course—out half the distance, and then back. Pat hit the halfway point still at a run and headed home, ignoring the incipient cramps that were invading his thighs. He made it to the 20-mile mark—the mile post that is most often associated with The Wall by marathoners—when his left hamstring finally clenched like a fist and wouldn't unclench.

"As soon as I bent over to massage the hamstring, I felt and even saw the muscles in my right leg cramp up and begin to pulsate every which way. I tried massaging them, but as soon as I would stop, the spasms would start up again," he wrote. "I could no longer run. I began to walk... In addition to my legs, my abdominal and even my neck muscles were cramping up. Every half-mile or so I found myself doubling over... Finally, at 24.5 miles, I reached back to massage my hamstrings and my stomach locked up so tight that I keeled over face first... I was now on all fours. It actually felt good to be down."

Near the end of a race, the runners' creed is, "If it feels good, don't do it." So Pat hauled himself to his feet, somehow walked a quarter-mile, and then started running again. And when Janice McKeown—a woman—caught him and started to pass, he discovered he could run even faster. He couldn't catch her, but he ran the rest of the way and actually sprinted to the finish line. By then, he was almost out of it, but he wasn't so far gone that he didn't check his time. He had predicted 14:30, and when he looked at the clock, it read 14:28:57. He'd made it with 1:03 to spare.

"I was far too exhausted for a show of emotion," he wrote. "All the same, I knew I had just completed the most important day of my life with a sprint. And how many people can say that?"

That might have been enough for most people. Not for Pat. He heard about a race called the Western States 100, a contest that is 100 miles as the crow flies, but if the crow has to run up and down the nine mountains on the course, it's much longer. He entered that and had finished about 30 miles when he got to a medical checkpoint. There a doctor looked at the bleeding mess that was his stump and disqualified him on the spot. Pat wanted to go on, but the doctor said that even if he finished, they wouldn't acknowledge it. When Pat heard that, he agreed to quit. It was the only race he ever quit.

His performance in the Cape Cod ironman got him into the 1985 Ironman in Hawaii. He finished that race and the next year's, too, bringing his personal best down from 14.5 to about 13.5 hours, which is just unbelievable. And all the while he kept running marathons and shorter races in between. Along the way, Timex, the watch manufacturer headquartered in Waterbury, signed a contract with him to sponsor their products, partly because he was a hometown hero, but mostly because Pat, like Timex, "took a lickin' and kept on tickin'."

I was delighted for him personally about the Timex deal. It allowed him to be a professional runner and freed him from worrying about where the next rent check was going to come from. His girlfriend, Robin Dowling, had moved in with him, and money was a little more important than it had been. At the same time, I was worried that when he finished his competitive running career, he would move into an executive position with Timex. My fears were totally selfish, because I wanted him to become the next president of Achilles, the one who would take over from me and take the club into the 21st century. He was perfect for the job, a terrific coach, an impressive presence to deal with potential corporate donors, a genuine hero who had been featured on many national television programs from "Wide World of Sports" to "A Current Affair"; in short, as fine a representative as any organization could hope for. He could be all that and be tough, as well. New runners who came to him for advice were met with a certain distance until they demonstrated that they were serious. Then he poured himself into their training. He could be moody and cantankerous without alienating people.

Once a loner, Pat began a relationship with Robin, a reading disability teacher, and in 1986 they got married. A year later they had a daughter. For the first time in his life, he had finally realized genuine happiness; he had a future beyond the next race, the next workout. He had a full life.

In 1987, he entered the Ironman Triathlon in Hawaii again. It was scheduled for October, just a few weeks before the New York City Marathon. Since he figured to be still recovering from the Ironman, he had decided to run the marathon as a guide with another runner rather than run it competitively. Meanwhile, he planned to go to Hawaii early to train there and get used to the climate.

Before he left for Hawaii, Pat, Robin, and Laura came to the City to spend the day and have dinner with Betsy and me. We went to a Spanish restaurant and he and I ordered the paella, which came in a huge dish. He was training heavily and packing in about 8,000 calories a day. When the paella came, he wolfed down about two-thirds of it and I got the other third. I remember being delighted to see someone who could grossly outeat me—and not gain weight. We had a good time that night, and when it was over, I wished him luck in Hawaii and went home feeling good. It was the last time I saw him alive.

Patrick Griskus died October 3, 1987, in Hawaii. He was training for the race, riding his bicycle with a group of fellow triathletes. As they rode along the side of the road, a cement truck passed them. The pouring chute on the back of the truck wasn't secured, and as the rear of the truck reached Pat, the chute swung around and hit him in the back of the head. He died instantly. None of the other athletes were touched.

So many images struck me when I heard the news. I thought about Pat and how he had come to Achilles like the Tin Woodsman, in possession of everything but searching for a heart. I had encouraged him to pursue his impossible quests and he had conquered them all. In the process, he had discovered the heart that was there all along.

I tried to think of his story as having a happy ending. I remembered an obscure radio serial I used to listen to as a kid during the 40s. I think it was called "Tennessee Jed," and it was about these people who had one trouble after another. Every half-hour, they'd overcome one test and the next week another, fresh torment, would be awaiting them. Then, in the last episode before it went off the air, they solved the last problem and rode off into that eternal sunset.

I saw Pat that way, riding off into the sunset on his bicycle, his problems and cares behind him. And I thought of how it was like the image of the Grecian urn that had struck me when I was in the hospital going into surgery, not knowing if I would come out alive. If I didn't, I would have been frozen on the urn on that hospital gurney forever, going in for an operation I would never quite get to. But Pat, for all eternity, is getting ready for his next Ironman Triathlon, riding his bike, feeling good, heading for a gorgeous sunset.

Pat died, but he'll never be gone. Each year, two Achilles runners, male and female, receive the Pat Griskus Award at the NYRRC awards banquet. But a more important legacy is the Pat Griskus Chapter of the Achilles Track Club at Gaylord Rehabilitation Hospital in Wallingford, Connecticut.

Gaylord, like the Rusk Institute, is an institution where people who have suffered disabling diseases or injuries go to learn how to do all the things that were taken away from them. Robin, Ted Mulvey, a young runner from that area, and myself came up with the idea and we got the chapter up and running about a year after Pat passed away. There was a running area at the hospital, and it has been our experience that running can help people recover from many different kinds of trauma.

About a year after we started the chapter, Gaylord got a

new patient who had come as close to death as you can come. The young woman was known in New York and around the nation as the Central Park Jogger. She was the woman who had been savagely beaten, raped, and left for dead by a gang of young thugs who waylaid her as she was running in the park. She had been a fine runner before the attack, but she had suffered severe brain trauma, and no one knew whether she would walk unaided again, much less run.

When she had gotten to the point where she could navigate a little with the aid of a walker, she joined the Pat Griskus Chapter. At first, she could do one lap—a quarter-mile—using the walker. By the time she was discharged and returned to her job with an investment firm, she was doing a comfortable five miles and there was general agreement that the running had been an important factor in her recovery.

I look at the Griskus chapter and the Central Park Jogger as part of a process of one generation empowering the next. If you went back 500 years to the days of Columbus and the voyages of exploration and discovery, you'd find ship's navigators were the most valued members of a crew. There were no standardized charts in those days, and each navigator made his own up as he went along. He guarded them jealously, storing them in sealed tubes that, to me, at least, are reminiscent of the baton that runners pass to one another during a relay race. The charts were his livelihood and they held the secrets of his trade. When the navigator grew old, he would take on an apprentice and teach the young man his craft, finally handing over the tubes with the charts to him to guard and protect. And he, in turn, would pass them on to the next navigator when he grew old. If he held on to them too long, or died young, the secrets were often lost with him, because navigators sometimes wrote in their own codes.

I like to think of Achilles as working the same way. We carry a baton in our own race, and when we have gone as far as we can, we hand it to someone who can carry it further. In that way, I handed my baton to Pat Griskus, and when he died, he handed it to the Central Park Jogger through his Achilles chapter at Gaylord. She, in turn, passed it to Toby Slocum, who was born with spina bifida and was inspired by the example of the Jogger to take up running himself. He now completes marathons on crutches. And each of us, by carrying the baton, was empowered to do things we had not been able to do before.

Today, new patients are taking up the baton at Gaylord. And as long as they do and as long as they take what they've learned out into their new lives and pass it along again, Pat Griskus will never perish.

*I've done a marathon. I'm not
tagging along anymore. I'm a leader.*
—Ann Applewhite

The first encounter I had with a disabled woman who
wanted to run the New York City Marathon was in 1979.
The deadline for entries to the race had already passed when
the Road Runners got a letter from a young woman who
said she was suffering from incurable brain cancer. Her name
was Rosie Ruiz and she said she only had six months or so
to live and she wanted to fulfill a life's ambition to run the
marathon. Could she please be allowed to enter the race?
She wasn't even sure she would be able to finish. But she
wanted to be in it. Fred called the woman and told her, of
course she could enter. I mean, how could he say no?

Rosie Ruiz entered the race, but found she didn't have
the stamina to finish it. She caught a subway to Central
Park, and was just trying to get to the gathering area beyond
the finish line when she found herself back on the course
and running through the finish line. Having taken the
subway, she was given a good time, and it made a nice little
story. It would have stayed that way except for what
happened six months later in the 1980 Boston Marathon.

Rosie's time in the New York City Marathon qualified
her for Boston, so she entered that race near the end of the
course. Jacqueline Gareau, a fine runner from Canada, was
leading the women's division of the race, and everyone was
preparing to welcome her as the winner, when Rosie, her
brain cancer apparently in full remission, came running
down the finish chute. She hadn't intended to win the race,
but only to slip in with the pack and cross the finish line.
But she had miscalculated the time and thrust herself into
one of the biggest scandals in marathon history.

Initially, she was a sensation, not just because she was unknown in Boston, but because she didn't look like a marathoner, which is to say she looked as if she had eaten in the past three days. But she had crossed the line first and she told the reporters an inventive story that had a lot of fuzz around the edges, and she was declared the winner.

Nine days later, the truth came out. When the Boston story emerged, her New York race was investigated and it was discovered that she hadn't run all of that one, either. If she hadn't wrecked it all by winning Boston, she might have gotten away with it. But because she was caught, the New York City Marathon in 1980 put video cameras at a number of locations throughout the race course to guard against future Rosie Ruiz wannabes.

Over the years a substantial number of runners have been disqualified because they didn't show up on the tapes at one or more of the video checkpoints.

The next woman runner I met who had cancer was as different from Rosie Ruiz as night and day. Her name was Ann Applewhite, and there wasn't a phony molecule in her body. She was 26 years old in 1985 when she came to us and she was suffering. Her troubles had begun as a freshman in high school when she had developed leukemia. She had fought through that and was doing okay until 1977, when she came down with a rare disease called herpes encephalitis. The disease put her into a coma, and when she woke up, she was paralyzed from the waist down. She fought through that, too, but then, in 1983, while undergoing chemotherapy for a recurrence of the leukemia, she went into neurological shock and again lost the use of her legs.

She had a job as a research data coordinator at Memorial Sloan-Kettering, where she was undergoing the chemotherapy, but when her workday was done, she would wheel herself across the street to her apartment and vegetate in front of the television. Finally, someone told her about Achilles and she came to a workout, as much to get out of the house as anything else. She was still undergoing treatment for the leukemia, and she was frail and kind of mousy. Self-confidence was not a word in her vocabulary.

She kept coming to the workouts, though, and one day she tried out another member's racing wheelchair. She had been using one of those big, clunky hospital models, and she couldn't believe how fast and maneuverable the racing chair was. It was like going from a station wagon to a sports car. She went out and got her own racing chair, and started working toward doing the 1985 New York City Marathon.

She finished the marathon, and she was changed forever. "It's changed how I feel about myself," she said. "I'm a different person than I was a year ago. I've done a marathon. I'm not tagging along anymore. I'm a leader." Ann wasn't mousy anymore, either, not by a long shot. She had become outgoing and vivacious and was, by consensus, the best-looking woman in any gathering. Most of the guys at the workouts noticed her.

The transformation in Ann after doing a marathon was a classic case of empowerment. "It was a tremendous self-confidence builder," she said. She looked at her life and realized that her research job was a dead end and that she wanted more out of life. She finally decided she wanted to be a physician's assistant, a paramedical position, and so she eventually moved to Texas where she enrolled in a program and is well on the way toward fulfilling her ambition. Now, instead of racing in the New York City Marathon, she does the radio commentary.

Ann Applewhite is just one of many people with cancer who, I am convinced, have lived longer and better through Achilles. Frequently, they do it despite the advice of their physicians. Cathy Bulboca, a courageous woman who is associated with Dr. Norman Vincent Peale's Marble Church and is the very embodiment of the power of positive thinking, is one of them. Actually, cancer is only half of the double hit Cathy took. The first thing she had to deal with, in 1988, was a stroke on the left side of her body. After that came liver cancer on top of a second stroke, and then a series of three or four mini-strokes. From 1988, when she had the first stroke, until 1990, not one of the doctors she went to suggested she try exercising. Instead, they advised against it. Finally, her psychiatrist told her about Achilles and suggested she might give it a try.

This is what Cathy wanted to hear. She had been active all her life. In college, she had been a fencer and continued that sport into middle age. She played softball and other sports, but had never been a jogger. She ran the idea past several medical doctors, "and they all said I'd be crazy to go out there," she says.

So she figured she'd be crazy. In August 1990, she showed up at an Achilles workout. As with so many others, it was slow going at first, but Cathy kept at it. Her goal was to run a four-mile race. "When you have a chronic illness, your goals are taken away," she says. "Setting a goal of doing a four-mile race may not be much, but it gives you motivation. And psychologically, it gives you a break from real life."

In 1991, she ran her four-miler. She had been in the hospital getting chemotherapy treatments Friday and Saturday before the race. On Sunday, without telling her doctors, she came to Central Park and entered the race. The last half-mile was like a hundred miles for her. But she made it across the finish line, an experience that she called, "the best feeling I've ever had in my life." Once she got across, she asked a race doctor to take her blood pressure. It was 180 over 120, high but not fatal.

When the doctor took the reading, he also told her what he thought of her adventure. "You people, I give you credit, but you do stupid things. You could end up with a stroke."

"All I wanted was my blood pressure, not a lecture," Cathy says. "When he said, 'You people,' I wanted to slap him in his face."

Achilles became a more central part of Cathy's life. She still worked and she still had friends, but her friends did not understand when she missed a date because she was simply too ill or too wrung out to make it. Achilles members always understood. They didn't put pressures on her or make demands. They just welcomed her when she came and helped her along.

"There's a strong sense of camaraderie," she said. "We've all got our problems. What your illness is isn't important. People accept you for what you are."

Cathy has become a crusader for the benefits of exercise. "I'd like to see more people with systemic illnesses get involved," she said. "But the doctors are afraid to tell people to be active. If you're a stroke victim, you're left for dead."

Being involved with Dr. Peale, Cathy believes in the power of mind over body. Running hasn't cured her, and she's had long periods when she hasn't been able to run at all. But she firmly believes that her involvement with Achilles has helped her fight her cancer. When you figure that in 1990 she had been given six months to live, and that in 1993 she's still going, it's hard to argue with her. One spring night Cathy came to a workout and suddenly felt very weak. I got her to my car and drove downtown. On the way she couldn't decide whether we should go to her hospital on East 20th Street or to the church a few blocks uptown. As we got closer, she choose the Marble Collegiate Church. I brought her up to the fourth floor and she took a nap in her minister's office. She was fine the next day.

Overall, we have a higher percentage of women members in Achilles than in the New York Road Runners. Our coaches, first Patti Lee Parmalee and now Helene Hines, who herself has multiple sclerosis, and Tricia Dorff, are women. Helene is a former high school athletic coach who was diagnosed with MS 14 years ago. Like a growing number of MS patients, she attacked her disease by throwing herself into physical conditioning. She does sets of 50 push-ups and does bench press reps with 135 pounds.

Three years ago, Helene joined Achilles and is the world record holder in the marathon for females with MS. This year, she had planned to run the Comrades Ultramarathon in South Africa, and as part of her training did a 50-mile run in February. Melissa Holden, her 25-year-old volunteer, had intended to go along for the first part of the race and ended up doing the entire 50 miles with Helene, the longest she or any Achilles volunteer had ever run. They took 11 hours, 14 seconds to complete the distance, and when they did, Helene also held the distance record for a female with MS.

As with most races, there was some comedy along with the pain. At one point, Helene's legs started cramping and she stopped to get a massage. The person massaging her saw by her T-shirt that she was an Achilles member and asked if she was running on an artificial leg. Helene was kind enough not to point out that the only thing harder to do than get a cramp in an artificial leg was to try to massage it out.

On May 31, Helene completed Comrades in less than 12 hours. The 56-mile run covered a number of mountain ranges including one stretch which was uphill for three miles. When she entered the stadium the crowd roared and tears came to my eyes. There were a few stories about the trip which were very amusing. While Helene was preparing for the race, she was also practicing the javelin for a track and field competition. Someone not very knowledgeable about the South African race asked if she would be carrying the javelin during the 56-mile run. I guess they expected her to defend herself.

As Helene started to run, she removed her fannypack and asked one of her volunteers to hold it. He blushed and explained that the term is not appropriate for South Africa inasmuch as it refers to the front of a woman's body rather than the back. (As a joke she sent him a box of Fanny Farmer chocolates after returning to the United States.)

After the event we went to a national park and saw literally thousands of animals, from giraffes and deer and monkeys to rhinoceri. At one point we were out with our Zulu guide, trying to find the black rhinoceros, which is a very dangerous animal. To the guide's chagrin, we discovered two standing some distance from each other, but both out in front of us, to our right and left. This meant that if the wind shifted, the rhino—whose sense of smell is superior—would discover us. The guide reached into his pocket and did what any modern-day Zulu guide would do: he held up his butane lighter and checked to see which way the wind was blowing.

The majority of the volunteers who run with our athletes and make the program possible are women. Maybe this is politically incorrect or sexist or both, but I would guess that we get more women volunteers because women are not as selfish as men when it comes to competition. Whereas many male runners wouldn't want to sacrifice their personal goals to run with a disabled person, women are more likely to get just as much fulfillment from helping others achieve their goals. You can argue with that, but the fact remains that at least 60 percent of our volunteers are women, and they are the backbone of the program.

One of our first two members, Linda Down, is a woman. Like Ann Applewhite, she was underemployed when she came to us. Actually, she wasn't employed at all and had just about given up finding a job. Besides being one of the first members, Linda was also the most loyal. In those early days of the disabled running class, when I never knew if anyone would show up for a workout, Linda was almost always there. Sometimes, she was the only one to show up. We ran a lot together, Linda and I. Her pace was easy for me to keep up with, but Bob Glover kept warning me that someday she would outrun me. Eventually, she fulfilled the prophecy. Now, she teases me by telling me she'll run circles around me, and in workouts, she does just that, running on ahead, then circling back and around me and then running on ahead again while I huff along trying to keep up.

Linda got a job working part time at a university on Long Island. I called around and talked to some people I knew and got her two job interviews with major corporations. But I couldn't get her a job. She did that herself, and the self-confidence she had gained by running the marathon gave her that special aura that got her two job offers and full-time employment.

Running, she once told Diane Hawkins of *New York Running News*, "changed the way I think about myself. Since it was a totally different territory for me, it became a big risk. I feel that it has helped me to take risks in other areas of my life... It means I am an athlete and gives me more of a sense of freedom."

I eventually asked Linda to serve on the board of directors of Achilles, a position she still holds. One of the reasons I asked her was because I thought that Achilles should have a disabled board member. I said that to someone who pointed out that I was disabled, and I had to admit I hadn't thought of myself as disabled. And when you look at what Linda has done in life, including running more than 150 races, it's hard to think of her as being disabled, either.

Another early woman member who has achieved a great deal is Paddy Rossbach. Paddy was born in England and it was there, at the age of six, that she was hit by a truck—a lorry over there—severely breaking her left leg. She lost a great deal of blood and was in a coma for three weeks. Like me, she developed gangrene in the leg and they had to amputate it, but below the knee. Unlike many others—myself included—who get sedentary after losing a limb,

Paddy was very active throughout her childhood. She was on the varsity cricket and swimming teams in her high school. She became a nurse in London, and, after a failed romance, came to the United States. She was then in her mid-20s.

For nearly two decades, she avoided disabled people. "I wanted very much to be like everybody else," she once told *Women's Sports and Fitness* magazine. "Then I met Dick Traum, and it was the most exhilarating feeling. I looked at all these people who would never go out into the park and run alone; everyone looked a little strange, one way or another. But the support was there, and the companionship. I realized that even if I don't need the support, I can offer it to others who do."

I met Paddy in 1984 when I was giving a speech on running at Memorial Sloan-Kettering, where she was working as a nurse in the critical-care unit. She had come to see if maybe running was something that would benefit her patients, teenagers who had undergone amputation for osteosarcoma, or bone cancer. Very few people she worked with knew that she was an amputee herself. She walked without a limp and saw no reason to mention it.

Paddy was an attractive woman in her mid-40s when we met. Twenty years earlier, she had been quite a looker and had nearly lost her job when an issue of *Playboy* came out with a nude pictorial of a woman who looked almost exactly like Paddy. She saved her job and stopped all gossip when she unveiled her artificial leg, demonstrating conclusively that the person in the magazine could not be her.

Although she came to my speech for her patients, Paddy joined Achilles herself. She was already an accomplished athlete, and with training she became the fastest female amputee marathoner ever with a time of just under five hours, a distinction she still holds. In 1985, after starting two hours ahead of the pack, she finished among the faster runners in the marathon. When she came across the line, race volunteers thought she was the 50th woman to finish and tried to give her an award, but she refused, pointing out that she had started early. The inspiration for her and several others to run harder in that race was Brian Froggatt, the above-the-knee amputee from New Zealand. She was as determined to beat him as he was not to get beaten by a woman, and the combination of competitive personalities led to some stirring stretch runs in races. Froggatt won, but not by much.

After Paddy joined us, I suggested that she set up a research project at Memorial Sloan-Kettering that would look at the effects of exercise and running on the recovery of kids with bone cancer. I started looking around for funding and the first place I called was Canada to talk to the people who were running the Terry Fox cancer fund. When I asked them for funding for an American program, they were extremely upset. "This money is for Canada," they told me in no uncertain terms, and that was the last time I looked for help north of the border. Then I called Al Gordon, my friend and a New York Road Runners Club director. Al is the honorary chairman of the board of Kidder, Peabody Group Inc., and was an original benefactor of Achilles. He has run three marathons since he reached the age of 80 and has run in others as an Achilles volunteer. I asked Al if he could help set up the program and he promptly wrote a check for $10,000 and sent it to Memorial Sloan-Kettering to start the program.

Paddy ran the program and called it ASPIRE, for Adolescent Sarcoma Patients' Intensive Rehabilitation with Exercise. Paddy has developed some of the very best amputee sprinters in the world through ASPIRE. Her project convinced others that it was much better for cancer patients to be active.

Paddy pointed out in an article in *New York Running News* that chemotherapy and cancer patients typically lie in bed and lose three percent of their strength each day for the first two weeks of idleness. "This is bound to lower someone's self-confidence and/or self-esteem because they begin to look and feel bad. It's what we call negative body imaging," she said. Once she started patients working out on treadmills, stationary bikes, or rowing machines, she said, "we began to notice a difference in the mental outlook and physical well-being of these individuals. It was quite remarkable." Betsy Haas, an Achilles member and cancer patient who specializes in sprints, added, "Running and cancer are a lot alike in that both are a physical fight."

As Achilles grew, I was constantly discovering new types of disabilities that could benefit from running, and in the process, meeting a succession of wonderful people. Sister Gladys, of the School Sisters of Notre Dame order of teaching nuns, is high on that list.

Sister Gladys was 41 years old in 1973 when her doctor told her that the sharp pains she was experiencing in her chest were from angina, which is caused by periodic episodes of oxygen starvation of the heart muscles because of constricted coronary arteries. She was stationed at a school on 62nd Street in Manhattan at the time, living in a convent and wearing a habit. With her tendency to having a well-upholstered physique, her angina kept getting worse until finally the doctor told her she'd have to do some kind of exercising just to keep the arteries open.

In those days, the Catholic Church did not encourage its nuns to shuck their habits, climb into sweat suits, and run around the neighborhood. But Sister Gladys figured it was either that or make an early exit from a heart attack. So she got a sweat suit and started getting up early to run around the schoolyard before morning prayers. Not knowing whether this was a sanctioned activity for a nun, she neglected to ask permission to start exercising. She just did it. "I'm sure I was the first one in my order to start running," she says. "It felt very funny at first. People would look at me. They had never seen my hair before." But she wasn't alone. Another nun from a different order who was staying at the convent and teaching in the same school turned out to be a runner, and when she saw Sister Gladys running, she joined her. Before long the two were leaving the schoolyard and running along the East River.

In 1981, Sister Gladys joined Road Runners and through them got into a group of cardiac patients who ran as a team. The founder of the club, Joe Michaels, lived on Long Island and had started running after undergoing quadruple bypass surgery. The group would meet at the Road Runners headquarters on 89th Street, and she'd go up there in her habit and change into her running clothes when she got there. Running opened up a new world for her. In her sweat suit and out in the park, she wasn't a nun anymore, but a runner. "People don't treat you like a nun," she said. "They treat you like another person. It's a wonderful feeling." As with all running clubs, she soon found herself entered in her first race, a five-miler in Central Park.

It wasn't an easy race. As she got within sight of the finish line at 90th Street, she was faltering badly and limping. I happened to be watching the race from the finish line and saw her struggling, so I ran down the stretch to her. "Do what I'm doing," I told her, and started hop-stepping toward the line. It's a gait made for a limp, and she did it and made it to the finish.

Sister Gladys didn't know who I was. She just knew I had helped her finish the race. "I didn't know he had one leg," she says. "He never said a thing to me. He just saw me limping and came out to help."

After we had finished, I introduced myself and told her why I was limping. She was as surprised as you'd expect.

Since Achilles didn't exist then, Sister Gladys continued to run with her cardiac runners club. She ran the 1982 New York City Marathon, an accomplishment which thrilled her fellow nuns, who decorated the convent with signs and banners that greeted her when she came home in triumph. She then got into the Boston Marathon, which she ran twice, setting her personal record of 6:14 in that race. But Boston, which had once told me that they didn't want me turning their race into a circus, wasn't excited about cardiac patients running, either. After Sister Gladys' second run there, they came up with a new rule that required anyone with heart trouble to run with a doctor. That was the end of her Boston Marathon career.

The running nun became something of a celebrity. When she was getting ready for her second New York City Marathon in 1983, ABC-TV heard about her and came to the convent to film a feature about her. They were taping her running around the yard when the convent's dog, a big and frisky golden retriever, slipped out of the convent and started running for the gate and the street. One of the other nuns yelled at her to grab the dog. When she did, she lost her balance and fell heavily on the pavement, bruising her knee and raising a big welt on her eye. When she collected herself, the television crew took one look and suggested that they finish the taping with shots taken from behind her.

Even with her knee swollen badly and running a fever from the knot on her head, Sister Gladys started the marathon. It was a rainy day, as miserable a day as we've had for a marathon, and after 16 miles, the fever and the knee proved too much for the feisty nun. She dropped out at that point, and it remains the only marathon she's failed to complete in a dozen starts.

Four years ago, Joe Michaels, the founder of Sister Gladys' running club, died. Wanting to keep running, she joined Achilles, and kept running races of all lengths, including five ultramarathons on Long Island, each one 30 miles or more in length. The running didn't cure her angina. She still suffers from it, and has undergone two angioplasties over the years to unblock arteries. These days, I have her race walking instead of running to guard her health. She chafes at the reduced pace, but in 1992 she finished her 10th New York City Marathon. She lives in an apartment now and dresses for work in a suit. After having taught every grade, she's now in charge of a pre-K class of four-year-olds, and loves her work more than ever.

"Mentally, it has helped me a lot," she says of her running. "You go out there with stress and strain and you come back feeling much better; a different person. Running makes you more aware of everything going on. It helps me when I teach the little ones gym. It gives me more stamina—and confidence."

The end of communal living and mandatory wearing of the religious habit aren't the only changes Sister Gladys has seen during her running career. When she started, she was almost always alone and considered more than a little eccentric. Now, her order encourages its sisters to exercise regularly. "Now I see people from the provincial council going out to run," she says.

Like so many others, she really doesn't need Achilles. She's been running for nearly two decades and knows what she's doing. But she enjoys the group and draws strength from it. "You see so many people with different things wrong with them," she says of her Achilles workouts. "You say to yourself, 'If they can do it, I can, too.' I look like the healthiest person in the bunch. They have some courage, I'll tell you. They certainly are an inspiration."

So is Sister Gladys.

As Sister Gladys introduced me to angina patients, another very special woman helped me learn about the role running can play for stroke victims. Her name is Andrea De Mello, and she is an Achilles Track Club legend.

Andrea was born in Rio de Janeiro, Brazil, the third daughter of a lawyer father and nurse mother. She was afflicted with cerebral palsy, but it was not a severe case, and her childhood was relatively normal until 1981, when, at the age of 13, her world and that of her family was changed forever. She had gone to an amusement park with her family and was enjoying one of the many rides when she suddenly blacked out. Her family rushed the unconscious girl to a hospital, where the doctors could find no explanation for her condition. They put her in a bed, and for 15 days she remained in a coma. The doctors couldn't tell her family whether or not she would wake up. Not willing to give up hope, her family stayed by her side until, on the 16th day, she awoke. But the girl who now lay in the hospital bed was not the same happy, active girl who had gone to the amusement park. She couldn't talk, couldn't eat, and couldn't move the right side of her body.

She had suffered a stroke, but the doctors were unable to diagnose it. All they knew for certain was that she was partially paralyzed and unable to talk. They suggested physical therapy for her, and told her family that it would be best if they put her in an institution for the severely disabled. There, they could visit her, but it was expected that they would see her less and less until they simply forgot about her and abandoned her to her fate.

This sounds cruel, but it was the way things were done in her country. Certainly, she couldn't go back to school because she was disabled, and in Brazil there were no provisions for such people. Disabled people were not accepted in society. "People look at you like you're not able to do anything," says her sister, Claudia.

Her family refused to put her in an institution and instead cared for her themselves. Her friends abandoned her, but her mother, Lourdes, would not. After exhausting all possible avenues of assistance in Brazil, Lourdes made a bold decision in 1984. She would bring her stricken child to New York.

There, perhaps the American doctors could tell them what had happened to Andrea and how she could be helped.

She took Andrea to Columbia Presbyterian Hospital, where a diagnosis was finally made. For the first time, Andrea's family learned that she had suffered a stroke. She was taken into surgery and a shunt was installed in her head to improve the blood flow to the damaged part of her brain. For the first time since the stroke, Andrea began to improve.

But the big improvement didn't begin for another year, when Claudia heard about the Achilles Track Club and took Andrea to one of our workouts. Claudia was her sister's constant companion. Andrea couldn't get on a bus by herself, couldn't navigate in the city. Both sisters still spoke only Portuguese, and they got their points across to me and the other athletes in sign language.

Andrea was fat—the result of an inactive lifestyle—when I first met her. She was painfully shy, and as slow as continental drift. I ran with her that first day, and she couldn't run—if that's what you could call her slow, painful progress—a half-block without stopping to rest. She helped support her paralyzed right side with a cane, which she still uses.

But she kept coming back and slowly she got better. After a year's steady effort, she could keep going for two miles, and to prove it, she entered a race of that distance in Central Park and finished it in an hour. It had been more than five years since her stroke, and it was the first time she had been able to accomplish something positive. And in New York, the crowds cheered for her and told her how great she was doing—a far cry from what would have happened in Brazil.

The two-miler gave her an enormous boost in confidence, and she went after her training with renewed enthusiasm. But now she wasn't thinking about a mere two-mile race. She was after the big one, the marathon. By the fall of 1987, Andrea De Mello, now 20 years old, was ready, one of 65 Achilles athletes who would run the marathon that year. She had lost 30 pounds since she began training and was so pretty she positively glowed.

On the day of the race, she started at 6 a.m., and for 20 miles she made decent enough time. Then her left leg—her good leg—started to go on her. The last six miles were torture, with Andrea stopping frequently for massages, and Andrea leaning heavily on her companion for support. But at 8:15 p.m., more than 14 hours after she had set out, Andrea De Mello crossed the finish line a winner. The members of the Achilles Track Club, every one of them an inspiration in their own right, voted her the most inspirational female in that year's race. And in the process of finishing the race, Andrea became the first female stroke victim to run a marathon.

When I first met Andrea and her sister, Claudia, they were like child and parent, with Andrea totally dependent on her older sister. But as Andrea became stronger, her confidence grew until she could come to the workouts by herself and the two sisters were equals. They even started having spats, as sure a sign of a healthy sister-sister relationship as there is.

Andrea's other sister, Valeria, is a physician and also lives in New York. She once explained that Andrea "says that she has an inner power that keeps her going and helps her have the feeling that she can overcome her disability. Her body is not as perfect as everybody else's, but she can do it."

Andrea herself doesn't converse well, especially in English, but she can get her points across. "Now, I'm more happy," she says of the difference between her life before and after Achilles. "Now my life is better."

She started running races every weekend. "This is my life," she says. "I started with Achilles and now I'm a full-time athlete."

Although she got stronger, marathons didn't get easier for her. In 1991, it took her more than 20 hours to finish the race. It was 2 a.m. when she finally pulled into the park from 59th Street to run the last stretch to the finish. As she and a small entourage struggled along, an Englishman in black tie and three ladies, all dressed in evening gowns, jumped out of a car and joined the parade. "Anybody still running this marathon, I'm going with them," the Englishman said, and he and his lady friends did just that, cheering Andrea along to the finish.

Andrea didn't stop at running. In addition to Achilles, she joined the American Cerebral Palsy Athletic Association, where she took up swimming and track. She swims every day, sometimes traveling to Yale University in New Haven, Connecticut, to use their 50-meter pool. She competes in the 50- and 100-meter freestyle, 50-meter butterfly, and two relays, and has won a roomful of trophies and medals. In 1992, she qualified for the Paralympics, the international games for the disabled held after the Olympics at the same venues used by the Olympic athletes. She went to Barcelona to compete, but once there, doctors discovered that her blood pressure was seriously elevated and kept her out of the games. It was a huge disappointment for her after all the work she had put in, but she was lucky the doctors caught it. Her condition was precarious, they felt, and she was admitted to a hospital back in the States. She missed the 1992 marathon as well, but the problem was brought under control and she's out and running again.

She's not going to quit and she says she'll never return to Brazil to live, and anyone who saw her before she started running knows why. Running has brought her to life and given her life purpose and direction. "In Brazil," says her sister, Valeria, "they told us to put her in an institution. Can you imagine that?"

I can't. Today, Andrea is reaping the pleasures of life. I couldn't be more delighted for her.

FINISH

Chapter 8

> *God appears to a Russian peasant and tells him he can*
> *have anything he wants—wealth, power, fame, all of the*
> *above—on one condition: Whatever he asks for, his neighbor*
> *will enjoy in double measure. This troubles the peasant, for,*
> *while he wants to be wealthy, he does not want his neighbor*
> *to have more than he. After thinking long and hard,*
> *he addresses God. "Lord," he says, "take one of my eyes."*
> —Russian folk tale

At first, I thought of Achilles as only a New York thing. But as word spread, chapters started to sprout up in other states. Then Brian Froggatt showed up from New Zealand and Anthony Philip, a man we found in New York, took the Achilles Track Club to his native Trinidad.

As I've said before, I've never chased publicity, but neither am I allergic to it. You have to have it to grow, and it was clear that the more stories that appeared in the media, the more members we got and the more new chapters were formed. It was just as clear that the surest way to get on television or in the newspapers was to have something new to give the reporters. I had learned on my second trip to Canada for the Terry Fox runs that the novelty wears off fast. So, when we started getting new runners first from outside the New York area and then from overseas, we knew we also had new stories.

I've never sent out a press release. I don't think it does much good. When reporters get releases, they know that 300 other reporters have the same release and it's no longer a good story for them. What I do is call certain reporters and tell them what's going to be happening at the next event. If we get a story, fine. If not, that's fine, too. And if there are four different papers in New York, I'll give each paper a different story, so each paper has an exclusive and no one has been left out.

The key is to keep getting fresh stories. And in 1987, I found an artesian well of material.

It started with a reporter, Leszek Sibilski, from Poland. Leszek is one of those remarkable people who has been successful in two entirely different careers. As a very young man, he was the top bicycle racer in Poland and in 1976 was ranked second in the world. After his competitive cycling career was over, he studied further, getting a doctorate and becoming one of Poland's leading sports journalists. He then got a job with the Polish equivalent of *Sports Illustrated* and somehow got himself assigned to cover sports in the United States from a base in New York.

I met Leszek in 1987 in Fred Lebow's office at the New York Road Runners Club headquarters. He had come to do a story on the club and to inquire about doing another story on a running club for the disabled that he had heard about. As our mutual luck would have it, I stuck my head in Fred's office during the interview and Fred introduced me to Leszek, who said he had been eager to meet me and do a story about Achilles.

I didn't know what to think of Leszek. At first, I was cool toward him because I figured that a Polish reporter who was working and living in New York must be a KGB agent. He certainly looked as if he could be, at least to my active imagination. Young, good-looking, and strong as an ox, he was an imposing presence of the sort I imagined a KGB agent to be. Still, a story's a story, and we made arrangements to meet and talk about the Achilles Track Club.

He wrote his story and in it invited people interested in disabled sports to write to him. The magazine got something like 60 letters in response to the article, which is an impressive number. Poland did have a ministry for disabled sports called START, but the response from his article was so strong that Leszek felt that more could be done.

It was rapidly becoming obvious that I had been as wrong as I could be about Leszek. He was and is one of the finest people I've met through Achilles, and he is dedicated to disabled sports. I learned one of his favorite books when he was a kid was about a Russian pilot who had lost both his legs in the war. After getting out of the hospital, the pilot went back into the Russian air force and continued to fly airplanes into combat. Ever since then, Leszek has had a great admiration for disabled people who refuse to be defeated. I think he saw that attitude in Achilles, and he has remained one of our greatest champions. Without him, Achilles wouldn't have nearly the presence it does internationally. And as for my suspicions that he was working for the KGB, I learned later that he had worked closely with Lech Walesa in the Solidarity labor movement. The man was solid gold.

Leszek and I talked about what we might do in Poland and we decided a good start would be to bring an Achilles member to Warsaw to run that's city's 1987 marathon. We happened to have a member who was perfect—Eddie Pazarecki, a Polish-American amputee who was a member of our New York chapter. Leszek made the arrangements, we went to Warsaw, and Eddie ran the marathon on crutches, getting a terrific response from the crowd. Eddie was the only amputee in the race, but I saw two Polish wheelchair athletes come across the line. With Leszek interpreting, I introduced myself and told them about Achilles. They became the first two members of the Warsaw chapter. A blind Polish woman had also run the race, and we recruited her, too, for a grand total of three members, or one more than I had started out with in New York.

To actually get the chapter going, though, we needed to set up a formal arrangement with START, the Polish athletic agency. Again, Leszek set up the meeting. That led to several days of dinners and negotiating. Basically, the Poles felt that if they were going to be part of Achilles, then Achilles should give them some resources to get things started. This was all new to me, but it made sense that they needed to at least have a telephone in an office somewhere, some stationery and money to buy stamps. At the same time, Achilles has never been rolling in money and I didn't have much to give them. So I said I could give them $500, 100 T-shirts, and 50 pairs of running shoes, which were donated by manufacturers. Everybody thought that was a good idea, so we signed the contracts and had a big dinner to celebrate.

I hadn't known what to expect when we went to Poland. I had traveled in Western Europe but had not spent significant time behind the Iron Curtain. What I expected to find pretty much conformed to the standard American stereotypes of Eastern Europe. When we first got off the plane in Warsaw, I wasn't disappointed in that regard. The airport itself was downright frightening. It was gray and cold and everywhere you looked were soldiers with guns. Even though I didn't have any reason to be concerned, when we got to customs, I couldn't help but worry that I could be arrested for something I wasn't even aware I'd done. I don't think I was an "ugly American," but I sure was an ignorant one.

The Polish people, I soon discovered, are wonderful and incurable romantics. Their economy was shot to hell, inflation was out of control, and no one knew where their next zloty was coming from, but even if they didn't have enough money to buy butter for their daily bread, they'd find a way to buy flowers. A Pole could have only one shirt to his name, but he'd give it to you off his back if he thought you needed it.

As in any country that has been run by a stifling bureaucracy, I ran into some situations that Americans would find utterly absurd. For example, there was a place to change money at the airport, but what money you could exchange depended on what they had on hand. Some days, you could change dollars into zlotys, but you couldn't change zlotys into dollars. That made a certain sense, because dollars are hard currency and they wanted to keep them. But the next day, if they were out of zlotys, they wouldn't accept dollars at all.

Some years later, they had an interesting situation with pay telephones, as well. Inflation had run way ahead of the phone company's ability to change the telephones, which had slots that accepted only a ten-zloty coin. If you had such a coin, this was great, because, with zlotys running something like fifteen thousand to the dollar, ten zlotys was virtually no money at all. But because the coins were worthless, they were out of circulation. So you'd have to go to a booth and buy a worthless coin from an official for maybe a thousand zlotys to work the telephone.

I guess it's the Polish equivalent of buying subway tokens.

Another interesting characteristic of Poland is the old-fashioned attitudes toward sexual equality. In the Warsaw Marathon the male winner received a color television set.

The female winner was given a clothes washer. This was considered entirely appropriate.

In some ways, the country is 100 years behind the Western World, and its people tend to live in the past. World War II is still very much a presence, as if it had ended only last year. People still put fresh-cut flowers every day in certain parts of Warsaw that had been bombed by the Germans during the war and not rebuilt.

I had read a couple of books about Poland and the war before I left, and I talked to the Polish people about what I'd read. They were very proud of the accomplishments of the Polish underground during the war. When I actually met some people who had been involved with the underground, I was thrilled. They were delighted to talk about their experiences, and were impressed with my knowledge.

So that first visit went very well, and before we left we invited several Polish runners to come to the New York City Marathon. When we got back to the United States, though, we realized we needed money to carry all this out. Leszek went to work and in short order had rounded up a donation from Pekao, a Polish trading company doing business in the United States, and one from Pole Foods, the people who bring you Krakus Hams. My original idea was to put the money—$12,000—in an account to draw from as needed, but when I told a Polish liaison in New York who was working on the project what I had, he wanted the money immediately. It was like seeing a starving wolf catch wind of a lamb chop. The donation was an enormous amount of money in Poland, more money that most ordinary people might see in a lifetime. I gave him both checks.

It didn't take long to realize that I had made a big mistake. I had assumed that some of the money would be siphoned off, but I figured that if half of it got to people who needed it, that was a lot of money in Poland. All I asked of the people I gave the checks to was an annual report of what they did with it. And they really could have told me just about anything. But a year later, they had no money and no reports, and as far as I could see, had made no progress. And it wasn't just the $12,000. As far as I could ever learn, none of the T-shirts or running shoes ever got to the people for whom they were intended.

There was miscalculation on both sides. I had assumed START, which was administering the program, would use the money to build Achilles. They assumed that I was a flash-in-the-pan who would be out of business in a year and then they wouldn't have to deal with me. On top of that, there was a simple clash of cultures. According to Leszek, START really did use at least some of the money for disabled programs. They just didn't necessarily use it for my programs in the way I had envisioned.

I didn't understand the perception people in other countries have of Americans. In telling them how to spend the money and asking for reports, I was doing what Americans are expected to do—throw their weight around and tell everyone what's good for them. But no matter how good your intentions are, people of other nations have their pride, and they resent being ordered around.

The bottom line was that I handled it poorly. But at least I learned a valuable lesson, one I didn't forget. The next year, when the Poles asked for another big check, I didn't respond. From then on, I never gave a new chapter a large amount of money. The most I provide is a couple of hundred dollars to get a telephone and work space. If they want more money, I help them get the means to earn it. One way I've done that is by getting a computer company to donate used PC's to Achilles chapters. This may not seem like a big deal to Americans, where personal computers are nearly as common as microwave ovens. But in Eastern Europe, computers are still rare, and even one PC can be the basis of a business. In Russia, one chapter rents out time on the computer and makes a nice income. In Mongolia, they are setting up a computer service operated by vision-impaired Achilles members using low-vision software.

Looking at it from the outside, I didn't really have an Achilles chapter in Poland—not right away, at least. All I had was one blind female runner and two guys in wheelchairs. They didn't have regular meetings or a clubhouse or much of anything. But to me they were a chapter. And when I brought them over to the United States for the New York City Marathon, I also had some new stories. Then, when they went back to Poland, there were more stories in the Polish press, which led to more members.

So bringing people to the United States to run was a great strategy. It was also a great adventure for the runners who came. Very few people in Poland have ever been to the United States, so someone who does make the trip is very newsworthy. They also go back considerably wealthier than they were when they left. This was something else I hadn't figured on. When we have runners in from foreign chapters, we usually arrange for their airfare, lodging, and a per diem payment for food. With the Polish chapter, Leszek would get tickets donated by LOT, the Polish airline. I'd put the athletes up at the West Side Y for the week of the marathon, and then I'd give them $20 cash per day for food.

Anyone who has visited New York knows that $20 can disappear in a hurry. But the Poles would bring bags of food with them and scrape by on a dollar or two a day. When they went home, they'd have maybe $130 in hard currency with them, which was really a lot of money—often a year's salary.

Athletes from different countries tend to use their meal money in different ways. When we got established in what was then the Soviet Union and started bringing athletes to the States from there, they would take their money and, instead of saving it, would add it to money they'd brought with them and buy consumer goods that were in high demand back home. They are among the truest capitalists I've ever run into. They buy low in the United States and sell high in Russia. They tend to specialize in electronics, but they will buy anything they think they can make a good profit on. The most memorable purchase I know of was made by a Russian who bought $600 worth of American prophylactics.

In the long run, the Russians end up with more money than the Poles do by taking currency back. The Russians are also the only foreign athletes who try to get more money. I had one Russian athlete come to me in New York with a horrible tale of woe about how $20 a day simply wasn't enough to live on in New York. The same athlete got on the plane to go home with several hundred dollars' worth of sound equipment. Having been raised in a society in which success depended on one's ability to work every angle and take advantage of every opening, the Russians are also the most likely to come back with the free pair of shoes you gave them, complaining that they don't fit quite right and asking if they could have another pair. Of course, they anticipate keeping the first pair, too, since they've already worn them. Put them one-on-one with a buffet line and the line goes home in their pockets. Where they come from, these are survival techniques. So, no matter what hard-luck story I hear, $20 a day is it. They can do anything they want with the money, including using it for eating.

One change I made in the way I handle the per diem in one Caribbean country is to distribute it almost daily, instead of all at once at the beginning of the week. That's because some of the athletes from this country don't save the money to take home and they don't buy consumer goods, either. They just go out and have a good time, and when I gave them $140 all at once, some would party the whole lot away in one night.

Some people wonder why I went into Poland and then to other Eastern European countries instead of trying to expand more in the United States or in Western Europe. The answer is simple: Achilles can do more good in Eastern Europe. In the developed countries of the West, the disabled have many strong advocates and many opportunities to be involved in mainstream activities. In the United States there are organizations for disabled golfers, skiers, water-skiers, glider pilots, basketball players, tennis players, and so on and on and on. There are also strong laws mandating facilities for the disabled and many advocates pressing for additional laws to make public facilities ever more accessible. Some advocates say we have a long way to go, and there are more things that can be done, but we tend to forget how good life is in this country because we don't have anything to compare it to.

In Eastern Europe and the Third World, however, life is considerably different. In some Third World countries, being disabled is like receiving a death sentence. Victims of quadriplegia seldom survive to attempt to rebuild their lives. Paraplegics and amputees are expected to either stay home and out of sight or to find a street corner on which to beg for what few pennies passersby are willing to toss at them. Not only are there few, if any, facilities for the disabled in schools, but the disabled are discouraged from even trying to get an education. If they do try, other children mock them, throw stones at them, and make their lives a living hell. Cosmas I. B. Okoli, the president of the Achilles Track Club of Nigeria, was one of those children. He was confined to a wheelchair by polio when he was young and it was only because his father was the headmaster of a school that he received an education. He dealt with bullies by becoming the smartest student in his class. When the other kids learned that Cosmas could help them with their studies, they accepted him and protected him. He was told it made no sense for him to go to college, but he went anyway. He became Africa's top wheelchair table-tennis player and started a company to manufacture affordable wheelchairs, crutches, and automobile controls for paraplegics.

Remarkable as it sounds, before Cosmas went into business, there was no source of something as simple as affordable, modern crutches in Nigeria. Modern prosthetic limbs are still not available at a price that the average Nigerian can afford.

This is the rule rather than the exception in much of the world.

When I went to Poland and later to the then–Soviet Union, I met many people confined to wheelchairs or using artificial limbs. A large number of the amputees who had lost legs during World War II were still getting along on legs which were at least 40 years behind ours. Racing wheelchairs or even lightweight everyday chairs were virtually non-existent. Those that did exist had usually been made by the disabled athlete.

Medical care for average citizens was also behind Western standards. During the Cold War, we used to hear so much about the wonderful Soviet health-care system and the innovative surgical techniques in use there that were years ahead of anything in the West. In fact, there were some pioneering techniques and highly skilled surgeons, but they were few. The average citizen had no access to them and instead was at the mercy of a state-run health-care system that was anything but state-of-the-art.

Before the Iron Curtain started to disintegrate, I would not have been encouraged to establish Achilles chapters in

Eastern Europe, but when countries began to cast aside communism for democracy, there was great receptiveness to new ideas. If you look at the progress of Achilles internationally, it follows the course of political change. The idea that new things are possible applies to the treatment of the disabled, as well. Achilles has expanded to Poland, Russia, Bulgaria, Lithuania, Mongolia, and South Africa.

On one of my early trips to Poland, I went to a rehabilitation center where I met a man who was senior administrator of a national organization that represented 20,000 blind people. This man wined and dined me and we soon became friends. When he told me he wanted to present me with a special medal for my work with the disabled, I was flattered. Leszek Sibilski watched the progress of our relationship and didn't say anything, but he knew that I was being set up. Once I accepted the medal, which is the most impressive-looking one I've ever seen, I learned that the man wanted to come to the United States for an eye operation to restore his vision. I should have seen this coming.

The man who gave me the medal in Poland knew that Achilles had an eye program. From the start of Achilles' international program, my goal had been to select athletes to come to the United States to run the New York City Marathon and at the same time to provide them with modern wheelchairs or prostheses, or, in the case of blind athletes, to see if their vision could be restored. The official who had given me the medal wasn't an athlete. He was an older man who had lost his vision approximately 40 years earlier, and a life of relative inactivity had left him overweight and out of shape. But he was the most important person in Poland's ministry for the disabled and he had given me this medal, so I invited him to come to New York and told him I would get a doctor to look at him and see if anything could be done.

The man was very excited about the possibility of regaining his sight. He had raised a family and now had grandchildren, and what he wanted most was to be able to see his grandchildren. We brought him to the States and had his eyes checked, and it was determined that he was a good candidate for surgery and restoration of his vision.

After considering the possibility of surgery a few months down the road, he went back to Poland. But before he could come back, he had a heart attack and died.

My feeling is that one of the reasons he suffered the coronary is because of the conflict that had been set up by his visit to New York and the promise of surgery. He was an intelligent man who had been involved with the Polish Communist Party from the early days. He had bought into the system, as I suspect I would have had I grown up under Communism, and he had worked all his life to promote it as the salvation of the working class. But when he came to New York and was told there was a chance his vision could be restored with a simple operation, he probably realized that if the system he had worked all his life to promote were any good, he could have seen years earlier. He may have found that he had worked all his life for something that wasn't any good. I think that he was wise enough to understand this and the psychological conflict it caused contributed to the timing of his heart attack and death.

The other side of the coin is that once it became known that I was taking selected athletes to the United States and getting them equipment or checking to see if their vision could be restored, everybody wanted to come. I had created a monster, and I was just lucky that Leszek was there to save me. He became the bad guy who spoke the language and would tell people that we couldn't take care of everyone. Or, when someone wanted an extra $10 during marathon week, Leszek would tell them they couldn't have it. It's a thankless job and people would come back to me to complain about the nasty guy who was working for me, which couldn't be farther from the truth.

With Leszek protecting me, I was like the character in *The Fantasticks* who, whenever she saw something unpleasant, would put on rose-colored glasses so everything would look beautiful. If someone was dying in a fire, the glasses showed only how pretty the flames were. That was me in Poland, seeing only the beauty, while Leszek was being roasted in the fire.

We look at people from a country like Poland coming to the United States for the first time and we think how naive they are. But we never think that we seem the same way to them when we go over there. I remember Kenny Carnes, a wheelchair athlete who went with us on one trip to race, going into a leather store to buy things for his friends back home. At that time, you could get for $20 a fabulous leather handbag that would cost hundreds of dollars in the States. Kenny saw the prices and basically said, "I'll take that whole shelf." Meanwhile, he was thinking that the sales clerk was probably thrilled because he was giving her so much business. In reality, she was probably hurt deeply because it would take her months of privation to save enough for the smallest bag in the store and here was this guy in a wheelchair buying more bags than Imelda Marcos.

Sometimes, we'd go into a store to make a lot of purchases and they'd make us wait. We'd stand there wondering, "What's wrong? I'm their best customer and they're making me wait. Aren't they happy?"

Yet Americans feel the same way when they hear about an Arab sheik or a Japanese businessman coming to New York and taking up an entire floor of a hotel, or buying Rockefeller Center. The businessmen probably think we should be happy to have their money, too, but we wind up resenting them.

Since I have realized this, when I go into a store in Eastern Europe to score some bargains, I buy only one or two items. If I want more, I bring someone with me to buy an additional item or two.

Buying in quantity isn't always a problem, though. One time where it is appropriate is at a party when you are buying the drinks. People in Eastern Europe don't feel guilty about drinking and smoking and it's still socially acceptable to get plastered now and then, especially when an out-of-town visitor arrives. Sooner or later—probably sooner—you're going to be in a situation in which someone pulls out the vodka and starts passing it around. You can refuse, but you do so at your own risk, because there's more going on than just having a couple of belts. Drinking together is not only an ancient bonding ritual, it's also a kind of test. The person who won't drink without a good reason—and there aren't many good reasons—is not to be totally trusted. The old Roman saying, "In vino, veritas"—literally, "In wine is truth"—is considered valid there. If you have a hidden agenda or character flaw, it's more likely to come out when you're four sheets to the wind. Beyond that, it's just considered impolite not to drink when everyone else is. Not drinking is like keeping your clothes on at a nudist colony.

One of my most memorable trials by vodka—what I remember of it—took place in the Polish city of Kalisz. My arrival called for a party, and I volunteered to be a good host and buy the drinks. There were 15 people there and the next morning I got the bill for 298 vodkas. Given the exchange rate, even that much vodka didn't come to $50. I'm not a big drinker and can't hold alcohol the way they can, and I probably hit the wall after about a dozen shots, so the rest of the party averaged over 20 shots a person. My fellow celebrants were kind enough to walk me up to my room and put me to bed, which I was in no condition to do by myself. I don't remember any of it, but the next morning when I woke up, I discovered that they had been thoughtful enough not only to help me get out of my clothes, but also to take my leg off. The funny part was that they not only took the shoe and sock off my good leg, they also thought to take them off my artificial leg.

When I go back to Kalisz today, people still mention that party.

One of the reasons I went to Kalisz was in pursuit of a long-standing dream of mine to establish a state-of-the-art prosthetics factory in the East. Kalisz is home to a jet aircraft engine manufacturer, and my idea was that since they made hydraulic assemblies there, they could use their equipment to turn out hydraulic knees for artificial legs. In the United States, the Veterans Administration owns the patent for the basic knee joint, and I believe they would have let the Poles make the knees without having to pay royalties. I figured that they could make for under $100 a joint that costs over $1,000 in this country. Building the rest of the leg is relatively easy, and if we had that joint, we could start outfitting people with good, affordable prosthetics.

The people at the jet engine plant agreed to work on the joint, and we brought engineers from the factory to the States to show them what we needed and how it was made. We sent them back with blueprints to make two pieces of the knee to see how it came out. They went back to Poland

and we waited for the pieces to come back. This was a golden opportunity for them to set up a joint venture to manufacture something they could sell throughout Europe and I figured it would take maybe 10 days for them to do the tooling to make the test pieces. But months went by and we heard nothing.

Finally, after about four months, they had the parts built. They sent them to us, and they were just terrible—utterly useless. They had botched the conversion on the blueprints we gave them from inches to millimeters, but when the pieces came out obviously wrong, they sent them anyway. I told them it wouldn't do and they said they'd try again, but that was basically the end of it. After decades of operating under the Communist bureaucracy, they had no concept of time and quality and no appreciation of the fact that the way you get business is to do a good job. The experience made me wonder just what we had been so terrified of during all the years of the Cold War. All we heard about then was how many missiles, planes, and tanks the Soviets had, but we never asked ourselves how many of them actually worked. My guess is not many.

I tried to set up a number of joint ventures in Poland, but none of them ever worked out. The basic problem was that there wasn't anyone over there on site to keep things moving. Unless you have that—a team—you're not going to get anywhere. So far, we haven't been able to establish that kind of partnership. They have their own projects and problems without worrying about mine.

One of my more unusual ideas was to export prisoners from the United States to Poland. People laughed at me when I suggested it, and I didn't pursue it enough to even find out if the Poles would consider such a scheme. Still, it's not as silly as it sounds. In fact, it makes a lot of sense on both sides. It costs around $30,000 a year to house a single prisoner in New York City. I estimated that the Poles could house the same prisoner for $5,000 and turn a profit. The savings in New York City alone would be enormous. The courts probably wouldn't let you just send prisoners over on the grounds that it would be cruel and unusual punishment to incarcerate them in a foreign country where their friends and relatives couldn't visit easily and where they don't have cable television, but you could offer incentives to the convicts to volunteer to serve their time overseas. For example, you could knock a year off a five-year sentence or you could pay them $3,000 a year for time served overseas. Then, if they had a 10-year sentence, they'd get out with enough money to get a decent start on a new life. Even if you paid $5,000 for housing and the $3,000 bonus, you'd still be saving $22,000 per year per prisoner.

Despite the fact that I could never set up any sort of joint venture, Achilles has done nicely in Poland. Each year at the Warsaw Marathon about 100 Achilles runners show up. I have no idea where they come from, but they're there. And over the years, approximately 50 Polish runners have made about 100 trips to the States to run in races in a number of cities. We send some to the "Run for Poland" and the Chicago Marathon each year, and the big Polish community there greets them like visiting royalty. We've had some great success stories along the way. The world's fastest marathon by a male stroke victim was run by a Pole, Jarioslaw Niewiada, and the first female double amputee to run a marathon on prosthetic legs, Elizbieta Gorgon, was also Polish. One of our blind Polish runners, Tomasz Chmurzynski, runs a sub-three hour marathon and once placed third in his age group in a marathon in Toronto. Malgorzata Ciesluk, another blind Pole, has won several races outright. And even though I have yet to get a prosthetics factory going in Poland, we have provided state-of-the-art limbs and racing wheelchairs to those runners we could best help and we continue to work with disabled Polish athletes.

In the spring of 1988, about a year after we went to Poland, an international bike race came through New York City. Leszek, who is fluent in Russian, covered the race for his magazine and struck up a conversation with a Soviet reporter, Vasilli Senatorov. Leszek told Vasilli about the new track club he had helped set up in Poland and asked if there might be interest in a similar club in Moscow. I hadn't talked about anything like that with Leszek, but he operates the way I do. If he sees an opening, he goes after it.

The Soviet Union was beginning to open up then under Gorbachev and his policies of *glasnost* and *perestroyka*, presenting the conditions that are conducive to introducing new ideas. Vasilli said it might be a good idea and Leszek brought me out to Kennedy Airport to meet Vasilli before he went back to Moscow. A series of international telephone calls followed, during which Leszek and I were funneled through the Soviet Olympic committee, which put us in touch with the Soviet officials in charge of disabled athletics.

To get things started, we asked the Soviets to send a group of disabled runners to the New York City Marathon, with Achilles arranging for their expenses. They agreed and sent half a dozen runners, most of them blind and none of them with prostheses or wheelchairs. They also sent a man who was famous throughout the country. His name is Valentin Dikul, and his fame was twofold. Professionally, he was the most famous circus strongman in Russia, and he was an imposing package. Standing only about 5-foot-8, he must have weighed 275 pounds and had muscles in such profusion you'd have thought he was growing them for export. In his act, he'd lift trucks and similarly impressive weights. One of his more theatrical tricks involved lifting a bar with two large boxes attached to either end. When he got it overhead, the boxes would open to reveal his wife at one end and his daughter at the other. The act made him a celebrity, but what made him a hero is the fact that he had once been paralyzed from the waist down. Somehow, he had hurt his back and he had been diagnosed as a paraplegic. But he worked at walking again like someone possessed and eventually recovered full mobility and resumed his career. His own success convinced him that paraplegia could be cured by dedicated exercise, and he had set up a facility with over 100 beds to help people overcome their paralysis.

Dikul's idea has some merit. Certainly, the more you are able to exercise, the more likely it is that whatever neural pathways remain after a spinal injury will regenerate and develop new routes. But limits exist and a severed nerve is severed forever. He was one of the lucky ones who did not suffer complete severance of the nerves, and the reality in his facility was that most people didn't recover as he did. I like Valentin a great deal, but he is not a highly educated man, and he felt that those who didn't regain the use of their limbs were guilty of not working hard enough and he would tell them that. I feel that's a cruel thing to tell people; that it's their fault they're still paralyzed. Just the same, it's impossible not to like Valentin.

One of our coaches was delighted when she found out the Russians were coming. Her politics are somewhat leftist, and she was thrilled that she was finally going to have an opportunity to talk to some genuine Russian Communists. It turned out to be a huge letdown for her, because it turned out they had no more interest in Communism than I do. To them it was a joke, not a way of life, which is one of the reasons it didn't work.

I took the Russian delegation out for drinks one night at the Helmsley Palace, which has a lounge overlooking St. Patrick's Cathedral. I thought of it as a kind of quintessential capitalist location. The subject of artificial legs came up, and they volunteered that they did not really have good prosthetic legs available for amputees. We had fitted one of their blind runners with a special contact lens that week and it had greatly improved his sight. So I suggested that if they would set up an Achilles Track Club in Moscow, we could bring some of the members over to get state-of-the-art limbs. In the Soviet Union, the idea of amputees running was virtually unheard of. Most of their legs were of pre-WWII technology. Some amputees literally got along on the sort of peg legs that I had assumed had gone out with pirate movies. We could start there, I said, and then investigate the possibility of setting up a modern prosthetics factory in Russia. Steve Wald, a longtime friend and Achilles volunteer, helped close the deal.

They agreed and the next spring sent seven amputees to New York to be fitted with new legs, and taught to use them, and then to run in a short race in Central Park. In the fall, they would come back and run the marathon. The group that came over included a 13-year-old boy, Ivan Panin, who had lost his leg five years earlier when he had fallen under a train, two soldiers who had lost legs in their country's guerrilla war in Afghanistan, a probable KGB agent named Anatoly, and a woman who had lost her leg in an auto accident. It was really a landmark occasion in the history of the disabled in the Soviet Union.

James R. Miller, a Soviet scholar, had told The *Washington*

Post at the time, "Disabled people in the Soviet Union remain in their homes because nothing is accessible to them in public places."

In truth, part of the problem was that their health-care workers handed out prostheses like toasters, with no effort to fit a limb to an individual. If one fit extremely badly, they'd give you another and ask if it felt better. Beyond that, there were no wheelchair ramps, curb cuts, elevators, restrooms, or anything else for the disabled. Five years earlier, the Russians would have denied vehemently that they had any problem at all. But *glasnost* had changed all that and made it possible for us to begin to introduce the disabled of the Soviet Union to the rest of society.

The large number of young men returning from Afghanistan without the standard number of limbs was a major impetus for the Russians to recognize that they needed to do something. They had sent these men to the Russian equivalent of Vietnam, and for an extra pittance—about $7 a month in combat pay—exposed them to high-risk combat conditions. And too many had had to give up their legs to get that $7.

Ivan Panin was near the age of my son, Joey. Ivan's favorite pastime turned out to be playing Monopoly. He could buy and sell and deal with the best of them and just wiped all of us out. When he was interviewed by *New York Newsday* he told them that when he grew up, "I want to be a businessman."

Most of Ivan's time and that of his compatriots was spent getting fitted and learning how to walk again. I had raised funds for the project, and enlisted the help of the Helen Hayes Hospital in West Haverstraw, New York, the Rusk Institute, Dr. Joe Fetto, the World Rehabilitation Fund, and prosthetist Carlo Morano in what was a major undertaking.

At the end of the stay, they all ran in a couple of races. Ivan ran the children's race, which was just a mile, but it was the first time he had run since he lost his leg. The others all finished a longer race with the exception of Anatoly, the reputed KGB agent, who got lost in Central Park after making a wrong turn. Here was a man who had been trained to survive in the jungle and the Arctic Circle. And now he was hop-stepping through the wilds of Central

Park on one leg and with no knowledge of English. People were coming up to him asking for money, he was dodging horses and skateboarders, and nowhere in his survival training had they told him how to deal with this. Happily, we realized he was missing, sent out a search party, and rescued him before he was scarred for life. His experience reminded me of the book and movie, *A Connecticut Yankee in King Arthur's Court.*

It takes time to win the trust of the Russians. Their nature in dealing with others is to always wonder, "What are they *really* after?" They have a natural knack for capitalism, but they do it individually, not having learned to trust others to the extent required for corporate capitalism. The folk tale about the man who asked God to take one of his eyes so that his neighbor would lose both captures the national mindset, while at the same time exhibiting the sense of humor that has served the country so well through so many trials.

After having failed to set up a prosthetics factory in Poland, I set out trying to get one going in Russia. Albert Gordon, one of my personal heroes, arranged for me to get a letter of introduction from Armand Hammer. (A dedicated runner, Al Gordon first ran the New York City Marathon as an Achilles volunteer at the age of 87. At 92, he was still running six-mile loops of Central Park without difficulty.) Hammer's letter was invaluable. He had been the first American industrialist to deal effectively with the Soviets, and had opened the door for others to follow.

Before I went I had arranged for Amoco to provide enough plastic to make the first 10,000 legs. In return, we would call them Amoco Legs and our slogan would be, "We run on Amoco." We would manufacture 3,000 legs a year and half of them would go to Afghanistan war veterans. The other half would be sold abroad for hard currency, which would pay off a $2 million loan we would need to get the operation started.

The critical element in the deal was $300,000 worth of stainless steel. It would be sold in the United States and used as collateral for a $2.7 million loan from a bank in England. We couldn't bring that in from the West because it was a strategic metal, and the Russian supply of stainless steel was controlled by the Soviet military. But we were working with a man named Vladimir Alkimov, who had been the Soviet equivalent of the Secretary of the Treasury and was now retired and involved with a health and rehabilitation organization. In America, the project would have taken off with that kind of backing, but in the Soviet Union, as in Poland, the bureaucracy became a player in the drama, and once that happened, nothing moved. No matter what we did, we couldn't seem to get the stainless steel, and without that, we couldn't do it.

Throughout the negotiations and the rest of my stay in the Soviet Union, which included a trip north of the Arctic Circle in Siberia, I was treated with the greatest deference. I had assumed that having a letter of introduction from Armand Hammer accounted for that, and I was partly right. The other reason for the respect I was shown was that somewhere along the line, Dick Traum had been rendered by a Russian translator as Don Trump. Evidently, the fame of Donald Trump as the ultimate capitalist had spread even beyond the Iron Curtain. Since they didn't really know anything about him, it didn't bother them that the "Donald Trump" they were entertaining was a somewhat rumpled middle-aged man with a bit of a belly and an artificial leg. While I wasn't aware of this, I realized I was considered important. After all, my hotel room was a suite that included three bathrooms.

We went to the Arctic Circle in Siberia through the courtesy of Oleg, a friend who was in charge of fur production in the Tumen area of Siberia. Several years earlier, Oleg had been an international bike racer and had competed against Leszek, who was with me on this trip. Oleg struck me as the sort of guy who, if he had been born an American, would be working for a large bureaucracy. Oleg took us to Nadym in Siberia, the site of one of the world's largest natural gas production facilities. Living in the land of the free and the home of central air-conditioning, I had grown up, like most Americans, equating well-being with a nice, cool home on a hot day. In Siberia, the opposite idea applied and the lap of luxury was being hot enough to take off your fur parka and woolen union suit.

There was a little hotel in Nadym, with about 20 rooms

and one waitress for the whole place. The waitress, I was told, moonlighted as the town prostitute. (Her success was evident when she smiled. She had several gold teeth, the Siberian equivalent of a diamond ring.) Before I went there, somebody had asked what sort of food I liked, and they were told pirogi. That wouldn't have been my first choice, but I guess it sounded good. Anyway, the whole time I was up there, almost every time I sat down to eat, mounds of pirogi were set in front of me. Since I suspected that they had specially prepared them, I couldn't very well say I would prefer something else. As I ate, groups of people would line up outside the restaurant, looking through the frosted windows to see what an American looked like.

I was told that I was the first American ever to visit Nadym and another town inside the Arctic Circle, and I'm virtually certain that I was the first American to be taken to visit the Nantsi Indians, a tribe of reindeer-herding nomads who haven't changed their basic way of life in centuries. Since they are nomads, just finding them is a trick. We took a helicopter and first looked for trees, then reindeer tracks, which we followed to teepee-like tents. The Nantsi are wonderfully hospitable and the Soviets don't attempt to govern them. As a result, they're only vaguely aware that they were part of the Soviet Union. It just doesn't affect them.

After we landed and were introduced by an interpreter, I asked whether I could look inside one of the teepees. The answer I got could have been given by my wife: "We weren't expecting company and it's kind of messy." They let me look anyway. It was like an exhibit of native Indians inside the Museum of Natural History.

Later, they asked me if I wanted to go hunting. Their idea was that they would catch a game animal—probably a wolf—and put it in a confined area where it couldn't run away so that I could be sure to shoot it. It seemed to me like shooting an animal in a zoo and I told them I'd rather not, since it didn't seem sporting. They said it wasn't all that unfair to the animal because I probably couldn't shoot well enough to hit it. They had me there, but I begged off anyway.

They fed me lunch, which consisted of some sort of red berries with a lot of sugar on them, and reindeer tongue, which they served with great fanfare. To them it was a great delicacy, and that meant I had to eat it. But I couldn't get over the feeling I was eating a part of one of Santa's reindeer. I guess reindeer tongue is an acquired taste. One item that was delicious was Siberian sushi, which is what I call the fish that they catch through the ice. When they pull the fish out, it freezes solid almost immediately in the minus-30 degree cold. They peel the skin off it and cut off chunks, which they douse with a hot sauce and eat raw.

We washed everything down with home-brewed vodka. On the way back to Nadym, the combination of unfamiliar food and home brew in my gut started to ferment until I simply had to pass gas. We had an executive of the natural gas operation with us, and I explained that I had some gas I'd like to sell him. We were all half sloshed, and he ended up paying me a ruble and I passed gas. So I can claim today that I'm the first American to sell natural gas to Russia. Our driver laughed so hard listening to the conversation, the price bargaining, and the sale of gas options, that he had to pull the truck over to the side of the road.

We finally left Nadym, but not before setting up an Achilles Track Club chapter. And when we left the Soviet Union, we had an agreement for more Russians to come to the 1989 New York City Marathon and for several American Achilles runners to participate in that year's Moscow Peace Marathon.

The Peace Marathon was a landmark event in the Soviet Union. The five Achilles Track Club members who entered the race were the first disabled Americans ever to compete in a marathon event in that country. Linda Down became the first woman with cerebral palsy to compete in and win a Soviet medal, and Terry Greenberg, a below-the-knee amputee from Colorado, became the first female amputee to do the same. Rafael Ibarra and Ken Carnes became the first two American wheelchair athletes, and they also introduced the Soviets to the remarkable speed that is possible in a sleek racing wheelchair such as the three-wheeled racing chair designed by original Achilles member Marty Ball.

The trip was an eye-opener in many ways. If you can imagine a government run like the average motor vehicles department in the States, you have an idea of what Russia is like. For Kenny and Rafael, it was an introduction to a society that made no provisions for wheelchairs. Used to being independent, they had to allow themselves to be carried and pushed up and down stairs and impossibly high curbs. In one restaurant, needing help to get down a long flight of stairs, they were almost attacked by the entire restaurant staff, all of whom were eager to help the Americans.

Muscovites also had their eyes opened. If people in wheelchairs went out at all in Russia, they kept to the sides of the streets and sidewalks, trying to blend in with the gray walls of buildings and be as inconspicuous as possible. The disabled were embarrassed to be seen, and, in fact, most of them had been relocated to towns outside the city. The prevailing attitude was exemplified by Tatyana Kuznetsova, one of the original Russian Achilles members. Tanya had lost a leg above the knee in an accident and got around well enough with a Russian prosthesis so that unless she told you, you wouldn't really know that she was an amputee. The point was that she felt she couldn't tell anyone outside of her closest friends. She most feared that her in-laws would discover her disability. If they knew their son was married to an amputee, she was certain they would make him divorce her. So for her to come out of the closet and run with us was as courageous a decision as any you'll see.

This, then, was the attitude of the Russians, and now they were seeing Kenny and Rafael in their rakish chairs, dressed in neon tank tops, and wearing sexy Oakley sunglasses. These men didn't stay to the shadows, but wheeled out into the middle of traffic. "It was interesting how strange the Soviets found us," they reported in a magazine article written by Kay Huffer. "It was apparent that they were checking us out. You rarely see wheelchair users on the streets. (This makes sense, considering the inaccessibility of the city.)"

If the Russians gawked at them just tooling around town, they gaped in disbelief on race day. The field for the Peace Marathon included 8,000 runners. I had negotiated a two-hour head start for Linda and Terry, and a five-minute head start for Kenny, Rafael, and the few Soviet wheelchair athletes. This was to save them from being tangled up in the opening stampede of runners. Kenny and Rafael wheeled off the line and never worried about anyone catching up. Where the Soviet wheelchair racers stayed to the side of the street, the Americans raced boldly down the center line as if they owned the road, and that day, they did. Trading the lead and drafting each other to conserve energy, they decided the race in a head-to-head duel down the last half-mile, with Kenny crossing first in 1:53:35, more than 20 minutes faster than the winner of the regular race. The crowd loved it, and no one who watched that day would ever again look at the disabled in quite the same way. The race organizers loved it, too, and the next year, we almost tripled our participation in the race, as we continued to invite Russians to run in New York. After the race, the Russians, especially the younger ones, lined up for half an hour to get Ken's autograph. They loved him.

One of those we asked to run the New York City Marathon was Tanya Kuznetsova, and here we ran into the fallout from that Russian folk tale again. Tanya had a coach in Russia, and when we asked her to come to New York, her coach expected to be invited to come as well. But we didn't invite him because we had limited funds and wanted to use them on athletes, not people who were just along for the ride. I didn't think it would make any difference, but he retaliated by advising her that she should stop running. This started in August, and by October, when she arrived to run the New York City Marathon, she was totally out of shape. The plan was for her to run the race on her Russian leg, and then afterwards we would fit her with a modern prosthesis. As far as I was concerned, she was going to run the race, no matter what condition she was in.

I will never force someone to run to the point of serious injury, and I won't endanger someone's health. But I also feel strongly that those we bring to New York owe it to the people who donated time and money to make the trip possible to do their level best to finish the race. So we sent Tanya out, and because she's an excellent athlete, she made 10 miles before she hit the wall. She told her volunteers, Patricia Dorff, who spoke Russian, and Bill Phillips, that her leg was hurting and she didn't know if she could continue, but Tricia nursed her along for two or three more miles. In patrolling the course, I found them around the 13-mile mark—halfway through the race. Tanya was in tears. She sat down and took off her leg and showed me where her stump was bleeding. "That doesn't look too bad," I said as nonchalantly as I could. At that point, she realized she had no choice, and she finished the race in about 11 hours, probably cursing me every painful step of the way. But when she finished, she became the first female above-the-knee amputee to complete a marathon. Then, and only then, she thanked us profusely for making her finish

One night, we went out to dinner, where she told us through an interpreter how she had lost her leg in a car accident. I then asked, "Did you find it?" It took the interpreter several tries, but finally Tanya got it and burst out laughing. It was the first time in the eight years since the accident, she told us, that she had been able to laugh about her disability.

As in Poland, Achilles took on its own life in the Soviet Union and later the federated republics. I don't know myself how many runners we have there, except that they keep showing up at races around the former Soviet Union. What took me by surprise, though, was a question from one of my Russian contacts about why I never invited anyone from the Sverdlovsk Achilles chapter to run in New York. I told him the truth. I had never heard of Sverdlovsk, but it turned out that we had a thriving chapter in that city. So at the next opportunity, we brought some of them to New York.

FINISH

Chapter 9

Now, I can do anything anybody else can.
—Cyril Charles

I don't like to think about failure, and I don't think we've had many in Achilles. So it's ironic that one of the few failures that we have had was responsible for one of our most touching success stories.

Among the many programs that the New York Road Runners operate is a running program for the homeless. Volunteers go to the various homeless shelters throughout the city and get the residents to come out to run. One day in 1985, they found a young man with an impressive running physique who happened to be an above-the-knee amputee. His name is Anthony Phillips and he is a native of Trinidad. They talked him into coming out to run, and when he showed up in the park, somebody else saw him running and suggested he join the Achilles Track Club.

Anthony took the advice and shortly after came with us to West Haverstraw, New York, to run in the annual 10K race sponsored by the Helen Hayes Hospital. He was about six feet tall and weighed around 170 pounds. If he had had two legs and somebody told you he was an Olympic athlete, you would have accepted that without question. But this was distance running where conditioning is more important than talent, and I decided to run the race with him. We started to jog, and he was obviously good. But I figured that I had more endurance than he and, being the president of the club, I felt obliged to let him know I was faster. So, when he had no trouble keeping up with my early pace, I picked it up. He kept up easily and I picked it up again, figuring that he would tire soon. Only he didn't tire in the least, and even started to outrun me. By then, I was hurting badly because I had pushed myself beyond my limits. I didn't want him to know that, though, so I said, "I can see you have the hang of it, Anthony. Why don't you run ahead and I'll check your form from behind."

Anthony became a regular runner, but he had a problem. He was an inveterate panhandler, the guy who kept hitting up all the members for money. Still, we put up with it, and when he decided to return to Trinidad for a visit, I asked him to help start an Achilles chapter there, which he did. With the help of other Trinidadian runners, Anthony gathered a group of six runners to come to the 1987 New York City Marathon. Transportation was arranged through British West Indies Airlines, which provided free tickets, and I reserved rooms at the West Side Y for the group. But Anthony told the runners there was a charge payable to him for their trip to New York. They could give him the money out of the $140 meal money I would give them on their arrival. (This is a trick a Russian official later pulled.) Anthony did, however, run a good marathon. The finish was captured forever with him and his volunteer, Fred Cook, crossing the finish line for an Imax movie called, *To the Limit*, which is shown on a screen four stories tall.

Off to a great start, Anthony kept up his pace after the marathon was over and it was time to go home. He had decided that he liked living at the Y, so he stayed in his room after he was supposed to have vacated it. After several days of trying to talk him into leaving, the Y locked him out. This apparently offended his dignity, and he hot-footed it down to the *New York Post* with a story about how he had run the marathon on one leg and we had thanked him by throwing him out of the Y without a job. The tabloid had a lot of fun with the story, all at the expense of Achilles. The fact that it remains the only negative story ever written about the club didn't make it any easier to take.

When I picked up the paper the next day and saw the story, I was furious. I called the reporter who wrote it. "Did you verify this?" I wanted to know. "Did you check with anybody else?"

"I didn't have time," he told me. "It was a good story, and it was on deadline and I had to run it before anybody else got it."

That's tabloid journalism for you, and the *Post* has written several good stories about us over the years. Anyway, I was most angry with Anthony for doing that. I was still fuming a day later when Anthony showed up at the workout and wasted no time asking for five bucks as if nothing had happened. "How could you make the club look so bad?" I demanded.

"Well, I was mad," he said, as if I were supposed to forget about it. "I'm sorry," he went on. "Can you spare $5?"

I threw him out right there, told him I didn't want anything to do with him ever again, never even wanted to see him. He was the first person I ever kicked out of the club. The only other person to be excluded was the gay blind runner who couldn't keep his hands off the volunteers. Of course, Anthony still shows up almost every year around marathon time, just in case I've changed my mind, which I haven't. From what I hear, he's living in the streets, roaming the subways, doing crack, and going nowhere. And it's such a shame, because here is a man with a great deal of talent but not a drop of ambition.

Still, Anthony did bring Cyril Charles to Achilles, and if you were to design a polar opposite of Anthony, it would be Cyril.

Cyril is the son of blue-collar, hard-working parents in the Trinidadian hamlet of Bell Vue, a mere 15-dwelling bump on the island's landscape. As a child he was bright and active in sports of all kinds, but he had been born with a congenital weakness in the corneas of his eyes. The condition gave him no particular problems until 1973, when he was nine years old. Then, one day when he was playing cricket with his classmates, the ball—which is the same size, weight, and hardness as a baseball—was thrown to him when he wasn't looking. It cracked into the right side of his head, knocking him out. When he came to, he felt a burning sensation in his right eye, but attributed that to the impact of the ball. "I'm all right," he told his classmates as he got up and waited for his head to clear.

About a month later, he noticed that the writing on the blackboard in school wasn't as clear as it used to be. His mother took him to a doctor who told her that the accident was for some reason causing his corneas to scar over. If he didn't go to Barbados for an operation, he would eventually go blind. The family didn't have money for eye surgery, though. They had no choice but to hope that the condition would correct itself.

Cyril moved to the front of the class so he could see what the teacher was writing, but eventually even that was not close enough. Once, he had gotten high grades. Now his grades dropped to failing and the teacher, thinking that Cyril was lazy, scolded him in front of his classmates. Cyril tried as hard as he could. By the age of 12, his right eye could tell only light from dark. His left eye could see blurred shapes, and he read by holding his books an inch away from his face.

Eventually, the family surrendered to reality and sent Cyril to a boarding school for the blind in Santa Cruz, a town near the capital city of Port of Spain. He learned to read Braille and resumed his studies, learning Spanish in addition to science and math. When he was 17, both his mother and father died within a month of each other, and he was left totally on his own. A teacher who had taken Cyril under his wing told the boy that he would pay his tuition to a school where he could learn to be a plumber.

Despite his limited vision, Cyril learned the trade and got a job in a housing project installing toilets. After work he played soccer, his great athletic ability and reflexes making up for the fact that other players existed as blurs of color and the ball as a dim blotch of white. Finally, he couldn't see even that much, and he had to give up soccer. It was the first time his condition had brought him to tears of despair.

He continued to work, though, until the day came when the contractors decided he was too blind to even install toilets. He asked for a chance to prove he could still do the work, and, as an article about him in *Reader's Digest* reported, the contractor sent him away, saying, "You blind people are always begging."

Cyril had always known what would come next, and he had fought against it as long as he could. But, unable to get work as a plumber and unable to see more than the vaguest of shapes, he went to the Blind Welfare Association of Trinidad and Tobago and took the only job left for him— weaving baskets. I have one of his creations, a beautiful lamp, which my son Joey uses in his room.

While he was working at the association for $35 a week, he met a visitor from the United States. Like Cyril, the man, Sharon Leacock, was a Trinidadian by birth. He was also blind. He had gone to the States in 1972 and had gotten a master's degree in music. He settled down in Philadelphia, where he taught piano and was the director of a music school. Listening to him talk, Cyril found hope that he might yet make something of his life.

Always looking for ways to earn more money, he heard about a race being sponsored by The Road Runners Club of Trinidad, an organization headed by Anthony Saloum. The race was just over two miles long around a track, and it offered a first-prize purse equal to two week's pay. He entered the race, and navigating by the dim shapes of the trees that lined the track, he won the race handily. Saloum was impressed by what Cyril had accomplished and took up his case. Not long after that, Anthony Phillips showed up in Trinidad with his mission of establishing an Achilles chapter. Saloum had been thinking along the same lines, and Achilles of Trinidad, our second international chapter, was born.

When it came time to select runners for the trip to the 1987 New York City Marathon, Cyril, now 24, was at the top of the list. He entered the race and finished in 3:47, a very good time for a rookie. After the race, Cyril went back to Trinidad, where Saloum gave him a job at the factory he ran. "Cyril really was a progressive young man," Saloum told a newspaper in Trinidad. "He wanted and tried to learn everything and had ambition."

He had enough ambition that he determined to leave his homeland and return to the United States. Screwing up his courage, he called up Sharon Leacock, the man who had inspired him several years earlier. Cyril asked Sharon if he could come and live with him in Philadelphia. Sharon said he could. Cyril got odd jobs doing whatever he could—and he could do a lot, including cutting lawns and working as a laborer. He got his high school equivalency diploma and all the while he commuted to New York once a week to run with Achilles.

It was now 1988, and suddenly an opportunity to change Cyril's life dropped on my doorstep. Dr. Richard Koplin, the director of the Eye Trauma Center at the New York Eye and

Ear Infirmary, came to me to ask if the infirmary could sponsor an Achilles race. He wanted publicity, and, as it happened, I thought he could give me something in return. I told Dr. Koplin that in return for the advertising we would provide, he would donate his services to any Achilles runner who couldn't afford vision-restoring surgery. He readily agreed, and the first person we had him look at was Cyril. When I told Cyril what I had planned, he remembered stories from when he was a boy and his vision had started to go bad. The corneal condition he was born with is relatively common in Trinidad, and others whose vision had deteriorated had gone for surgery and come back totally blind. But what the heck, he thought. He could see very little as it was, and eventually he'd be totally blind anyway. He may as well try it.

Meanwhile, Cyril wanted to run another marathon. He could have waited for the New York City Marathon, but he decided to run the Rochester, New York, Marathon about three weeks earlier, and then the New York race. He knocked nearly a half hour off his time in Rochester, finishing in 3:21, but when he tried to come back in New York and break three hours, his legs cramped up and he limped home in 3:37. "Next year, I'll be the first blind runner to go under three hours," he announced after the race.

That was not to be, however, because the next year, he wasn't blind. On January 19, 1989, Dr. Koplin's associate, Dr. John Seedor, transplanted a new cornea to Cyril's right eye, warning Cyril, "We can't tell how much, if any, sight you'll get back."

The next morning, Dr. Seedor stood by as an Oriental nurse removed the bandages. Some drops were put in the eye, at which Cyril blinked, and gasped.

"What happened?" the nurse asked anxiously, seeing a look of shock on Cyril's face.

"I can see you," he said. He could not only see her, but he saw her in crystal-clear detail—her face, the color of her eyes, her smile. The nurse replaced the bandages to let the eye heal, and left the room. When Cyril was sure she was gone, he snuck into the bathroom, lifted the corner of the bandage, and looked at himself in the mirror for the first time in 15 years.

Cyril's goal had been to run the marathon in under three hours, but now he changed that. He came to me and told me that he wanted to run the 1989 marathon not for himself, but as a guide for another blind runner. "Now it's my turn," he told me. "I must be a giver, too."

Cyril positively blossomed in the succeeding months. He had met a nurse, Carol Darlington, who was visiting in Philadelphia from Trinidad. He proposed marriage and she accepted. He learned to drive and enrolled in college to become a physical therapist. That fall, I set him up with Matt Densen, a 20-year-old college student from New Jersey, who had been blinded at the age of 12 by a brain tumor that cut off his optic nerve. Matt's goal was to break four hours in his first marathon, and Cyril brought him in eight minutes under their target. Along the way he had a wonderful time describing all the sights of the race to Densen, just as his volunteer had described them to him the previous two years. In gratitude, Densen's father promised to raise $10,000 for a scholarship for Cyril to pursue his college degree. On the heels of that news came the article in *Reader's Digest*, followed by word that there was interest in making a television movie about Cyril's life.

"Whatever he achieved, he did on his own," Anthony Saloum told the *Trinidad Guardian*. "There are disabled people who assume that handouts are a must; but contrary to this they should take advantage of opportunities to get up and get busy. It is about time we view disabled persons as normal people," Saloum concluded, with Cyril Charles firmly in mind as his example.

Besides going to school, Cyril helps out at Achilles in whatever way he can. He got together with Bob Glover to help run a children's running program. He has a son of his own now and just loves working with kids. Bob says that it's as if he got gypped out of his own childhood and is reliving it through the children he works with. And when they get together for a training session, it's hard to tell who's having more fun.

"Now," Cyril told the *New York Post*'s Dave Hanson, "I can do anything anybody else can do."

Cyril was the first but not the last person treated free of charge by Drs. Koplin and Seedor at the New York Eye and

Ear Infirmary. By 1993, they had looked at more than 100 athletes from all over the world, helping as many as they could. They are not alone. Dr. Murray Wiesenfeld, a New York podiatrist who had treated me in the past, also donates his services. It had started as a joke the first time I saw him in 1977. "If I only have one leg, do I get treated for half price?" I asked him. "No," he said. "Our policy is that all people with one leg get charged nothing." That was the beginning of a wonderful friendship. And Murray has held to his word. To this day, he's never charged an Achilles athlete, no matter how many I send to him. He even provides orthotics—inserts that go in your shoe to correct various foot and knee problems—free of charge. My dentist and fellow runner, Dr. William Horowitz, also donates his services to athletes who come from Third World countries and have dental problems. As far as I know, he's only balked once at a request, and that was from a female runner who came in for a checkup and asked for a new set of teeth. It came as no surprise that the woman was a Russian, working the angles again.

Among the many professionals who have helped Achilles athletes from around the world are Dr. Morris Hartstein at the Veterans Administration, who has donated services to many blind runners, and Dr. Ken Sherrick, who has fitted others with special contact lenses. Dr. Joe Fetto at New York University has donated his time evaluating amputees for artificial legs, and prosthetist Roger Chin has donated his time making the limbs. If special spinal surgery is appropriate, Dr. Mark Weidenbaum at Columbia Presbyterian Hospital has volunteered his services. Dr. Tom Einhorn—an Achilles board member—at Mt. Sinai, also volunteers.

We Americans don't realize how generous we are. So many people volunteer for so many things we have ceased to notice it. When I ask visiting Achilles athletes from other countries what most surprises them about America, the most frequent response deals with our great generosity with our time and services. The Achilles runners cannot believe that 300 Achilles volunteers run the New York City Marathon without getting paid. They do not understand the concept of volunteerism.

We have had many success stories among blind athletes. Tom O'Connor, the boy from Brooklyn who lost his sight through a pressure buildup in his skull, started by running a marathon, and, armed with the confidence he gained from that feat, went on to college where he excelled, as well as becoming the fastest blind triathlete. Matt Densen is currently teaching and continues to enjoy success in running. But after Cyril, my favorite story is that of Tuul Nyambullign, or, as he is known to one and all, just Tuul, Mongolia's premier marathoner.

As with most of my stories, there's not a trail that leads directly to Tuul, but rather one that gets there the long way around the mountain. In this case, the story begins in China, and, as with all of our Eastern European and Asian chapters, it involves my good friend, Leszek Sibilski.

We hadn't intended to go to China. It just worked out that way because to get to Mongolia, we had to go to China first. When we asked for permission for the trip, the Chinese figured that if Mongolia was going to get involved in this Achilles thing, they should, too. They asked us if we would come there to establish chapters, and we agreed. We made two trips to China, the first to talk about what might be done and to set up a chapter in Chanchun, the second to establish chapters in Beijing and Shanghai.

The first visit came in June of 1990, one year after the Tienanmen Square massacre of Chinese students. Nerves were still raw and the authorities were more distrustful than usual of foreigners. We were told when we arrived that we would be assigned a "guide." Even though the guides lived in the city, they stayed in the same hotel with us. On every floor of the hotel was an employee whose job it was to tell the guides when somebody left his room. If we went outside, we'd be watched, because they were afraid that we could be sneaking out to stir up trouble.

It was politically incorrect to go to China at that time, but, again, an opportunity had been offered and I felt that I could do more good by going there than I could by staying home. Naturally, when I got to the hotel, I changed into my running clothes and went out for a jog. The hotel was two or three miles—about a half-hour's run for me—from the famous square, so that's where I set out for. A long avenue, mobbed with people, led from the hotel to the square.

I had hardly set out before a man running one of the bicycle-powered rickshaws that do much of the work of taxis stopped and offered me a ride. I don't speak Chinese, but I got the impression that he wasn't looking for a fare, but simply wanted to help out this foreigner who had one leg. I thanked him but declined the offer and set out on my run. In the half hour it took me to run the length of the avenue, I must have passed 100,000 people. That remains my one overwhelming impression of China. No matter where you go, the streets are crowded with people. And as I ran, those who looked at me gave a thumbs-up signal to let me know they approved of my efforts. I don't think there was one person who did not notice me running. Heads would turn as bikes passed. When I finally got to the square, I stopped and noticed that the man with the rickshaw I had just passed had pulled up behind me. I looked at him and he had tears in his eyes. My feeling was that he was impressed by the fact that this guy with one leg had beaten him down the avenue. Of course, he could have been thinking about his lost fare.

Our hosts took us out of the capital to the northern city of Chanchun. The city had a man-made lake with a beach and we decided to go swimming. Before we could get in the water, a man timidly came over and asked if he could touch the hair on Leszek's chest. Leszek said he had no problem with that, and the man kind of brushed the hair gingerly and then let out a squeal and scampered off. This is the sort of thing that one of us might have done when we were 10 years old and seeing someone of a different race for the first time. But in China, the sight of foreigners, especially one like Leszek who is about twice the size of the average Chinese, is still rare.

The other thing about the Chinese, as well as the Koreans and Japanese, is that they think they are racially superior to Caucasians. One of the proofs, they think, is that Orientals have very little body hair, which to them is a clear indication that they are further removed from apes than hairy white people.

We went to a school for the deaf in Chanchun and the kids there kept coming up to me and politely indicating their wish to touch the hair on my arms. I let them, and they would sort of play with it to see if it was firmly attached. To explain how the hair got there, I bent down so they could see my bald spot and made motions to show that I had taken the hair from my head and put it on my forearm. They thought that was pretty funny.

We made the usual number of mistakes in dealing with cultural differences. At one dinner, Leszek was presented with an award by an attractive young Chinese woman. Leszek kissed her as thanks. Apparently, to the Chinese, this was the equivalent of someone in the States thanking a woman by grabbing her breast. The guides who traveled with us were required to write reports about everything we did and to note our transgressions. This kissing was a major no-no, but Leszek's guide agreed that Leszek's sin was the result of ignorance. After all, he was from Poland.

Considering everything else we did, that was a reasonable explanation, one that had the added benefit of being true— and he didn't report us.

If you go to China as a guest of the government, the one thing you can count on is a minimum of one banquet per day. And in China, the way they show hospitality is to order much more food than the group can conceivably eat. The theory is that if all the food is eaten, then they didn't order enough and that would be impolite. It reminded me of my grandmother, who, during the Depression, always kept a covered pot of water simmering on the back burner of the stove. It was only water, which was about all she had to put in the pot, but she kept it there so that if anyone came calling they would think she was making soup and that the family had food.

We hosted a couple of banquets ourselves, and I ordered just enough food to go around. First, I don't like to see food wasted, and, second, I didn't see any need to impress anyone like that. Then I found out that everyone mentioned that we hadn't ordered enough food. Later, when we had a group from China come to New York, I took them out to eat and, bowing to culture, ordered more food than we could eat. When we were done, I had it put in a doggie bag and gave it to Ann Stauber, an Achilles volunteer who had lived in China and was our translator. I found out they thought that taking the leftovers home was just as coarse as not ordering enough food. I tried to explain that if we were friends, and we were, there should be no need for me to impress them.

Speaking of doggie bags, we went to a Korean restaurant to eat when we were in Beijing. We ordered a dish that consisted of raw meat that we would cook at the table. Near the end of the meal, we found out it was dog meat and I was able to fulfill a lifelong dream by asking for a doggie bag in which to take home the leftovers. But they didn't offer that option and the joke didn't translate, so it was kind of a loss.

Another thing we learned is that prophylactics in China come in three sizes—large, extra large, and imperial. I thought these would make great souvenirs, so Leszek and I, together with our guide, marched into a pharmacy and asked for a dozen of each size. But the lady behind the counter said she didn't have any. We knew that wasn't true. When we asked what was going on, our guide explained that the saleswoman must have assumed that we meant to use the condoms in China, and they don't like the idea of foreigners consorting with the locals. So we went to another store and sent the guide in by himself. He came out with the goods, which made a nice conversation piece when we got home.

The Chinese made good sports wheelchairs and also had an up-to-date prosthetics factory that had been donated with the help of Jimmy Carter. Unfortunately, I never saw anyone running the equipment. But they did make decent prosthetics elsewhere and had a knee that wasn't as good as a hydraulic knee but which cost only $5. At some point, I hope to make that joint available to other countries when I finally get a prosthetics factory up and running.

On the basis of that visit, we invited the Chinese to send some runners to the States, and, in the spring of 1991, they sent two blind runners to participate in the Boston Marathon. We attempted to get Achilles runners from America into the Beijing Marathon, but the timing wasn't right. We did, however, set up our own race in which Polish Achilles athletes ran with Chinese Achilles athletes. We have three chapters in China, but participation is still small. But if China ever embraces the Achilles idea, I have no doubt that we will have thousands of members in very short order, because once the Chinese decide to do something, they do it with a great deal of dedication. I really think the Russians could learn a lot from them. Although China does not have nearly the vast resources of Russia, they make much more efficient use of what they have. We even visited one factory where Chinese workers were making fur hats for sale to Russia. If there's one thing you'd think the Russians could make in endless supply, it would be fur hats, but they actually import them from their neighbor.

When we made our initial contact with China, we also contacted Mongolia. One of the reasons we did this was because if we told the Chinese we wanted to go there to get to Mongolia, they would be more likely to welcome us. If we had approached the Chinese directly, I don't think we would have gotten as warm a reception, if we would have been allowed in at all. But knowing that we were interested in Mongolia piqued their interest. They wanted what the neighbors were getting.

But I was also very interested in Mongolia, because that country was going through exactly the kind of changes that would make it receptive to new ideas. The old Communist system was changing and a representative government was coming in. And, I was pretty sure that there were many people in Mongolia who could benefit from the Achilles program. But to get to Mongolia, you had to fly through China, so the two countries were very much connected.

Leszek made the contacts in Mongolia through his contacts in Poland, who had good relationships with Mongolia. Leszek saw to it that the appropriate officials received copies of the many favorable articles that had appeared about Achilles in both the Russian and Polish press. In addition, they knew about Achilles through Russian television, which has covered Achilles on a number of occasions. All of this gave us credibility, and, when we asked if they could send three disabled runners to the 1990 New York City Marathon, they agreed.

This was all done by phone, fax, and mail, so we really didn't know who we would be getting until the runners arrived in New York with a government official. But the trio that was sent couldn't have been better chosen for the program. And, unlike those of some other nations, the

Mongolian officials never made any effort to take advantage of us by using the program as an excuse to get a free trip to New York.

In addition to Tuul, the other runners were Batsaihan, who had had severe burns on his hands, arms, and legs, and Gambold, a physician who is a below-the-knee amputee. Gambold was perfect for the program, since, being a doctor, he was more qualified than anyone we had ever had to oversee the kinds of programs that I hoped to start in Mongolia, including my long-cherished goal of starting a prosthetics factory. Batsaihan was a somewhat unusual case for Achilles, but then, we make a living on unusual cases. As part of the rehabilitation for his burns, he had started to run for his legs and then was told to draw, to develop movement in his hands and fingers. When he began drawing, they discovered that he had real talent as an artist. He later returned as a scholarship student at the Art Students' League.

Tuul joined the ranks of the disabled in 1979. He was just 21 and had a construction job in Ulan Bator, the capital city, when one day a hose carrying cement under pressure blew up in his face. The caustic lime in the cement burned his corneas, blinding him. At the time, the Soviet Union was the only place he could go for surgery to restore his vision. But after two cornea transplant operations failed, the Soviet doctors gave up and pronounced Tuul blind for life.

In 1981, Tuul was given a job in a workshop for the blind. He went on with his life, meeting a woman whom he later married and fathering two daughters. Unsatisfied with a sedentary life, he took up running with a guide to keep in shape and then went on to trekking, a popular sport in Mongolia that involves trips lasting as long as seven days through the rugged country with a full backpack. Tuul became foreman of his workshop and had 37 people working under him. He was such a good salesman that he soon had 20 of his workers out trekking with him.

When Tuul arrived, we took him to see Dr. Seedor at the New York Eye and Ear Infirmary. Dr. Seedor's diagnosis was that it might be possible to restore Tuul's sight, but it would be risky. Since Tuul had already undergone two unsuccessful transplants, a perfect match would have to be made. If it didn't take, Tuul would almost surely be blind for life. But

Tuul's first concern wasn't his vision. He had come to run a marathon and had had only one month to get in shape for a distance he had never run. He had gotten in the best shape he could during that time, getting up at 6 a.m. and running every day before work until he had built up to 12-mile training runs, but that was still not even half a marathon.

The Mongolians were perfect guests, and it's kind of a shame that Gambold, on his first day on the streets of New York, came across a street-corner game of three-card monte, the modern-day equivalent of the old shell game. Fascinated, Gambold stopped to watch and promptly got his pocket picked. When he realized what had happened, he started shouting and some good New Yorkers—yes, there is such a creature—ran the thief down and brought him back. Gambold understands English, and the thief, being a New Yorker, threw himself on the mercy of the court, laying down a real three-hanky tale of lost jobs, starving children, evil landlords, and whatever else he could think of. He had just needed the money that day to buy food for his poor children, he said, and if he could only have it, he would repay Gambold the next day, when his ship was going to come in. Being a doctor and a humanitarian, not to mention unschooled in the ways of the big city, Gambold told him to keep the money and repay him the next day. At this writing, three years later, the next day has yet to come.

On marathon day, the three-runner team acquitted themselves well. Tuul, carried along by the roaring crowds who were seeing the first Mongolian nationals ever to run the marathon, finished in under five hours.

The marathon turned out to be the easy part. Finding an exact match for Tuul proved to be a lengthy process, probably because there isn't a lot of Mongolian genetic material floating around the United States. Tuul lived in the Mongolian mission and continued to run while he waited. Finally, in January, Dr. Seedor found a cornea that he felt would work. "We are going to give you blue eyes and return you home. The blue eyes may be from a lady," Dr. Seedor told him.

Tuul was pretty sure it was a joke, but he wasn't completely sure until he was assured that his new eye would match the old.

When Tuul finally returned to Mongolia, he told the newspaper *Peoples Freedom* about the operation. The story was headlined: "A MONGOL WITH AMERICAN EYES." This, in a Mongolian-supplied translation, is how he put it:

Tuul: Just think about it. The cornea, meaning "the flower," in my eye was gouged out and replaced by another cornea from another human being. It is needless to say that this is a major undertaking.

Interviewer's question: It must be a very miraculous experience for you to suddenly regain sight after ten years; a rebirth not only physical but spiritual.

Tuul: Needless to say, that is true. I do not believe it. I was operated on January 18th. That day, after the completion of the operation, the doctors and all the people that helped, such as nurses who I had come to know by sound, came before my vision. As I began to see the people who had helped me, I found myself before people with blue eyes and golden hair... I regained the dimension of sight through literally the hands of American people by gaining an eye of an American and thereafter I set my eyes on the American people.

The way Tuul told it and the way the newspaper wrote it, it sounded as if we had given him an actual eyeball instead of just a cornea. Added to the fact that the Russians had twice tried and failed to restore his vision, this presented quite a public relations coup for the United States. Tuul also told the newspaper that all the expenses had been picked up by Achilles and added:

This is an association that is very humanitarian in their work, and, needless to say, this is a very Buddhist concept. They are "boo in tay"—people that are God-sent to do God's work and spiritual merit.

To *Running Times* magazine, Tuul had this to say about America: "Before I came to the United States... I thought Americans were very aggressive, but it has been just the opposite. They have been open-minded and full of goodwill."

Tuul stayed a total of six months in the United States. Since he was here in April, we sent him to run for the first time as a sighted guide for a blind runner in the Boston

Marathon, which that year accepted an Achilles contingent for the first time.

When it was finally time to go home, Tuul was very excited about seeing his wife and daughters who greeted him at the airport. They were the most beautiful people he had ever seen.

The success with Tuul earned us an invitation to visit Mongolia and set up a program, and now our previous work in China began to pay off. We set up another visit there, which allowed us to catch a plane to Ulan Bator and to keep the Chinese chapters rolling. Actually, calling the thing we were expected to board an airplane was a stretch. I'm not good on airplane models, but I'm pretty sure this was a DC-3, a twin-engined propeller plane that went out of production after World War II but is still in service in various remote corners of the planet. To get on, you climbed up a little stairway, which meant you had to walk past the plane before boarding it. This process didn't inspire confidence. The plane was all rivets and wrinkled metal with grease stains streaking the engine nacelles. The tires were beyond bald and their fabric belts showed through the rubber. But it was the only plane available, and it flew (we hoped) only once a day, so it was this or nothing. Although it had 44 seats, once those were full, another 15 people got on and sat on the luggage and crates that were piled in the center aisle. For atmosphere, someone brought a couple of goats along, just in case the dense clouds of smoke raised by the cheap cigarettes everyone smoked wasn't enough.

At least they didn't serve lunch.

Besides setting up an Achilles chapter and beginning talks about my prosthetics facility, we also took a side trip to the Gobi Desert, which is as barren a slab of landscape as exists. I liked to tell the Mongolians we met that before the Communists took the country over, it had been the Gobi Sea. And it had been, except I didn't mention that that had been millions of years earlier. We drove in a jeep out to a tourist facility consisting of about two dozen yurts. (Yurts are the tents the nomads live in.) From there, we took excursions further into the wasteland.

We kept driving a long time, until finally we saw some dots on the horizon. As we got closer, the dots got bigger

until we recognized them as a herd of Bactrian camels—
that's the two-humped variety. We got close to the camels
and were watching them when a man riding another camel
thundered up and said something in Mongolian, which I
took to be, "What the heck are you doing here?" Our
translator explained who I was, and to my amazement, the
man had heard of me on the radio. They may live a lifestyle
that hasn't changed in half a millennium or more, but they
do have radios.

The man took us to his yurt, and we got down to a
vodka-and-camel's-milk party. The Mongolians are wonderful
people, generous to a fault, brimming with hospitality. It's
the rule of the nomad that when someone passes by, you
feed and house him because there is nowhere else to go.
These particular people were camel herders, and they
followed herds of camel around the desert, stopping to set
up their yurts wherever they could find a patch of the coarse
scrub that passes for forage. They made what little money
they needed by selling the camels. This was supplemented
by charging the tourists who came through for camel rides.
What really struck me, though, was that a boy who couldn't
have been older than 10 was in charge of a big herd of
camels which he handled with total confidence and
competence.

There was a baby camel outside, and they proposed
roasting the little fellow in my honor. I would have accepted,
but we didn't have the time to wait the several hours until
it would be done—and they didn't have a microwave.

An interesting thing about the way of life there is that
the people live in perishable houses but they build a large
number of temples. Their philosophy is that it doesn't make
sense to build a house that will last longer than they will.
But a temple, being dedicated to God, should last forever.

Although very religious, they still have the fierce pride
and bearing that, under Ghengis Khan, made them the
masters of Asia. The Great Wall of China had been built to
keep them out. When the Russians had taken over the
government of Mongolia, they painted Ghengis Khan as an
evil oppressor. When the Mongolians regained their
independence, they restored him to a place of honor in
their rich history.

Much of their artistic heritage was stripped by the Russians, who still keep Mongolian treasures in the Hermitage Museum in St. Petersburg, and elsewhere. One of my fondest dreams is to get those treasures back for the Mongolians. The Russians, of course, won't part with them for anything, any more than the English will give the Elgin Marbles that were taken from the Parthenon back to the Greeks. But Mongolia has something the Russians would like to have. In the Gobi, there are rich fossil fields which many years ago yielded the first fossilized dinosaur eggs ever discovered. Today, the Mongolians are guarding in the desert another fossil of a type that has never been studied. The Russians would like to have it, and I am suggesting a deal that would give the Russians the fossil in return for the Mongolian art treasures. So far, the Mongolians are interested in the exchange. Now for the Russians.

Tuul came back to New York to run the 1991 marathon and he reduced his time by almost two hours—to the three-hour range. That gave me another idea. It struck me rather late, but in 1992, I wondered whether Tuul might represent Mongolia in the Summer Olympics being held in Barcelona. Leszek and I contacted the Mongolian Olympic Committee through their embassy in New York and proposed the idea. They said they'd like to, but they didn't have the money to send another athlete. They were sending only two or three athletes on their own, one of whom was a world-class wrestler. It came down to the $5,000 to pay for Tuul's passage to Barcelona. Board members helped with the funds, and Andy Tisch helped with the details. With less than two weeks to go before the Olympics, it still hadn't been finalized, and it wasn't until a day or two before the opening ceremonies that all the strings got pulled and Tuul was actually on a plane to Barcelona as a full-fledged member of the Mongolian Olympic Team.

I understand that he had a pretty good time in Barcelona. Next to the athlete's village, which was built on the Mediterranean, was a topless beach where the athletes of the world unwound after a hard day of sweating for the motherland. There has probably never been a beach like it, because it was populated almost entirely by young people who were among the healthiest in the world. Certainly, athletes from such countries as Mongolia had never seen anything like it. It was on these tepid beach excursions that Tuul was most appreciative of having his vision restored.

The men's marathon was the last event of the Olympics, and it was timed so that the winner would finish in the Olympic Stadium on Mont Juic about an hour before the start of the closing ceremonies. Once the ceremonies started, none of the runners still on the course would be allowed on the track and would have to finish instead on a practice track outside the stadium. All week before the race, I worried about whether Tuul would make it to the finish line. Barcelona was hotter than the hinges of hell, the air was thick with pollution from the horrendous traffic, and the marathon course itself ended with a difficult upslope that culminated with a climb up Mont Juic that would rip the heart out of a mountain goat. It was so brutal that the winner of the race collapsed on finishing and was carted off the field on a stretcher. I sent instructions to Tuul through Leszek, who was there, and a sportswriter I knew, to take it easy and not try to do anything foolish like keep up with the lead pack, which would be made up of the 20 or 30 fastest marathoners in the world.

I needn't have worried. Tuul hadn't trekked blind through the mountains of Mongolia and come all that way to Barcelona to quit on his country in the world's biggest track meet. He didn't make it into the stadium. He finished an hour too late for that. But he finished, and although he was last among the survivors, many runners with better credentials quit along the way. And he didn't finish alone. As he entered the practice stadium for his last lap, with the Achilles T-shirt I never asked him to wear (honest!) soaked with proud sweat, the NBC cameras were waiting to flash his courageous image around the world

A *Sports Illustrated* photographer was there as well to take his picture for an article that ran the next week. There was no crowd like those in New York to scream and cheer for him, but the cheers were there just the same. They were the cheers for a man who had made the supreme effort.

And Tuul, the first Mongolian to run the Olympic race, rode those cheers to the finish line!

FINISH

Chapter 10

We are all in the gutter,
but some of us are looking at the stars.
—Oscar Wilde

It must have been some party that Andre Francis went to. I wasn't there, but I saw the results. Apparently, everyone was drinking and getting increasingly boisterous. I don't know what Andre did, but whatever it was, some others at the party took exception to it. To straighten him out, they picked him up by the heels and dropped him on his head. Right then, Andre stopped being a nuisance and the party stopped being fun.

Andre's neck was broken, and by the time they got him stabilized in the hospital and got done with the tests, the diagnosis was grim. He was a quadriplegic and would spend the rest of his life in a wheelchair. He had a little movement in his arms, but not a great deal. They put him in New York's Coler Hospital for rehabilitation, and eventually in their long-term nursing facility. It was really warehousing. Andre had nowhere to go and nothing to do when he got there.

One day a man named Jim Beckford, who was coaching Marty Ball and other wheelchair athletes, stopped in at Coler, looking for victims to deliver to the Achilles Track Club for liberal applications of exercise. He had met me at the finish line of the New York City Marathon when I watched Marty finish the race and went up to him to introduce myself. Marty became one of our first members, and Jim became a recruiter and coach for us. One of the places he went was Coler; one of the people he brought back was Andre Francis.

Jim took an interest in Andre probably because Andre was one of the more difficult people he had met and Jim enjoyed a challenge. Somehow, he talked Andre into coming to our workouts. Jim would go to the hospital and drive Andre over to Central Park, then take him back after the workout. I guess Andre came because it got him out of the hospital, but he wasn't really interested in trying to propel his wheelchair more than a few yards. It was hard work, and he couldn't see that any good would come of it.

Still, Jim kept bringing Andre out and Jim and I and the rest of the club kept working on him until he could actually go a mile in his wheelchair. This was a remarkable accomplishment considering the lack of strength and range of motion he had had when he came to us. (I'm not sure Andre looked at it that way. After all, he still had no reason to want to go a mile other than to get us off his back.)

At Coler, the long-term patients were allowed to take excursions in the neighborhood if they were capable of it. And now Andre was at least able to go outside and wheel around a bit. Because of his workouts, he also knew exactly how far he could go before he had to turn around and come back. And this is where going a mile turned out to be important, because one half-mile from the hospital was a liquor store. When Andre made this discovery, his life changed. Suddenly, there was somewhere to go and something to do.

Andre didn't have any money, but other patients in the hospital—patients who couldn't get out and about—did. When Andre told them he could get to a liquor store, they collected enough money to get a bottle of liquor to bring back to the ward. Now liquor was forbidden in the hospital, and to make sure none got in, the hospital had employees who checked patients returning from outings to make sure they weren't carrying any contraband. But Andre had a trick hidden up his sleeve, or, more accurately, his pants leg. Being a quadriplegic, Andre had no bladder control and was fitted with a urine collector that drained down a tube into a bag. So, before going out on his run, Andre disconnected the collector and got a clean, empty bag. When he got to the liquor store, he poured the hooch into the bag, which the guards never thought to check when he came back.

This system worked quite well. The patients in the ward got to kick back a few drinks to break the boredom of hospital life and they paid Andre for his labor by letting him keep half the bottle for his own considerable thirst. Meanwhile, Andre kept coming to Achilles workouts, and now he had a reason to work out to increase his distance. As he got stronger, it meant that he could make two runs a day instead of one. Then it was three runs a day. Without realizing it, Andre was getting in shape.

What Andre had done was to get a job as a liquor wholesaler. It was against the rules, but it's really hard to fault these guys. Being in a hospital and confined to a wheelchair is like being in prison. There's nothing to do and if you can get drunk, it's a good way to kill half a day. It does have its dangers, though, and those showed up when Andre started making multiple runs. When he could bring back only one bottle, no one could get really drunk. But when he could bring back a lot, they could. One day the inevitable happened and some of the patients got so drunk they were falling out of their wheelchairs. This is not only dangerous, it's a hell of an inconvenience to the nurses and orderlies. The hospital officials knew the men were drunk, but they couldn't figure out where it was coming from. Since no one would tell, they eventually took away everyone's wheelchairs for a few days as punishment. They still tell stories about it.

Although Andre was drinking, which is how his troubles had started, he kept coming to Achilles. He had really gotten into the program. Progress was slow, but the more he worked out, the greater the range of motion of his arms and the more strength he had in his hands. After a year he felt ready to attempt the annual Helen Hayes 10K race. No quadriplegic with Achilles had ever attempted to go six miles before, and when people saw Andre laboring along, he became the hero of the race. It took him 2.5 hours to finish, but many spectators stayed, cheering and applauding. The roar of the crowd is a powerful stimulant, and Andre had never heard people cheering for him like this. Over the last stages of the race, his hands and fingers were torn up and bleeding and officials kept asking him if he wanted to stop. But he was Rocky now, running up those stairs in Philadelphia, and he insisted on finishing under his own power. When he did, Helen Hayes herself greeted him at the finish line and told him his was the most courageous performance she had ever seen. She gave him a great big kiss, and he glowed with delight!

Six months later was the New York City Marathon, and Andre, no longer resigned to his limitations, determined to enter it and finish. Andre was still a quadriplegic, but a funny thing was happening. His range of motion and strength kept improving even though that was supposed to be impossible. Call it the Valentin Dikul effect or call it a miracle. But some time later, I ran into one of Andre's doctors at a cocktail party. He told me that if he had known I was going to try to train Andre to run a marathon, he would have probably stopped it. He would have told me there wasn't a chance in a thousand that Andre would make it.

"I would have told you that all you were going to do was frustrate him because this guy was a high quad and there wasn't any way he would ever be able to do it. Sometimes," he went on, "it's really good that people like you don't know what you're doing. If you had known, you wouldn't have tried."

And maybe that's the point. We didn't have the benefit of the medical wisdom that says Andre couldn't do it. All we knew was that getting out of the hospital and getting some exercise couldn't do Andre any harm and could be fun. I've said before that you can't predict success or hold failure against someone, but neither should you not bother trying just because an alleged expert tells you it can't be done.

Andre is proof that it can be done!

He entered the marathon and he finished it in about eight hours. Carl Landegger went with him as his guide, and when they came over the 59th Street Bridge and turned up First Avenue in Manhattan, where the biggest crowds gather, Carl had on a T-shirt that said, "My friend's name is Andre." So now, all the way up First Avenue, hundreds of thousands of people were cheering and clapping and yelling, "Go, Andre!"

At one point, Carl leaned over and said to Andre, "You know you could be elected mayor today?"

Andre beamed through the sweat and effort and said, "I know."

And I know that Carl, who has made millions of dollars and done countless wonderful things and been hailed around the world, felt just as good as Andre. Even though he knew the applause was for Andre, he probably also felt that some of it was for the nice volunteer with him.

After the marathon, Carl called me up and asked what we could do to get Andre a job and a life outside the hospital. We came up with the idea of getting Andre driving lessons, and eventually a job as a taxi driver. If it worked, Carl would have bought a medallion and permitted Andre to purchase it from him out of his earnings. It was a good idea, but Andre didn't go for it. He did, however, accept Carl's offer to help him get an apartment on the upper East Side, where he could live on his disability payments.

Andre moved out of Coler and continued to work and to get better. He even got married and had a couple of kids. Like Valentin Dikul, he got to the point where he could walk a little, and by working at it, eventually could walk without a cane for short distances. He still loves to run, which he does in his wheelchair, and continues to compete in the marathon.

Best of all, he gave up alcohol; swore off it completely. Along the way, he had gotten religion, and in the process had decided that strong drink was evil. So on the one hand, you have a case where alcohol did some good in that it gave Andre incentive to increase his abilities. And then you have a case for the benefits of religion because it got Andre off alcohol when he had become hooked on it.

Most of all, you have the benefits of hard work. No one can explain how Andre regained the use of his arms and legs, but I've seen it in Andre, Valentin, and others. I'm not a medical doctor, and no one's really researched this thoroughly, but my suspicion is that you can go through rehabilitation in a hospital and after a while they declare that you've gone as far as you're going to go. After that, you may exercise some each day, but it's like vitamin C in the sense that, if you eat an orange each day, it's really a small amount and you may not see the benefits of it. But if you take vitamin C pills, which some people swear by, it's like eating a bushel of oranges and then you see an effect in greater resistance to colds. Training for a race is like taking that vitamin pill. You're working hard for several hours a day. This increases the blood flow and circulation, and the enriched blood supply may bring nutrients to areas that have been starved by injury. We've seen people with brain injuries—like the Central Park Jogger—make similar dramatic improvements through sustained exercise.

This admittedly is speculation, but until someone comes up with a better explanation for Andre Francis, I must believe there is something to it. I feel certain that when someone gets around to doing a real study on the phenomenon, they'll confirm my anecdotal experience. And just because it doesn't work all the time, doesn't mean it doesn't work some of the time.

As Andre Francis also showed, a regular running program can even help people with alcohol or drug problems. We've had a number of runners who came to us with habits or addictions and who found the self-esteem and fulfillment in running that allowed them to kick their habits. Andre is one. Pat Griskus and Kenny Carnes are two others. But, as with paralysis, it doesn't help everyone.

The saddest story—and at the same time, one of the happiest stories, at least for a while—I've been involved with centers around a man who couldn't beat drugs. I've talked a little about John Paul Cruz, one of the first members of Achilles. But I haven't told you his story; not all of it.

John was about 20 years old when I met him in 1982. I was just starting the running classes that would lead to Achilles, and one of my employees had run across John in Bryant Park by the New York Public Library. My employee and friend, Dr. Joe Cody, had gone for a lunch-time walk and saw John among the many small-time drug dealers who frequented the park. What set John apart was that he had one leg. He had been born that way in his native Puerto Rico. His mother had taken the anti-nausea drug, thalidomide. If he had been born with two legs, he would have been a wonderful athlete. Even on one leg and one crutch, he could beat a lot of able-bodied people in a game of basketball.

Knowing that I was starting a running program, Joe told John about it and suggested he come to Central Park to give it a go. I guess he came because no one had ever asked him to join a track club before and he figured he ought to at least check it out. It turned out that he and Achilles were a perfect fit. He loved the athletic challenge and he was so bright and handsome and outgoing that everyone just fell in love with him. I liked him immediately, not only because of his personality, but because he ran on his crutches at just about the same pace that I ran on my prosthesis. So we naturally ran a lot together and would talk and talk. We quickly became good friends.

He continued to sell marijuana in Bryant Park, which gave him a little bit of money and also provided him with grass to smoke himself. I'm not judgmental about drugs or about many things. My concern was to keep him in the Achilles program and get him to run a marathon. Maybe other things would grow from that.

As our relationship progressed, I offered him a job with Personnelmetrics. He was bright and could have learned just about anything, but he just had no interest in a full-time job. He'd come in when he needed a few bucks and work for an hour or so or run an errand for me, but if I gave him a job that involved two or three hours of Xeroxing, he just couldn't do it. He had to be moving.

John stayed with the running and in the fall of 1983, he was among the first six Achilles members to run the marathon and the first one-legged person ever to run the distance on crutches. His was, as I suspected, a terrific story, and after the marathon, when the White House called Fred Lebow to ask him if the winners of the race and one of the inspirational runners could come down to be honored by President Reagan, Fred and I both felt John would be perfect.

Reagan made a lot of noise about stopping the drug trade, but I never considered that in sending John to meet him. As far as I was concerned, the two were unrelated, although I'm not sure the President would have been as enthusiastic about having John visit if he had known what he did for a living. But the way I saw it, John Cruz deserved the honor. We bought him a suit for the occasion and sent him to Washington, and it was quite probably the greatest moment of his life.

It was like George Bernard Shaw's story, *Pygmalion*, or *My Fair Lady* as it became when Hollywood was done with it. Only where Eliza Doolittle was selling flowers when Professor

Henry Higgins found her, John was selling grass. But they both applied themselves and they both made it to the highest level of society, Eliza to the ball and John to the White House. And both fit right into those situations. And when they returned from their moments of incandescent triumph, both had to face the question of "What next?"

Unfortunately, John didn't have a Hollywood scriptwriter to pen his ending.

John was a hero, but it didn't make him rich, or even self-sufficient. Eliza got married, but John went back to selling grass. He didn't have a permanent address, but instead moved from friend to friend and relative to relative, staying for a week or a month or however long it took to wear out his welcome. Then he'd move on. The only constant in his life was Achilles.

Since John didn't need help running, I used him as a volunteer and companion for others. One of the people I sent him out with was a woman who came down from Connecticut. She had lost a leg to cancer and was very slow. John was perfect for her because he was so upbeat and, unlike others who are more competitive, didn't mind moving along at a pace slower than his own. I'd send them out together into the dark winter nights and they would have a good time. One day I got to talking to her and she told me how amazed her friends in Connecticut were that she would go into New York and run around in dangerous Central Park at night. I didn't have the heart to tell her that the kid she was running with who made her feel so safe and secure was a drug dealer.

After John's success in the marathon and his visit to Washington, his life became a little more hectic. He was invited as a guest of honor to a fund-raising dinner at which they showed a short film of John running. I had rented a tuxedo for him for the occasion, and he looked like a million bucks when he stood beaming in front of all these people who were cheering their heads off for him. When the dinner was over and the applause had died, all the patrons got in their nice cars and drove home.

John stepped outside with me and asked for a buck so he could get on the subway and go home.

He needed a regular job, but even though I offered him

employment, he didn't accept. He said he liked the lifestyle he had in Bryant Park, taking it easy, selling a little grass, smoking a little grass, not worrying about anything. The trouble was that he was a celebrity now, and the people for whom he sold grass figured he was too important to waste on nickel bags of marijuana. So they graduated him to selling cocaine, and he graduated to snorting it.

Whatever problems marijuana had caused for John were nothing compared to those brought on by coke. If John smoked a lot of grass, it would eventually put him to sleep. It was a self-limiting drug. But cocaine gives a much briefer and more intense high. When an addict gets hold of some, he doesn't do a little now and a little later. He does it all and doesn't pass out until it's gone. This is what happened to John, and he found that he couldn't support his own habit on what he was making by selling the stuff. After a while, he had used up all his credit with the suppliers and they informed him that things would get very unpleasant for him if he didn't come up with the couple of thousand dollars he owed them.

Right about then, John decided that he really wanted to go to Miami. He had relatives there, the weather was nice, and, anyway, he didn't want his one leg broken. When John got to Miami, he resumed hanging around and dabbling in drugs. But he enjoyed running, and he loved kids, and that combination led him to get involved with starting a running program at a school for the retarded. That was the beginning of the Achilles Track Club of Miami, and the following October, the club sent runners to New York to do the marathon. One of the people was Scott Wagner, an adult with Down's syndrome who became the first person with Down's syndrome to run the marathon. Scott recently died of cancer, but his last years were very happy ones. He called himself, "King of the Road."

No matter how many successes John had and how many people he helped, he still couldn't help himself. He got deeper into drugs, but he kept coming back to New York to run the marathon and to visit. He continued to live mainly in Miami, where he also ran and was the subject of newspaper feature stories. Around 1987, he met a woman named Susan, who was a letter carrier for the post office and delivered

John's mail. She recognized him from an article she saw in the paper and was smitten by this brave young man with the ready smile and warm personality. Before long they were living together and it wasn't very much longer before she was pregnant and delivered a baby.

Susan was the great love of John's life and he of hers. He asked her to marry him and she said she would on two conditions. First, he had to get off drugs, and, second, he had to get a job. But John couldn't do it.

It must have hurt Susan terribly, but she told John he had to leave. The measure of John's addiction is that as devastated as he was to lose her, he couldn't quit using to get her back. But he still loved her, and when he happened to come across Susan one night with a new boyfriend, he snapped. They were in a car when John spotted them, and he went up to the car as if to say hello. But instead of chatting, John hauled the boyfriend out of the car and beat him severely with his crutch. He didn't beat Susan, but he screamed at her, calling her a whore and threatening to kill her.

The attack was so severe that Susan and her boyfriend pressed charges and John was sentenced to a year in jail for assault and battery. After several months, he was released on probation with the condition that he not use drugs. But as soon as he was out, he was back on cocaine. He might have gotten away with it, but John is one of the most honest people I've ever met, and when his probation officer asked him routinely whether he was doing drugs, he said he was. That got him thrown back in jail for the rest of his one-year term.

Through it all, he kept in touch with me. We talked a lot on the phone about what had happened, and he was still angry about Susan going out with another man. I tried to point out that he went to bed with other women and it was the same for Susan. He didn't have a franchise on her. But he had a double standard on such matters. What was all right for a man was not all right for a woman.

The one good thing about jail was that they had a drug-rehabilitation program there and John couldn't get more cocaine while he was in. To boost his spirits, I sent him a copy of the photo of him and President Reagan, which he put on the wall of his cell. Jails are full of people with all sorts of tales of past glory, but John could prove his.

John came to New York when he got out and went right back to drugs—only by now he had graduated to crack, the most pernicious form of cocaine. Over the years I tried everything I could to get him off the habit. His running idol was Grete Waitz, the great Norwegian runner and winner of nine New York City Marathons. So I contacted Grete when she was in town and she dropped everything to come to breakfast with John and me. She spent a couple of hours telling John very pointedly that she wanted him to get off drugs. To prove her sincerity and to give him incentive, she gave him a beautiful crystal vase she had been given for being the first woman runner to cross the Polaski Bridge. (This is the kind of person Grete is.)

Even that didn't do it. He was on this great emotional roller coaster now, and had been for some time, alternating between euphoria and horrible depression. Starting about two years after his White House triumph, he would turn on me from time to time in rage. "What are you fucking with my life for? Why didn't you just leave me out there in Bryant Park? I was happy until you came along and put me through all these situations and now I can't be myself."

And then he'd blame me for his unhappy situation.

Maybe he's right.

Here I am a behavioral scientist working as an industrial psychologist, which basically means that I have a doctorate in manipulating people to change their behavior. The only difference between myself and a clinical psychologist is that the clinical person tries to change individuals and an industrial psychologist tries to change the behavior of groups.

John's anger on these occasions was the same as Eliza Doolittle's toward Professor Higgins. I had picked him out of the gutter and made him into this wonderful character, and from his point of view, it was all for my own amusement.

Maybe I was, in effect, making reality fit my fantasies—producing a movie without a camera. And John was a wonderful movie. He had one leg, he was handsome and bright, he was Hispanic, and all of that played well.

None of this was done consciously, but there it is.

And all I can say is that I tried in every way I could to make it come out right. I opened every door I could for him, and he simply didn't want to walk through. So many others have grabbed at opportunity. John didn't.

But he remained my dear friend, and I suspect that he both loves me and hates me. He can't get away from me, nor I from him. And despite his feelings about me when he was down, he was always there to help when I needed him. And I have tried to help him.

In 1989, after he had gotten out of jail in Miami, he came around at marathon time, and I sent him out to show Tanya, the Russian amputee, New York. John was wonderful in these situations, and he took Tanya out along with another Russian woman, Vera, and stopped in a store to buy each of them a scarf. The scarves were quite nice and he paid about $20 for both of them, which to the Russians was a month's income. They asked him what he did for a living to have that kind of money and he cheerfully replied that he was a beggar.

Tanya and her friend didn't believe him, they thought he was joking. So he took them down to his favorite territory in one of the better sections of town, got a cup, and, as they watched from a little distance, worked the crowd for an hour and collected another $20. In the immortal words of Yakov Smirnov, the Russian comedian, "What a country!"

At that time, John still looked presentable enough to be able to work a crowd, but his continued dissipation soon took that away from him. To work a good neighborhood, you have to look good yourself, and John got to the point where he was unshaven and unkempt. Now, when he came to New York, he crashed on the Bowery with a lower class of bum. That's where he was when we brought the Chinese over.

Now among the things that the Russians and Chinese particularly want to see when they come to New York are Harlem and the Bowery. They have been drilled so much on the poverty in the United States and on our racial problems that they want to see for themselves. I oblige and drive them up to Harlem, where they roll up the windows, lock the doors, and gape at the passing scene. They're amazed to see people living normal lives because it doesn't jibe with what they've been told. But there's no way they'll get out of the car. On occasion, I will jokingly say, "Okay, we'll get out now and shop." The reaction is one of utter fright.

They have been drilled all their lives about the desperate

poverty in the United States, and it blows them away to see all these big cars—Lincolns and Cadillacs—in the midst of what is supposed to be a poor area. The fact that some of the cars are 10 or 15 years old means nothing to them. While such cars have little value here, in Russia, the value of a car is determined not by its age but by its size. As far as they were concerned, a 15-year-old Continental must belong to a rich man.

They also had trouble dealing with the vast amounts of fresh produce piled up on tables outside of produce stores. In Russia, the fruit wouldn't last. Yet in America, oranges and apples and fruits they had never seen, like kiwis, were standing unattended, and no one was stealing them. Where was all this crime they had been told about?

The Chinese were particularly interested in the homeless, since that was very much in their newspapers. Knowing that John was in town and about where he was, I drove down to the Bowery and quickly spotted him. Stopping the car, which was frightening enough to my passengers, I called him over, which was probably terrifying for them. He came over and was as pleasant as could be, answering their questions through an interpreter and refusing to blame anyone for his situation.

I believe that this encounter was the most exciting part of the Chinese team's trip to the United States.

There is no happy ending to the story. John continued to go in and out of jails in New York and Miami. He'd dry out in jail, then fall deeper into his drug trap when he got out. He started injecting drugs.

His future, which could have been so bright, is almost extinguished. Two years ago he fell ill and was taken to a hospital, where doctors discovered on his heart cysts of a type that are associated with AIDS. They tested him for the disease, but he didn't stick around to get the diagnosis. He'd rather not know.

After this, John told me that he thought you could only get AIDS by using an infected needle intravenously. He thought if he just injected drugs under his skin, he would be safe.

I still think of him almost as a son, except a son wouldn't call me as often as he does. His story is sad, but it is not as difficult for me to watch as you might think. I know that I've tried and that he's tried just as hard. He's doing what he wants to do and, as his friend, I have to accept that.

What I have difficulty accepting is that part of the reason he's in the condition he is is because the drugs he cannot give up are illegal. He's been through practically every program you can imagine and he's tired of trying. He wants to be left alone to do his drugs. I truly believe that some people, and he is one of them, have a medical problem— call it a disease—that cannot be cured. If I had the power, I would make drugs legally available to people like John Paul Cruz. They would be given to him under medical supervision and by prescription. And if the drugs were legally available and responsibly supervised, the illegal demand would be reduced and the profit motive that drives the drug trade would then decline.

As it now stands, the illegal drug trade will not be stopped and people like John will live on the streets.

Whenever you intrude in someone's life and change that person's behavior, both positive and negative things happen. For most members of Achilles, the effects have been overwhelmingly positive. For John, they have been negative. How much of that is due to Achilles, I don't know. Maybe it would have happened anyway.

But no matter what happens, he did see the stars, and for one moment, he was close enough to touch them.

Is it better, as the poet said, to have loved and lost than never to have loved at all?

I think it is.

FINISH

Chapter 11

> *Heroism, the Caucasian mountaineers say,*
> *is endurance for one moment more.*
> > —George Kennan

They asked me what I wanted and I told them a beer—
that's *piwo*, pronounced PEE-vo, in Polish. I had dreamed
about that beer for the better part of a day, fantasized about
it as a teenager in full hormonal overdrive might fantasize
about a pop star. One perfect, cold beer, biting deliciously at
my taste buds; nothing more. Oh, I did want a nice hot
bath at some point, and something to eat, but those things
were secondary. First, I wanted that beer. It had been waiting
for me at the finish line in downtown Kalisz, calling out to
me like a siren. And now at last I had it in my hand and I
couldn't drink it.

That was how it ended. I had the only reward I really
wanted, and I couldn't get it past my lips! You can't tell me
God doesn't have a sense of humor.

It had started 25 hours earlier, in the chilly October
twilight. The race was straightforward—two 50-kilometer
loops of the farmland surrounding Kalisz, a Polish city of
about 100,000 and famous for its piano factory—but not
easy.

On the starting line, with a handful of other Achilles
runners, I knew it would be a long and grueling test, but I
had no idea how hard it would be. Unless you've done
something like running 100 kilometers—62 miles—there's
no way of knowing. And now that I've done it, I can assure
you, you really don't want to know. If you get as far as the
starting line, you'll find out soon enough.

The one question I didn't ask myself on the starting line
or at any time during the next day, was what I was doing
there. I knew that much. The idea had been planted half a

lifetime earlier, when I had been 24 years old and lying in a hospital bed at the Rusk Institute. One of the orderlies, a former officer in the Israeli Army, had told me how every Israeli soldier had to be able to travel 100 kilometers—the width of the country—in a single day. "I'd like to do that someday," I said offhandedly, which probably sounded funny coming from a guy who was flat on his back with one leg sawed off and the rest of his body encased in plaster up to his neck.

I had said it and then forgotten it as I went about the business of pursuing a career. I didn't even think about it when I first started running in 1975. Then, in the summer of 1976, when I was training for my first marathon, I was sitting in a steam bath after a workout at the West Side Y. Bob Glover, my coach, was in there with me, and he was talking about a 50-mile race he had just run. He called the race an ultramarathon, and it was the first time I ever heard that word, which applies to any race over the marathon distance of 26.2 miles. I loved the way it sounded—ultramarathon—the word gave me a special tingling sensation; the word would never be forgotten.

I pushed him to describe in minute detail how he ran the race. My feeling was that the 26 miles I was planning to run was about the equivalent of his 50 miles, at least in the length of time it would take, and I could pick up some pointers from him.

I ran that first marathon, and when I was done the old conversation with the Israeli orderly came back to me. Maybe I would run 100 kilometers one day. But it wasn't going to be soon. I still felt I had a lot of room to improve in the marathon before I went after longer distances.

By 1980, it had become apparent that I wasn't going to lower my time any further in the marathon. I had gotten it down to 6:44, and I was 40 years old. A few years later, when Brian Froggatt arrived from New Zealand, I wasn't even the fastest above-the-knee amputee anymore, and I wasn't going to regain my title. Now the ultramarathon became more than a casual thought. The day when I would run one was getting nearer. I knew that.

The New York Road Runners ran several races longer than the marathon distance. There were 50- and 60-kilometer races in Central Park and a 100-mile race around a one-mile loop in the parking lot of Shea Stadium. But the shorter races weren't that much longer than a marathon and the 100-mile race was too long.

The idea continued to percolate until I met Leszek Sibilski and Achilles went to Poland. Leszek was from a town in Poland not far from Kalisz, and he told me about the 100-kilometer race that was an annual event there. We proposed to the Polish organizers that an Achilles team be allowed to enter the race. When they agreed, the die was cast.

I had a lot of reasons for choosing 1988 and Kalisz, Poland, for what would be my last big race. On a personal level, Joey was 12 and on the verge of young adulthood. I'd want to spend more time with him, which meant less time on running. I also wanted Betsy to be able to spend more time with her painting, an avocation she had taken up about 10 years earlier and pursued with a great deal of enjoyment at the National Academy of Design. She paints because she enjoys it, and it was traumatic for her when one day someone wanted to buy one of her works. She liked it so much she didn't want to sell it to someone else, but I convinced her that she was a painter and should sell it.

Personnelmetrics, meanwhile, had shrunk steadily from its heyday in the early 1980s. The services I had once provided were increasingly available in-house as business computers became standard office equipment. They couldn't get the same custom-tailored work I did, but they could get a program that would handle the job well enough for their purposes. I had moved to smaller quarters. Eventually, I would move out of those offices as well, finally leaving my trusty old dinosaur of a computer, Emm, behind.

When my business had first started to contract, I had pursued new accounts aggressively, but I came to the conclusion that it was neither profitable nor useful to do that. I kept a few valued old customers and concentrated on serving them. In return, I made enough money to live comfortably. And I also gained a great deal of time to put into Achilles. The club that had begun as a hobby was now my business, and my business had become my hobby.

But before I could move on, I wanted to run my 100-kilometer race. I had put it off long enough. Before too many more years passed, I probably wouldn't be able to do it physically. And this 100K was perfect. The course was flat and it would be run in October, when the temperatures would be cool. Anyway, I would be almost 48 years old by the time of the race. By my way of reckoning, that was the end of my second trimester of life.

When the idea of dividing my life into segments had first come to me I was 24 and recovering from my accident. I realized that the first trimester of my life, which I had devoted to my education, was over. The second 24-year trimester would probably be given over to my professional life. The final trimester would be ending my professional life and then enjoying retirement. I was giving myself 72 years, which, statistically, was probably less than I could expect. But my father had died at 65 and I figured that if I lived longer, the years wouldn't be as productive, and I didn't want to look back and think about what I hadn't done.

Life has to be lived. So many people go through life moping around, grousing about everything, being as unhappy as they can make themselves. Some of them are the type who would die and then complain that the coffin's too dark inside. It's almost as if they think they'll do all the things they really want to the next time around. But then you've got to believe in reincarnation, and if you die and it turns out you don't get to do it again, you're going to be awfully disappointed.

So, for me, it was do it now or go through the rest of my life knowing I had been handed an opportunity and had dropped it.

Now, if I was going to attempt to run 100 kilometers, it also made sense to do it somewhere far away from New York. If I didn't make it, no one would know about it. I could do it in privacy. Also, we had just started our Polish chapter and were moving into the Soviet Union. The publicity that could be generated by a team of Achilles runners taking on the ultimate race would be invaluable in furthering the cause of the disabled behind the Iron Curtain.

Jerzy Kosinski, the Polish émigré who became a great American novelist, once wrote a book called *The Painted Bird*. The title refers to a custom of putting a painted bird in a field of crops. The other birds come and peck the painted bird to pieces because it's not like them. When I first came to Eastern Europe, that was the image I had of the disabled. They were the painted birds of society, taunted and abused by the able-bodied. But if we fielded a team and ran this mighty race that very few able-bodied people would think to attempt, our differences would be a source of respect and admiration, not scorn.

Finally, there was the simple desire to achieve something difficult. Some of us simply have to accomplish things. Al Gordon is like that. He had reached his 90s having accomplished every imaginable goal in business, athletics, and charity. You'd think he'd be satisfied, but he took up running and now holds world records at different distances for his age group. Then there's Bill Phillips, who was the CEO of Ogilvy and Mather, who, in his 60s, goes around the world climbing the most difficult mountains, some of which have never been climbed before. Ted Rogers, a partner in American Industrial Partners and formerly CEO of NL Industries and our first sponsor, does the same sorts of things. One week he climbed Mt. Elbris, a difficult peak in Russia. Three days later he joined us for the Moscow Marathon.

Some call people like these romantics. In my line of work, they're need achievers and no matter how much they've done in their lives, they have a continual need to find new challenges that are so difficult that it's not a given that they can do it.

The 100K was that to me—a challenge that required planning and nerve and preparation, a challenge that I couldn't get from the marathon anymore. And even if I prepared perfectly, there was no guarantee I would make it. No other above-the-knee amputee had ever run so far. Maybe none would. It was something I'd have to find out. Non-runners look at us taking on these challenges and wonder why anyone would want to put themselves through so much pure torture. Runners know the answer is because it's fun. It's also fun to attempt what may be impossible.

I trained all through the summer of 1988 for the race. It was a horrible summer, filled from end to end with 95-degree heat and near 100-percent humidity. This turned out to be a blessing. The biggest single problem in running long distances is staying hydrated, and running in that heat, I had to learn how to get enough liquids in me just to be able to train. Training itself was totally different from training for a marathon. I ran fewer miles, but ran them in bigger chunks. Every weekend, I'd go out and run anywhere from 20 to 30 miles, which essentially meant I was running all day. Then I'd have to take two or three days off to recover and run a couple of short training sessions of five miles or so during the week. John Cruz showed up in New York that summer and ran many of those miles with me, which made it a lot more bearable. Training is hard enough, but training alone is almost impossible, and I was lucky to have John there to help. I was also lucky that Betsy put up with me, because for four months, every weekend was consumed by my training, and after running 25 miles on a Saturday, I didn't feel like going out Saturday night.

Besides keeping my liquids up, I concentrated on what I call low-pulse running. By that, I mean trying to maintain a steady pace at as low a pulse rate as possible. My theory is that if you can do that, you won't get tired as rapidly and should be able to run longer and farther. To do that, I'd sing nice, slow folk songs and show tunes to myself.

Taking one big training run a week and laying off three days is not the ideal way to train. But a side benefit of that schedule was that I didn't lose weight and went to Poland still pleasantly plump. You have to carry some body fat into an ultramarathon, just as you need it in an ironman triathlon. Marathoners can run with almost no fat, but if you go much further, you need a source of extra energy, and fat is where it's at. For me, this was especially critical because of my stump. If I lost too much weight, the stump would get smaller and sink into the socket of my prosthesis. Eventually, the prosthesis wouldn't stay on.

Finally, it was time to go to Poland.

I had gathered a team of 10 other Achilles athletes, including Ken Carnes, our superior wheelchair racer; Irene Hecht, who was blind; Ev Hall from Ohio, who has cerebral palsy but is ambulatory; Bill Reilly, who has cerebral palsy and with whom I had trained during the summer (He runs by kicking his chair backwards.); and Sandy Davidson, who has had a stroke. A similar group of Polish Achilles athletes entered, so that we had about 15 Achilles runners, which was impressive considering that there were only 100 able-bodied runners in the race. Four or five days before the race, we got to Warsaw. From there, we bused about a hundred miles west and south to Kalisz.

The race was scheduled to start at 5 a.m. the following Friday, but those of us who weren't going to set speed records needed an earlier start so we'd at least finish the same day as the fast runners. We decided a 10-hour early start was about right, so the group of us who were anticipating a long, slow race, prepared for a 7 p.m. start the evening before the main start. We tried to sleep in, and then spent the day relaxing and napping. I took a last nap in the afternoon, went out for a big meal heavy with carbohydrates about an hour before the start, and then we were on the starting line.

Every runner had a team of volunteers. My actual guides would be two Polish teenagers. One, Bartoz, would take me through the first 50-kilometer lap, and then the other, his 16-year-old cousin, would go the rest of the way. We also had Patti Lee Parmalee, our coach, with us along with Dr. Tom Einhorn, an orthopedic surgeon from New York who was one of the first doctors to take a serious interest in Achilles. Patti and Tom toured the course in an automobile, stopping to visit with each runner or group of runners and to give whatever help was needed. Tom also ran many miles with me.

By the time the gun went off, we were awash in adrenaline. This was new territory for all of us. And for the first few kilometers, we jogged along in a great, noisy gaggle, babbling in two languages.

For 10 kilometers, that was fine. It takes me a long time to warm up, and I was just starting to fall into a rhythm in that first six miles. But during the next 10 clicks, all the chatter and socializing started to get annoying. I realized then that this wasn't a party. This was probably my only shot at this race, because I sure didn't want to have to do it again, and if I was going to finish, I had to go at my own pace. The group I was with was going too slowly for me, so I picked it up and set off on my own into the Polish night.

It was around midnight. Earlier, we had been greeted in

the small towns we went through by bands playing folk songs and polkas. Small children gave us flowers, which presented a problem, because you didn't want to throw them away after a child had given them to you, but you also didn't want to run 62 miles carrying a bouquet. So we'd carry them until we reentered the night and then drop them. But even in the countryside, we sometimes had company. People came out with torches at all hours, even at 4 a.m., to watch us come and go and to jog along beside us for short distances.

It was eerie when we'd finally break into long stretches of farmland. We were running by moonlight on paved roads that carried little traffic. You knew there were farmhouses along the road, but you couldn't really see them. To pass the time and calm myself, I started singing songs to myself. I started with "This Land Is Your Land," which gave me a chuckle because here I was an American, singing this song in Poland. Since I'm a big fan of folk music and Woody Guthrie in particular, I would sing a number of his songs. Then came show tunes from *Brigadoon*, *Carousel*, *Oklahoma*, and *The Fantasticks*.

I didn't sing out loud, however. It wouldn't have been polite to inflict that kind of noise on a peaceful country.

After going through my repertory of songs, I'd fall into movie mode. This was a system I'd learned in the hospital while under the influence of Demerol. I believed that the staff were showing movies on the inside of my eyelids. So I played back those ancient movies in Poland. One I particularly remember for some reason had Eddie Cantor in it. He was gliding through a beautiful field as if in a canoe on water. All the movies involved other restful scenes, but only that one starred Eddie Cantor.

The one thing you do when you get in a race like this is think. And basically, you start reviewing your life. It starts with the obvious question: "What am I doing here?" So you go back and you figure it out. I thought about losing my leg. I thought about the funny things that had happened because I only had one leg. I thought of the day I was standing outside a grocery store in my grungy clothes and on crutches, when a nice little old lady saw me and my one leg and gave me a quarter. I thought of saying, "Thank you.

I can use this to pay off my apartment," but I simply pocketed it, gave her a smile, and let her think she had done a good deed.

I mentally ran through my catalog of awful jokes, like the one I tell people when they ask what to call someone who's lost part of their leg. "We're de-calf-inated," I tell them. Or the story I heard in Poland about the three-legged pig. "Why does that pig have an artificial leg?" the straight man asks. "With the price of ham so high, you don't eat a pig all at once," is the punch line.

The story of the Wizard of Oz came back to me and the idea of quests. I switched from that to Peter Pan and the boys who wouldn't grow up, and wondered if I was one of them. I thought of my own version of the ages of man, sometimes chopping it up into my trimesters, and then thinking of it in 10-year increments. Now I was nearing the end of my fifth decade, and I had gone from businessman to apostle of running.

After dividing up my life, I divided my running career. First I was like a child, concerned with personal achievement. I had graduated to the role of parent, teaching others to run, urging, correcting, cajoling. Now, it seemed, I was ready to become a grandparent, being able to nurture without having to correct; devoting myself to encouragement and giving the coaching over to others.

And thus the miles passed, and the night with them. Instead of thinking of the race as 100 kilometers, I made it a 20-mile affair. The course was marked with a sign every five kilometers, and those were my mile-posts. It made the distance seem smaller and more manageable.

I finished the first lap in about 11 hours, still running in the dark. We ran past the start-line and out into the countryside again. My first volunteer, who had spoken a bit of English, dropped out and his cousin took over. Since he spoke not a word of English, I could turn totally inward. Meanwhile, the other runners were finally starting behind us. Again there was a burst of noise and excitement. You could tell the relative talents of those going past by the noise they made and the shape of the bodies. The first runners were lean and hard, and the women looked firm going away. They ran quietly, their thoughts consumed with winning. The slower runners followed, and the farther back they were the broader were their beams and the more noise they made. For them, winning was out of the question. They were there for a good time, and they were having it.

It had been getting progressively lighter as dawn neared. Now I had something else to occupy my thoughts, as I followed the hour-long progression from the first graying light to the streaks of pink and purple and then red. Meanwhile, I was being serenaded by what seemed like every rooster in the world, as they alerted the farmyards that it was time to get on with another day.

The course had regular stops, where they had water, warm tea, and food that consisted of slabs of bread and hunks of cheese and kielbasa, with which I supplemented the stock of Milky Way bars I had brought with me. In addition, I had brought a crate of bananas from the States for all the runners, and the race organizers had distributed them around the course. At one of the food stations, around the 60-kilometer mark, I finally stopped and sat down for the first time since I had started. My stump had been chafing, as it inevitably does, and Dr. Einhorn thought it was time to take a look. In the back, where the top of the prosthesis hits it, it had rubbed through the skin and was working on the muscle underneath. Tom was concerned about my developing an infection if it rubbed too deeply into the muscle, but we slathered it with Vaseline—1 1/2 jars!—and I put the leg back on and got back to running.

I wasn't running so much as walking now. But I was moving and the fact that I could see the countryside I had gone through during the night helped. It was lined with neat single-story, thatch-roofed farmhouses that reminded me of Hansel and Gretel and the nursery tales of childhood. The children who came out to watch were bright and happy with blond hair and rosy cheeks. But their parents somehow had lost the brightness of the children and all looked worn by work and care and immune to the charms of nature all around them. I was getting a bit silly as fatigue and pain began to dominate my progress. I started talking to the cows and ducks and horses along the way, and my Polish volunteer, I'm sure, thought I was nuts.

I wasn't bleeding too much, but the raw spots on my stump were oozing clear blood serum. The serum has a distinct smell to it that brought back even more vividly my days in the hospital just after the amputation when the stump was oozing quarts of this stuff and I thought I was going to die. It wasn't a problem running-wise, but it wasn't a smell that I enjoyed.

I got to the 75K mark, and now it was getting down to that time when athletes and coaches start talking about digging down deep, sucking it up, and all those other clichés that carry you through when you can't carry through. I took the leg off again for Tom to check it. When I sat down to do that, it struck me that I was really tired. I'd been going about 18 hours at this point, and my body was shutting down on me. I didn't have any choice, didn't have the option of fighting it. It was as if someone had pulled a switch. I struggled to get from the chair I was sitting on to the pavement. I laid down and passed out immediately. I was only out for five or 10 minutes, but it felt like a full night's sleep. As quickly as I had fallen asleep, I revived, my eyes snapping open like a pair of window blinds. I looked up, and 50 or 60 people were standing around me, staring at me as if they were debating whether I were dead. I felt like Gulliver looking up at them.

I put my leg back on, got up, and jogged off down the road, and as I did, the group that had been looking at me burst into applause. That little nap and the applause gave me a surge, and I felt absolutely terrific for the next 10 kilometers. I thought of Ted Corbett, a Road Runners Board member, friend, Olympic marathoner, and ultramarathoner. He used to talk about the 85-mile mark in a 100-mile race as the wall. But at the 85K mark, my adrenaline-rush had been exhausted and I was back to walking again. The sun was starting to go down, and that made it even tougher. But I kept going to the 90K mark and sat down again.

I knew I was going to make it. I had known that all along, if only because I didn't ever want to have to try this again. But I had whittled the race down to a 10K, just 6.2 miles, the basic weekend road-race distance. I had done more 10K races than I could count. It was a distance I knew. I just had to collect my energy for the last push.

As I sat there, Jeff Pledger, one of our blind runners who had started that morning, came down the road. I hailed him and he stopped to exchange condition reports. "I'm tired," he said. "Me, too," I offered. "The last 10 kilometers are always the worst." He agreed and took off down the road. Jeff was the first blind president of an Achilles chapter, the Westchester Chapter.

That gave me another boost. Maybe one-third of the runners who entered didn't finish the race at all. Several Achilles runners had dropped out at the 50-kilometer mark and a few more had made it past halfway before packing it in. Jeff let me know that Irene Hecht had made it, becoming our first blind female 100K finisher.

Now I knew Jeff would make it. The one person I wasn't concerned about was Ken Carnes, the wheelchair racer. He finished the race in under six hours, losing the wheelchair championship—in a sprint to the finish—to Zbigniew Wandachowicz, a Polish Achilles athlete who was known to all of us as Zibby. Zibby was really remarkable. He was pushing a clunky, homemade, $30 wheelchair and beat Ken, who had a Marty Ball racing chair. The following year, Ken came back for revenge and whipped Zibby by an hour, finishing in a world wheelchair record of just over five hours. After that accomplishment, he gave Zibby his racing chair, and Zibby thanked Kenny by breaking his record in the new chair the following year. Zibby won by refusing to let Ken draft him. He even stopped to wait for Ken to go ahead, and then would draft. Ken was learning, but at a high price.

Kenny recovered from losing quickly enough, though. He had met a beautiful, young, Polish woman with wonderfully striking blue eyes. She was waiting at the finish line to console him. At first I couldn't figure it out. Everywhere we went in Poland and Russia, Kenny was surrounded by hot young women. Then Kenny told me his secret. When he was paralyzed from the waist down, he had lost his ability to get an erection. So he had surgery to have an implant that he could inflate so he could have sex. The irony of this was that before Kenny was paralyzed, he had been very selfish sexually, interested primarily in pleasing himself. After his accident, he couldn't feel anything, but with the implant, he could give his partner unmatched pleasure. And he found that it was more gratifying to be able to give pleasure than it had been to take it. The Polish and Russian women had discovered this, and they gave him all the companionship he wanted. He liked to tell about the night his unusual ability was so sought after that the next morning he was actually black and blue. What the heck. It didn't hurt.

At this point in my race, I was beyond thinking even of that for diversion. From here on into Kalisz, it was a matter of getting from one stride to the next. As I slogged along, though, a group of people started to latch on to me, and that helped a little. I knocked off a mile, and now, I thought, it's just a five-mile race. Then it was a four-mile race and then we were actually entering Kalisz and the streets were lit and more people were around.

There were also bus stops about every quarter-mile on the streets. Now, I stopped thinking about miles and kilometers, and started thinking about bus stops. I'd aim for the next one down the street, and when I got there, I'd stop to bend over and stretch the cramps out of my leg. Everyone else who was going to finish had finished by now and all anyone had to concentrate on was the last, one-legged runner dragging himself through the final five kilometers.

My mind was grabbing hold of anything it could to keep from thinking about the pain. A young woman, our translator, joined my little parade and walked very close to me, encouraging me. She was well-endowed and as I swung my arms they brushed against the side of her breast. She may well have been oblivious to the contact, but I kept thinking about how nice it was of her to pep me up like that. I could even close my eyes and think about breasts as I walked, and then open them to see if the next bus stop had gotten any closer.

When I passed the 95K marker, I translated it to mean that I had two loops around the Central Park reservoir, and I could do that. Then it was one loop around the reservoir. I was in a fog and really moving slowly. The gathering crowd was encouraging me, telling me to pick it up, as if there were anything left inside. There wasn't, or at least I didn't think there was until one man who had a snootful of vodka got real close and started telling me how swell I was doing. The whiff of his breath was like the breaking of an ammonia capsule under my nose, and I got the last little boost I needed.

The finish line was just ahead. Patti Parmalee, who had told me before I started that she gave me at best a one-in-three chance of finishing, was there along with the rest of our crew. Leszek, who had checked on me throughout the race, came out from the crowd of hundreds of people waiting for me to finish. "Make sure you put your hands up and smile when you finish," he reminded me. Any experienced marathoner will tell you the same thing, and it doesn't matter how destroyed you are, you can always manage at least a jog for those last few yards and you can always get the hands up for the finish-line picture.

I don't know where I got the strength, but I managed a little jog and struck my pose. When I crossed, I heard the sweet cheers, and then a band waiting there struck up the Polish National Anthem. Then they sang "Sto Lat," which means one hundred years. The song in effect wishes long life. During this trip, a famous Polish general from World War II died at the age of 99. One of the stories that circulated was that, when they sang this song, he realized that they were only wishing him just one more year! As everyone joined in singing, I realized I had made it.

That's when they asked me what I wanted and I told them a beer. Almost immediately, I had one in my hand. I looked at it and imagined drinking it. I tried to drink it and knew I needed to drink to replace the fluids I had lost. But it wouldn't go down, so I stood there holding it, thinking about how good it would taste if only I could drink it.

I had no idea how I was going to get back to the hotel. I had been given the presidential suite, and it was 1,000 square feet of the finest accommodations Kalisz—or any other city—could offer. That's where I wanted to be, but Leszek loaded me into a car and drove me to the awards ceremony.

Leszek had to help me up the steps of the building, but when I got inside, I caught my second wind. The race officials called the various winners up one by one. The winning male got the keys to a new car. The winning woman got a carpet. (The following year, they got a little bit more with the program. Instead of giving the female winner a carpet, they gave her a bicycle. The male winner still got a car!) They saved me for last, and they gave me my medal and a special award. They also brought out a huge, sinfully rich chocolate cake that must have weighed 10 pounds. It really looked good. I'm sure it tasted delicious. But I couldn't even imagine eating the smallest slice. So I gave it to my two young Polish volunteers, who couldn't believe that I was giving them that whole, wonderful cake.

After they gave me the medal and cake and everyone stood and cheered me as I had never been cheered, Leszek told me I had to give a speech. I could barely remember my name, but Leszek saved me again. He stood next to me and whispered what I should say and whom I should thank. He'd whisper and I'd say the line, then he'd translate it into Polish, and if I missed anything, he put it into my translation and everyone agreed it was a wonderful speech.

This whole time, I was hanging on to my beer. It had long since gone warm, but I didn't care. It was like a talisman that would keep me from harm. If only I could drink it. In the States, they probably would have put me in a hospital and hooked me up to IV bottles, but I was on my own in Poland. I knew I had to get liquid into me, but I just couldn't.

After the ceremony, Leszek took me and my pet Polish beer back to the hotel. I ran a bath and crawled into the tub, but that wasn't as good as I had imagined it would be, either. Finally, I went to bed, but although I was as utterly and completely exhausted as I had ever been in my life, I couldn't sleep. I felt as if I were a prisoner of war who was undergoing sleep-deprivation torture.

My body had simply shut down and was unable or unwilling to follow any more of my directions. I had convinced it to run this ridiculous race and look what that had done. I could tell it to sleep, drink, eat, anything. My body didn't care. It was done listening to me.

I was suffering as I had suffered when I lost my leg. And it did feel just as if a truck had run over me. But at the same time, it was a good feeling because I knew I had run my race and I wouldn't ever have to do it again. Yes, it had been torture, but it was only for 25 hours, and now I would be able to talk about it for the rest of my life; to tell my grandchildren about it and to bore untold hundreds and thousands of people.

Then, magically, I was asleep, and I slept the sleep of the dead. Someone got me up at seven the next morning. I had to figure out how to get out of bed and get dressed, but by eight o'clock we were at the aircraft factory talking about my prosthetic leg project over breakfast. They had prepared an extraordinary breakfast in my honor, and I found myself sitting in front of a big shank of veal. And, like the chocolate cake, I couldn't eat a single bite. I felt bad that they had made such a special dish and it would go to waste, but then someone told me not to worry. Food didn't get thrown out in those parts, and someone else would be glad I wasn't hungry and would finish it for me.

We stayed a couple more days in Poland, and I spent most of the time walking around with a beer, still trying to get more than a few sips down my throat. It took those two days before I could keep much down. And it took weeks before I felt anything near normal. I had really gone to the limit of what a man with one leg could do.

It changed my thinking about encouraging others to try the same distance.

Only half our group had finished, and after that, I have strongly discouraged other Achilles runners from trying the 100K distance. A marathon is perfect both in terms of the effort involved and the rewards that come from finishing it. And it's a doable distance. The drop-out rate for Achilles runners in marathons is very low.

When you start trying to do an ultramarathon, you cause all sorts of problems. Doing the marathon is conquering the impossible. The risk of failure there is low. But once you've done it, you no longer accept not finishing a race. This is dangerous. It's like the karate experts who try to break big piles of bricks with their bare hands. If they do it, they're fine. But if they don't, there's serious pain involved. The ultra is like that. If you don't finish, you're wracked by self-doubt. Am I a wimp? Did I fail to train properly? Do I lack the will? And when I look back, I realize that I was lucky to finish. Even having prepared thoroughly, I could have cramped up at the end and simply been unable to move. Then, all the will in the world wouldn't have gotten me to the finish line.

But I did finish, and it was a great moment in my life. I could finally put competition behind me. In running, I had no more conquests I cared to attempt.

I didn't know it, but I had one more test before I got back to New York. It was on an airline flight, which was filled to capacity. The only seat I could get was in the smoking section, which was the right side of the plane. Now, I'm a tolerant guy and don't object to smoke. I used to be a serious pipe smoker. But I was still destroyed from the race, and when the man in front of me lit up one of the terrible Eastern European cigarettes they smoke, I couldn't tolerate it. I leaned forward and asked him if he could please not smoke. He replied that this was the smoking section and that's what he intended to do.

"I'm not fooling around," I said, "I'm sick. Will you please not smoke?"

He replied by puffing harder, raising a cloud of noxious fumes that could fell a horse. If that's the way he wanted to play, I had a response. I rang for the stewardess and told her I couldn't breath and needed oxygen. On an airplane, if a passenger says he has to have oxygen, they can't refuse, so she brought me a small tank and a mask and I started breathing it.

Of course, when someone's using oxygen, no one can smoke near him, and the stewardess told my tormentor he had to put his cigarette out. He did, and I took off the mask. Seeing that, he lit up again, and I put the mask back on so he'd have to stub it out.

"Look," I told him. "Every time you light up, I'm going to get the oxygen." He didn't smoke again the rest of the flight.

My final surprise came when I met my wife and son at the airport back home. "What happened to you?" Joey asked in shock.

I knew I had lost 15 pounds during the run, but his amazement drove home the fact that my entire body had changed during those 25 hours. My clothes hung on me strangely. Everything was rearranged.

I was, quite literally, a new man.

FINISH

Epilogue

I'll never get faster, but I can help others.
—Dick Traum

Every time a disabled person joins Achilles and begins the long, hard road that leads to running a marathon, it is a victory for humanity. Every time a volunteer takes time out of her or his busy schedule to help another human being, it is another victory. As we have seen, one victory leads to another, and people who had thought their lives were narrowly circumscribed by their disabilities have gained the courage and the self-confidence to become more fully involved in the mainstream world and to reach closer to their full human potential.

My work with the Achilles Track Club is wrapped up in disabled issues, but this really isn't about disabled people. It's about people—all of us. There are many victories for mankind, both large and small, to be won. As Americans, we should be truly proud of how much we already do for others. We in this country tend to get down on ourselves, to focus only on the negatives. But as I have seen with the thousands of volunteers who work with Achilles chapters everywhere, there is much good in the American spirit. We need to recognize that, build on it, and export it around the world. When you are disabled, you learn very quickly that we are all brothers and sisters on this planet. Race, religion, gender, political orientation, and ethnicity all evaporate in the shared experiences of the disabled. The greatest victory of all will come when the able-bodied population realizes what the disabled have known all along.

This is one of many reasons that I will continue to spread the Achilles ideal around the world. In 1992, we welcomed South Africa, Nigeria, and Italy to the family. We're operating in Mongolia, Bulgaria, Lithuania, Colombia—in more than

20 countries overall. We will continue to expand around the world, but now it's time to go beyond just running.

This is how I see things as I go into what is probably the last decade of my prime. Because if we don't begin reaping the benefits of what we have started, it won't survive. And I want the Achilles Track Club to continue after me, not because I started it, but because I think it's important. We have just begun to touch the surface.

During the week before last year's marathon, I gave a speech to a group of medical doctors who run. My message was this: Running is good not just for the able-bodied, but for the disabled as well. I went down a list of specific disabilities that I have seen respond to running. Arthritis is one. In my own case of that debilitating joint disease, the pain virtually disappeared during 15 years of regular distance running. Doctors have traditionally told arthritis patients not to exercise, but I believe that is a mistake.

Cancer is another. I don't think it's a coincidence that Fred Lebow defied the predictions that he would die within six months of the discovery of his brain cancer. As soon as he could, Fred started running laps on the roof of Mt. Sinai Hospital. He continued through debilitating chemotherapy sessions and by the end of 1992 had run a marathon and was gaining strength by the day. I have seen others with cancer survive far longer than they were supposed to after they took up running. I have tried to get the medical professionals at Memorial Sloan-Kettering to study the links between running and survival in cancer patients. Fred has helped raise over a million dollars for the hospital. The Board of the New York Road Runners Club asked me to encourage the hospital to use these funds for research of interest to runners.

Victims of brain trauma—strokes, head injuries, and aneurysms—have improved dramatically once they have taken up a running program. Paraplegics and quadriplegics have likewise shown remarkable improvements in their range of motion and strength once they have joined Achilles and stuck with it. A few have gotten out of their wheelchairs. I'm sure that extensive exercise is responsible, and when someone studies it, we'll know why.

Other disabilities may not be cured by running, but people

with multiple sclerosis have stayed active longer by maintaining the strength in unaffected muscles. The blind have discovered the thrill of racing and the joy of comradeship. The list goes on. But old attitudes, particularly in the medical establishment, are hard to break. Not enough doctors are telling the disabled to get out there and be active.

I go back to the Wizard of Oz and all those people who think they lack courage, heart, or brains. We need to show them what is inside, to encourage achievement. I think that should be emphasized at all levels of life, particularly in schools. We need to encourage people to seek achievement instead of accepting mere survival. We need to teach it, not just in this country, but around the world.

I am particularly interested in the Third World, where so much needs to be done and where the many programs and advocates we have in America do not exist. As the world prospers, so do we. Recently, the Achilles Track Club has begun to work more closely with the World Rehabilitation Fund. Through the fund, my dream of establishing a prosthetics factory in Mongolia to provide good, inexpensive limbs to the Third World, should shortly become a reality. We are also expanding our program of distributing personal computers with low-vision software to our chapters around the world and teaching them how to use the computers to generate funds. We hope to set up workshops in which disabled people will repair and manufacture wheelchairs. Finally, we are establishing an exchange program to bring doctors and technicians to America to learn how to correct vision defects, make prosthetics and inexpensive wheelchairs, and run the computers. For any program to be successful, it needs someone who will take over the local operation and make it work.

From this start, we can establish a university of programs to teach the disabled how to work in the construction trades, to care for AIDS victims and the elderly, to work in facilities for unwed mothers. In the health-care areas, I think the disabled can be compassionate and effective workers because they are disabled. They establish bonds of empathy that the able-bodied cannot build, and they represent a resource that is virtually untapped.

Achilles runs on a tiny budget, and very little of it goes to offices, executives, or fund-raising because, other than my own office, we don't have any of those things. Ironically, that puts us at a disadvantage in the charity sweepstakes in which too many organizations with charitable purposes spend enormous amounts of money on administration, salaries, publications, and perks. Some of the abuses in the charity business are a national disgrace. If people donate to charity, they should not have to wonder whether their money is going to the people who need help or to the chief executive's chauffeured car. We need to establish a means to measure how effectively the funds are used.

Finally, we, the disabled, must start concentrating on fundamental discrimination. When we demand elevators in every subway station, we only turn off the general public, which has no desire to part with the tens and hundreds of millions of dollars it would cost to provide such facilities in New York City alone. We need to do what women and blacks have done and focus on the basics of jobs and housing. We may not be able to walk, but most of us have nothing wrong with our brains. We need opportunities and empowerment.

Empowerment is what Achilles is all about. We don't work with magic spells. We just go out and run, and in doing that, we discover that we do not have to sit quietly at home and dwell on our disabilities. We do it for fun, and before we know it, we're on the starting line of a marathon, and then we're actually running a marathon, hearing the cheers that we thought weren't for us, getting the medal that confirms that we can do things that too many people told us we couldn't.

I say we because, even though losing a leg didn't prevent me from being successful, I didn't begin to really drink in life until I took those first uncertain running steps around the West Side Y gym. Since then, Achilles has changed not just my life and the lives of the disabled, but the lives of the thousands of volunteers who have helped us over the years as well as the lives of people who don't even know we exist. Every time human beings realize more of their potential, all of society benefits.

I've done it both ways. For the first half of my life, I was a taker, consumed by my own success. For the second half, I've turned to giving, consumed with passing that on to others. If you want to know the truth, life has never been more fun.